HOMEWORK HELPERS

English Language & Composition

MAUREEN LINDNER

CAREER
PRESS
Franklin Lakes NJ

Copyright © 2005 by Maureen Lindner

HOMEWORK HELPERS: ENGLISH LANGUAGE & COMPOSITION
EDITED BY JODI BRANDON
TYPESET BY EILEEN DOW MUNSON
Cover design by Lu Rossman/Digi Dog Design
Printed in the U.S.A. by Book-mart Press

To order this title, please call toll-free 1-800-CAREER-1 (NJ and Canada: 201-848-0310) to order using VISA or MasterCard, or for further information on books from Career Press.

The Career Press, Inc., 3 Tice Road, PO Box 687,
Franklin Lakes, NJ 07417
www.careerpress.com

Library of Congress Cataloging-in-Publication Data

Lindner, Maureen.
    Homework helpers. English language & composition / by Maureen Lindner.
      p. cm.
    Includes index.
    ISBN 1-56414-812-2 (paper)
     1. English language--Composition and exercises--Handbooks, manuals, etc.
  2. English language--Grammar--Problems, exercises, etc. I. Title: English
Language & composition. II. Title

PE1408.L5596 2005
808′.042--dc22

                                          2005042070

A determiner or adjective modifies the noun. For instance, *bike* modified with the possessive pronoun *your* becomes *your bike.* When a possessive pronoun acts alone, it is substituted for a noun, such as: You ride *your bike,* and I will ride *mine.*

Examples

My favorite teacher likes lemons.

In this sentence, the pronoun *my* is the singular first-person possessive case.

She lives in her house. We live in ours.

In this example, *her* is a determiner and *ours* replaces the noun *house.*

There is one common error associated with possessive pronouns. Be careful to avoid this error.

Do not use an apostrophe in the possessive forms of personal pronouns.

Example:

Incorrect: The dog woke up from it's nap.

Correct: The dog woke up from its nap.

Example:

Incorrect: Her's is the car with the dent.

Correct: Hers is the car with the dent.

Pronouns are also used to replace nouns in sentences. They frequently take the place of the specific nouns to either serve as shorter forms of the nouns or to give variety to the sentence. The nouns that these pronouns replace are called **antecedents.** Pronouns must always match the antecedent it replaces.

Examples

The teacher writes on the board as the teacher lectures to the class.

This sentence is awkward. By replacing the antecedent teacher with a pronoun, the sentence flows better.

The teacher writes on the board as she lectures to the class.

Here, the antecedent *teacher* is replaced with *she.*

The team won <u>its</u> first game.

Its (third-person singular possessive) replaces the antecedent *team* because team is a collective noun.

> Before the <u>dancers</u> took the stage, <u>they</u> stretched <u>their</u> legs.

In this example, *dancers* is the antecedent for *they* and *their*. *Their* also acts as a possessive pronoun determiner for *legs*.

Exercise 1-4

For each of the following sentences, underline the pronoun(s) and write the antecedent(s) in the space provided.

Example: The student passed <u>his</u> exam.   *student*

1. The girls play in their backyard. _____

2. After dinner, Eric and I played cards in our room. _____

3. The committee adjourned its session. _____

4. My cousins like their new home. _____

5. There is food for whoever wants it. _____

6. The playground had its equipment painted. _____

7. The team lost interest when its coach yelled. _____

8. The bride and groom danced their first dance. _____

9. Later, the two people enjoyed their time alone. _____

10. Arnold gave his wife a ring. _____

Reflexive and Intensive Pronouns

Reflexive and intensive pronouns refer to the *subject* of the sentence or clause. They end in *self* or *selves*. The chart on page 23 shows the correct reflexive or intensive pronoun.

The difference between *reflexive* and *intensive pronouns* is subtle. A **reflexive pronoun** indicates that someone did something to himself.

Examples

> The avid gardener bought <u>himself</u> a new hedge clipper.

Himself shows what the antecedent *gardener* did.

Reflexive/Intensive Pronoun Case			
Singular		Plural	
Antecedent	Reflexive/Intensive Pronoun	Antecedent	Reflexive/Intensive Pronoun
I	myself	we	ourselves
you	yourself	you	yourselves
he	himself	they	themselves
she	herself		
it	itself		

After dinner, the girls treated <u>themselves</u> to a refreshing swim.

Themselves refers to the *antecedent* girls.

The hiking group lost <u>itself</u> in the majestic scenery.

Itself is the reflexive pronoun for the collective noun *group*.

An **intensive pronoun** emphasizes the noun or pronoun to which it refers.

Examples

The restaurant manager <u>himself</u> served the coffee.

In this case, *himself* still refers to the antecedent *manager*. However, *himself* here helps to emphasize the subject.

The landlord painted the apartment <u>herself</u>.

In this sentence, *herself* is the intensive pronoun that emphasizes the antecedent *landlord*.

There are a few common errors with reflexive pronouns. Be careful to avoid these errors.

Do not substitute a reflexive pronoun for a personal pronoun in the nominative or subjective case.

This is a common mistake in speech. Do not make it in your writing.

Example:

Incorrect: William and <u>myself</u> never eat veal.

Correct: William and <u>I</u> never eat veal.

Example:

Incorrect: Gary brought the plate to Mary and <u>myself</u>.

Correct: Gary brought the plate to Mary and <u>me</u>.

Do not use *hisself* or *theirselves*. Neither is a word.

Example:

Incorrect: He dressed <u>hisself</u> for the meeting.

Correct: He dressed <u>himself</u> for the meeting.

Example:

Incorrect: The owners <u>theirselves</u> fixed the roof.

Correct: The owners <u>themselves</u> fixed the roof.

Exercise 1-5

For each of the following sentences, fill in the appropriate reflexive or intensive pronouns.

Example: The problem resolved *itself*.

1. The young boy bathed _____.

2. People who find _____ lost should get directions.

3. I know you consider _____ an expert in mathematics.

4. The team roused _____ before the big game.

5. We treated _____ to a new dishwasher.

6. She told the students, "Be good to _____."

7. I bought _____ a new car.

8. Annie never lets _____ feel gloomy.

9. Tom's dog scratched _____ on the ear.

10. The teacher frequently spoke to _____.

Indefinite Pronouns

Indefinite pronouns refer to unspecified nouns. They include the pronouns *anybody, anyone, each, everybody, everyone, nobody, no one, one, somebody,* and *someone.* These indefinite pronouns are **singular.** This means a gender must be determined by using *his, her,* or *his or her.* People tend to use plural pronouns with indefinite pronouns to avoid the awkward choice of he or she, but this is incorrect. For instance, you might hear "Each student needs *their* notebook." Remember that the verb is already conjugated as singular, so this idea must be continued throughout. The pronoun must match the antecedent.

Examples

Each of the men takes his trash to the curb.

Each is an indefinite pronoun and takes the singular *his* as a personal pronoun.

No one brought her jacket to school.

Her is the singular pronoun for the antecedent *no one.*

The most common error associated with indefinite pronouns is the lack of pronoun-antecedent agreement.

A personal pronoun must agree with the singular indefinite pronoun.

Examples:

Incorrect: Everyone carries their plate to the dishwasher.

Correct: Everyone carries her plate to the dishwasher.

Incorrect: Why did someone put their hat on the table?

Correct: Why did someone put his hat on the table?

Choosing a singular pronoun can become an issue when trying to avoid gender bias. Here are a few suggestions for avoiding this problem.

Avoid the awkwardness of choosing a gender by changing the subject to plural.

This solution allows for correct grammar, yet is less obvious than *he or she*.

Examples:

Incorrect: Everyone needs his coat today.

Correct: All travelers need their coats today.

Incorrect: Did each student bring her pencils?

Correct: Do all students have their pencils?

Another method for avoiding any hint of gender bias is to drop the pronoun altogether.

Examples:

Incorrect: Everyone needs <u>his</u> coat today.

Correct: A coat is necessary in this weather.

Incorrect: Did each student bring <u>her</u> pencils?

Correct: Are the students prepared?

Exercise 1-6

For each of the following sentences, choose an appropriate pronoun and write it in the space provided.

Example: Someone in the class has <u>*his*</u> headphones on.

1. Anyone can succeed if _____ tries.

2. Everyone must clean _____ work area.

3. No one needs to worry if _____ is prepared.

4. The room was cold today so nobody took off _____ coat.

5. Did the kids leave _____ socks on the floor?

6. Anybody who leaves the room must wear _____ nametag.

7. I need somebody to bring _____ copy of the documents.

8. Nobody move from _____ seat!

9. Can anyone feel _____ toes?

10. When one makes eggs, _____ should watch for shells.

There are also a few **plural** indefinite pronouns. They include *both, few, many, several, most,* and *some.*

Example

Trees come in several varieties. <u>Some</u> are conifers.
<u>Many</u> produce fruit.

In these sentences, *some* and *many* are plural indefinite pronouns that replace the plural noun *trees.*

Demonstrative Pronouns

Demonstrative pronouns are used to identify a specific person, place, thing, or idea. These pronouns can be used as either determiners in front of a noun or in place of a noun. They can be singular or plural and include *this, that, these,* and *those.*

Examples

This shoe is dirty. Those need shoelaces.

This refers to one specific shoe and is therefore a determiner. *Those* replaces *shoe.*

That plant needs watering. These need sunlight.

That is a determiner for *plant. These* refers to several specific plants so it is plural, but it still replaces the noun *plant.*

There are several common errors associated with demonstrative pronouns. Be careful to avoid the following errors.

Do not use demonstrative pronouns to replace articles.

Example:

Incorrect: I learned this new dance.

Correct: I learned a new dance.

Do not use *here* or *there* after a demonstrative pronoun.

Example:

Incorrect: This here sandwich is delicious.

Correct: This sandwich is delicious.

Do not use *them* when you mean *those.*

Example:

Incorrect: You should have bought them video games.

Correct: You should have bought those video games.

Interrogative Pronouns

Interrogative pronouns are used to ask questions. They include *who, whom, whose, which,* and *what.*

Examples

Who would like a cookie?

Who is an interrogative pronoun as the subject of the sentence.

I will give the reward to whoever deserves it.

I is the subject of the sentence, but *whoever* is also nominative because it is the subject of the dependent clause. Notice also that *it* replaces the antecedent *reward*.

Give it to whomever you choose.

In this sentence, *you* is the subject. *Whomever* is the object of the clause and is therefore in the objective case.

To whom are you speaking?

In this example, *whom* is the direct object and takes the objective case. *You* is the subject of the sentence, and therefore it takes the subjective case.

Which game shall we play?

Which is an interrogative pronoun as the object of this sentence.

Exercise 1-7

For each of the following sentences, correct the demonstrative or interrogative pronoun error.

Example: I can dance with whoever I want.
> *I can dance with whomever I want.* (Whomever is the object of the verb *want*.)

1. To who do you wish to speak?

   _____

2. The story is about this boy who wants a puppy.

   _____

3. This here problem requires a solution.

   _____

4. By the time we saw that there traffic jam, we were already stuck.

   _____

5. Who is Alison trying to find?

   _____

6. Patty was wearing this black dress.

   _____

7. Her child had this angelic face.

   _____

8. During them long classes, the students became tired.

   _____

9. For who is this message?

   _____

10. If you wish to learn more about that there event, consult the newspaper.

   _____

Relative Pronouns

Relative pronouns relate the subordinate or dependent clause to the rest of the sentence. They are used at the beginning of the subordinate clause to relate the subordinate clause to the main clause. Relative pronouns include *who, whom, whose,* and *that.*

▶ **Who**

When referring to people, always use who and its related forms. Who is used when the relative pronoun is the subject of the clause. **Whom** is always used when the relative pronoun is the object a verb or preposition. **Whose** is used to show possession.

Examples

Patty is a person <u>who</u> never complains.
Who is the subject of the dependent clause and connects it to the rest of the sentence.

Patty, <u>who</u> never complains, was nicknamed "the martyr."
Who is the subject of the dependent clause, even though it is in the middle of the independent clause (Patty was nicknamed "the martyr").

The friend <u>whom</u> Betty met for dinner was Allison.
In this sentence, *whom* is the object of the verb *met.*

Allison is a person with <u>whom</u> Betty is comfortable.
Whom is the object of the preposition *with* in this sentence.

▶ **That, Which**

When referring to things, always use that and which. In speech, people frequently make the error of using that or which with people. Avoid this error; always use forms of who when referring to people.

Examples

Her favorite pet store <u>that</u> carried exotic birds was closed on Sundays.

In this sentence, *that* begins the subordinate clause, even though it is in the middle of the independent clause.

The store was located in the mall, <u>which</u> opened in 2002.

Which connects the subordinate clause to the main clause.

These are the two main errors associated with relative pronouns:

Do not use *that* or *which* when referring to people. Always use *who* or *whom*.

Example:

Incorrect: Michael is a man <u>that</u> likes pizza.

Correct: Michael is a man <u>who</u> likes pizza.

Do not use *which* unless the antecedent is clear.

Example:

Incorrect: The computer crashed, which started from a virus. (What is the antecedent?)

Correct: The computer system malfunction, <u>which</u> started from a virus, crashed the computer.

Reciprocal Pronouns

Reciprocal pronouns refer to individual parts of plural antecedents. They include *each other* and *one another.*

Example

The game was lost because the players worked against <u>each other</u>.

Each other is the reciprocal pronoun for the plural antecedent *players.*

Special Problems of Case

It is important to always make sure your pronoun matches your antecedent. There are times, however, when this becomes complicated. For instance, there are special singular antecedents. They include *each, either, neither, every one,* and *one.*

Examples

Neither of the boys had his bat.

His is a singular pronoun for the antecedent *neither.*

Every one of his books had its pages torn.

Its is a singular possessive pronoun for the antecedent *every one.*

Another special case is the **compound subject.** If there is more than one person or thing represented in the antecedent, then the pronoun must be **plural.**

Example

Mary and Alison like their new car.

Mary and Alison is a compound subject as an antecedent and therefore takes a plural pronoun.

When using a pronoun in a *comparison,* the case can be problematic. Either the nominative or the objective case might be correct. In order to be certain, complete the comparison and choose the appropriate pronoun. One hint: In most cases, the nominative case is used following the verb *to be.*

Examples

Her daughter is as lovely as she.

To complete the comparison, you would say: Her daughter is as lovely as *she* (is). Therefore, the nominative case is appropriate.

The problem affects Andrew more than him.

To complete the comparison, you would say: The problem affects Andrew more than (it affects) *him.* Therefore, the objective case is appropriate.

In the previous sentence, if the pronoun is changed to the nominative case, the meaning of the sentence is changed.

Example

The problem affects Andrew more than _he_.

To complete the comparison, you would say: The problem affects Andrew more than _he_ (affects Andrew). As you can see, the meaning of the sentence has completely changed. Always be precise!

Exercise 1-8

For each of the following sentences, write the correct pronoun in the space provided.

Example: The award was more important to my mother than to _me_.

1. One of the children lost _____ toys.

2. Firefighters and police officers frequently donate _____ time.

3. Chris is older than _____.

4. Either of the parents can show _____ identification.

5. Neither can of peas is worth _____ cost.

6. The gift means more to Stephen than to _____.

7. Ella and Patrick brought _____ suitcase.

8. We sometimes feel others are smarter than _____.

9. She is just as funny as _____.

10. After studying, every one of the girls closed _____ books.

Lesson 1-3: Verbs and Verb Phrases

Verbs are words that show action or being. A verb phrase contains the main verb and its auxiliary verbs. Alone or in phrases, verbs determine tense and /or other implied meanings.

Examples

We _work_.

Work is a verb. The verb is conjugated in the present tense, first-person plural.

He _tried_ to ski.

In this example, the verb is conjugated in the past tense, third person singular. *To ski* is the infinitive form and acts as the object of the verb.

These sentences contain a simple subject and a main verb in its base form. Sometimes verb phrases are needed to provide more detail. In these cases we use **auxiliary verbs** (also called **helping verbs**). Auxiliary verbs include forms of *be, do*, and *have*, which are also used as main verbs, and modals, which include *can, could, may, might, must, shall, should, will*, and *would*. Auxiliary verbs are used with a base form, present participle, or past participle to create verb phrases. The most common auxiliaries are forms of have, be, and do, which are used to create different tenses, the passive voice, emphasis, questions, or negative comments. Modal auxiliaries are used to form questions or to show future action, possibility, necessity, and so forth. Therefore, make sure each word is necessary so your sentence is precise. (For more information about tenses and different verb forms, consult Chapter 3.)

Examples

I <u>have</u> my dessert.

In this sentence, *to have* is the verb. This sentence is in simple present tense.

I <u>will have</u> my dessert.

In this sentence, *to have* is the main verb and *will* is the modal auxiliary. By adding the word *will,* the tense changes from present to future tense.

She <u>has</u> my dessert.

In this example, the main verb is still *to have*. However, the verb is conjugated to match the subject. In each sentence, the subject and verb must agree in person and number. Notice how the sentence sounds when the subject and verb do not agree: She *have* my dessert. When using all types of verbs, make sure the subjects and verbs agree.

Exercise 1-9

For each of the following sentences, identify and underline all of the verbs and verb phrases.

Example: By next year, I <u>will have been boxing</u> for seven years.

1. I should clean the house.

2. We do need a rug.

3. Margaret does read well.

4. Jerry could have been a rock star.

5. She has been driving for three hours.

6. He will like the movie.

7. Marcus would not be happy.

8. David can dance.

9. It would be fun.

10. Mark never eats dinner.

Linking Verbs

A linking verb joins a subject with a **subject complement,** a word or group of words that identifies or describes the subject. If it *identifies* the subject, the complement is a noun or pronoun and is sometimes called a **predicate noun.** If it *describes* the subject, the complement is an adjective and is sometimes called a **predicate adjective.** (For more about adjectives, see Lesson 1-4.)

Examples

William is an engineer.

William is the subject. *Is* acts as the linking verb. *Engineer* is the subject complement (predicate noun) that identifies William.

He seems intelligent.

Seems is the linking verb. *Intelligent* is the subject complement (predicate adjective) that describes the subject.

Linking verbs include forms of *be* when used as the main verb, *appear, become, feel, grow, look, make, remain, seem, smell, sound, stay,* and *taste.*

Exercise 1-10

For each of the following sentences, identify and underline all of the linking verbs.

Example: The wool feels rough against my skin.

1. Emily is an experienced chef.

2. She seems adept at many things.

3. Her food smells appealing.

4. The dishes are appetizing.

5. It all looks delicious.

6. Watching her cook has become impossible.

7. I feel ravenous.

8. Her friends are impressed with Emily's talents.

9. They look proud.

10. Emily feels satisfied.

Transitive Verbs

A transitive verb is a verb that takes an object. In other words, the verb is not complete on its own. A transitive verb needs a **direct object.** The direct object identifies *who* or *what* receives the action of the verb.

Example

Sarah <u>makes</u> <u>movies</u>.

Sarah is the subject. *Makes* is the transitive verb. *Movies* is the direct object. Notice that without the direct object, the sentence is incomplete.

A direct object may be followed by an object complement. This may be a word or word group that describes or identifies the object. Object complements may be adjectives or nouns.

Examples

I <u>consider</u> <u>Sarah's movies</u> <u>artful</u>.

I is the subject. *Consider* is the transitive verb. *Sarah's movies* is the direct object. *Artful* is the objective complement (adjective) that describes the direct object.

Her movies <u>make</u> <u>her</u> <u>an artist</u>.

Her movies is the subject. *Make* is the transitive verb. *Her* is the direct object. *An artist* is the object complement (noun) that identifies her.

A transitive verb may also take an **indirect object.** The indirect object answers *to whom* or *to what,* or *for whom* or *for what* the action is done.

Example

Sarah's movies make the studio money.

In this case, *Sarah's movies* is the subject. *Make* is the transitive verb. *Money* is the direct object. *The studio* is the indirect object. Sarah's movies make money *for* the studio.

Intransitive Verbs

An intransitive verb expresses a complete action and therefore needs no object.

Example

Children play.

Play in this case is an intransitive verb. It does not require an object to complete the action. Be careful though: Some verbs can only be transitive or intransitive, but others can be used both ways.

The boy studied.

Studied is the intransitive verb.

The boy studied math.

In this sentence, studied is transitive and the direct object is *math*. In most situations, it is not necessary to label verbs as transitive or intransitive. It is only important to complete the action.

Exercise 1-11

For each of the following sentences, identify and underline all of the verbs. In the space provided, write if the verb is *linking, transitive,* or *intransitive.*

Example: The child remains seated. *linking verb*

1. The couple enjoys dancing. _____

2. They never tire. _____

3. They are charming on the dance floor. _____

4. Dancing is fun. _____

5. After dinner, other couples will dance. _____

6. They seem youthful. _____

7. The music sounds beautiful. _____

8. The couple gracefully crosses the floor. _____

9. The music ends. _____

10. The couple opens the door. _____

Verbals

Verbals are verb forms that do not function as verbs. Instead, they function as nouns, adjectives, or adverbs. There are three types of verbals: participles, gerunds, and infinitives.

The **participle** functions as an **adjective.** The present participle is the *–ing* form of the verb (dreaming, watching, and so on). The past participle usually ends in *–ed* (dreamed, watched, and so forth), but there are many irregular past participles (ate, been, saw, and so forth).

Examples

The mother woke the <u>sleeping</u> child.

Sleeping is the adjective (present participle) that modifies child.

The <u>expelled</u> student found a new school.

Expelled is the adjective (past participle) that modifies student.

The <u>lost</u> wallet was recovered.

Lost is the adjective (irregular past participle) that modifies wallet.

The **gerund** has the same form as the present participle (ends in *–ing*), but it acts as a noun. A gerund can be both a subject and an object.

Examples

<u>Camping</u> is my favorite hobby.

The present participle *camping* is the subject of this sentence.

I enjoy <u>camping</u>.

Camping in this case is an object. In both sentences, they are gerunds.

The **infinitive** is the *to* form of a verb (to cook, to eat, and so forth). It can function as a noun, an adjective, or an adverb.

Examples

He wanted <u>to cook</u>.

To cook is the object of the verb and therefore a noun in this sentence.

He wanted time <u>to cook</u>.

Here, the infinitive modifies the noun *time* and therefore acts as an adjective.

He was ready <u>to cook</u>.

In this sentence, the verb phrase *was ready* is modified by the adverb *to cook*.

Exercise 1-12

For each of the following sentences, identify and underline all of the verbals. In the space provided, write if the verbal is *a participle, a gerund,* or *an infinitive.*

Example: I want <u>to meet</u> your friend, Devon.   *infinitive (noun)*

1. Gardening is Alice's favorite hobby. _____

2. Every year, she looks forward to planting season._____

3. First, she likes to weed her vegetable garden. _____

4. She knows when the soil is ready to produce. _____

5. She waits for the right time to plant. _____

6. She can be found sowing seeds in her yard. _____

7. Dried seeds are scattered._____

8. Birds like to eat the seeds. _____

9. Tending her garden keeps Alice happy. _____

10. The blossoming produce provides nourishment. _____

This section has dealt with the terms *adjective* and *adverb*. Let's review those now for better understanding.

Lesson 1-4: Adjectives and Adverbs

Adjectives and adverbs are both modifiers, but they modify, or describe, different parts of speech. The same word can act as an adjective or adverb, depending on its place in the sentence.

Adjectives

Adjectives modify nouns and pronouns. They do this by describing, identifying, or quantifying those words. Adjectives can include numbers, articles, and pronouns. They are used to make comparisons and to show degree.

Examples

The <u>brazen</u> student asked <u>rude</u> questions.
Brazen and *rude* modify the nouns *student* and *questions*.

<u>That</u> person needs to stand up.
That identifies which person.

We saw <u>two hundred</u> ships.
Two hundred quantifies ships.

The <u>balloon</u> parade was the <u>smallest</u> in <u>our</u> town's history.
Balloon describes the parade. *Smallest* shows a degree. *Our* identifies which town.

Notice that the placement of the adjective is not consistent with each sentence. Adjectives can come before the noun, as in the example <u>balloon</u> parade, or after the noun and a linking verb, as in the example was the <u>smallest</u>.

Just as a proper noun is, a proper adjective is capitalized.

Example

My favorite beverage is <u>Colombian</u> coffee.
Colombian is capitalized because it is a proper adjective.

Exercise 1-13

For each of the following sentences, identify and underline all of the adjectives.

Example: The <u>hungry</u> dog ate <u>three</u> biscuits.

1. The slender child sat on a large precipice.

2. The beautiful sky became cloudy.

3. Inclement weather can be dangerous.

4. After several hours, his mother became worried.

5. She telephoned the local police to report the wayward child.

6. An alert officer noticed the helpless child.

7. Although they faced extreme danger, they took a calculated risk.

8. The daring officers rescued that child.

9. Fortunately, the child learned an invaluable lesson.

10. The remorseful child discovered a newfound appreciation for police officers.

Adverbs

Adverbs modify, identify, or quantify verbs, adjectives, other adverbs, or clauses. They are used to tell when, where, how, or to what degree. Many adverbs end in *ly,* but some do not (always, never, not, well, and so on). Also remember that some adjectives end in *ly* (such as friendly and lonely). The five basic kinds of adverbs are adverbs of time, adverbs of place, adverbs of degree, adverbs of manner, and sentence adverbs.

Example

Matthew <u>recently</u> completed school.

Recently modifies the verb *completed.* This sentence demonstrates an **adverb of time.**

Some other common adverbs of time include:

again	first	now	usually
always	forever	once	weekly
before	late	sometimes	yearly
finally	never	tomorrow	yesterday

Example

Joshua sat <u>nearby</u>.

Nearby modifies *sat.* This is an **adverb of place.**

Adverbs of place tell about position or direction. Some common adverbs of place include:

above	downward	here	out
anywhere	east	left	past
away	everywhere	near	sideways
back	forward	nowhere	upstairs

Example

This was a <u>completely</u> unexpected event.

Completely modifies the adjective *unexpected*. This is an **adverb of degree**. It shows to what degree or extent the event was unexpected.

Some other common adverbs of degree include:

absolutely	greatly	otherwise	scarcely
almost	hardly	partly	somewhat
certainly	only	rather	too

Example

The onions for this recipe must be <u>finely</u> chopped.

In this sentence, *finely* modifies *chopped*. This is an **adverb of manner**. It explains how the onions must be chopped.

Other adverbs of manner include:

| adeptly | awkwardly | manually | officially |
| angrily | hilariously | mechanically | skillfully |

Example

<u>Fortunately</u>, the couple had tissues.

Fortunately modifies the independent clause *the couple had tissues*. This is considered a **sentence adverb** because it modifies the entire sentence.

There is also a group of words called **conjunctive adverbs.** Conjunctive adverbs modify an entire clause and express the connection in meaning between that clause and the preceding clause or sentence (however, likewise, and so on). They are commonly used as transitions between sentences. (For more about conjunctive adverbs, consult Lesson 1-6.)

Example

Matthew graduated from school. <u>However</u>, he needs to return his textbooks.

However shows the connection between the two independent clauses.

There are two common errors that occur with adverbs. Always check your work to avoid these errors.

> **Avoid double negatives. Only use one negative word to express a negative idea.**

Example:

Incorrect: I <u>never</u> ate <u>none</u> of those cookies.

Correct: I never ate <u>any</u> of those cookies.

> **Place adverbs of degree as close as possible to the words they modify. Misplaced modifiers make sentences confusing.**

Example:

Incorrect: He has <u>almost</u> completed <u>all</u> of his chores.

Correct: He has completed <u>almost all</u> of his chores.

Exercise 1-14

For each of the following sentences, identify and underline all of the adverbs.

Example: <u>Usually</u>, I <u>hurriedly</u> read the morning paper.

1. Very recently, I accepted a demanding job.

2. Realistically, I never should have taken this position.

3. The unusually stressful nature of the job left me completely exhausted.

4. This job quickly became tiring.

5. I very nearly collapsed one day.

6. I no longer felt well.

7. I reluctantly decided to respectfully resign.

8. Therefore, I needed more stimulating employment.

9. I happily entered the employment office.

10. Thankfully, they strategically solved my problem.

Comparatives and Superlatives

In addition to their basic form, many adjectives and adverbs have two other forms: the comparative and the superlative. The **comparative** form of an adjective or adverb compares *two* persons or things.

Examples

Barry is <u>more creative</u> than Rachel.

More creative compares two people.

Flying is <u>faster</u> than driving.

Faster compares two things.

The **superlative** form of an adjective or adverb compares *three or more* things.

Examples

Barry is the <u>most creative</u> of all the designers.

In this example, Barry is being compared to a group and deemed the *most creative*.

Flying is the <u>fastest</u> form of transportation.

Here, flying is compared to many other things.

Paula's wedding day was the <u>happiest</u> day of her life.

In this sentence, one day is compare to the rest of her life.

There are a few simple rules to form the comparative and superlative cases:

▷ If an adjective or adverb has one syllable, add *–er* to form the comparative or *–est* to form the superlative.

▷ If an adjective or adverb has more than one syllable, form the comparative by using *more* or form the superlative by using *most*.

▷ If an adjective ends in *y,* change the *y* to *i* and add *–er* to form the comparative or *–est* to form the superlative.

Look at the following chart for some examples.

	Adjective	Comparative	Superlative
One syllable	fast	faster	fastest
	hard	harder	hardest
	small	smaller	smallest
More than one syllable	beautiful	more beautiful	most beautiful
	talented	more talented	most talented
	wonderful	more wonderful	most wonderful
End in y	happy	happier	happiest
	lonely	lonelier	loneliest
	crazy	crazier	craziest

We must remember there are always rule-breakers. The most common here are probably *good* and *well*. *Good* is an **adjective** and uses *better* for comparative case and *best* for superlative. *Well* is an **adverb** but still uses the same *better* and *best* for comparative and superlative cases. Always be on the lookout for these anomalies!

Absolute or Incomparable Adjectives

There are some adjectives that are not capable of having a greater or lesser degree because they designate a state or condition. These adjectives are sometimes called **absolute adjectives.**

Examples

The Wooly Mammoth is <u>more extinct</u> than the Dodo bird.
One thing cannot be *more extinct* than another.

The tennis ball is <u>rounder</u> than the basketball.
One thing cannot be *rounder* than another.

Other absolute adjectives include:

absent	circular	dead	impossible
infinite	lost	missing	perfect
pregnant	square	white	unique

One important thing to remember is that although these adjectives are absolute, they can still be modified with adverbs such as *almost* or *nearly*.

There are two common errors that occur with the use of comparatives and superlatives. Be on the lookout for these errors.

Do not make a double comparison. In other words, do not use two forms of either the comparative or the superlative.

Example:

Incorrect: Our high school is <u>more bigger</u> than our middle school.

Correct: Our high school is <u>bigger</u> than our middle school.

Do not make an incomplete comparison. Use *other* or *else* when you compare one member of a group to the other group members.

Examples:

Incorrect: *The Deer Hunter* was better than <u>any</u> movie. *The Deer Hunter* is a movie.

Correct: *The Deer Hunter* was better than <u>any other</u> movie.

Incorrect: The girl earned better grades than <u>anyone</u>.

Correct: The girl earned better grades than <u>anyone else</u>.

Exercise 1-15

For each of the following sentences, change the adverb in bold to both the comparative form and the superlative form.

Example: A **frequently** attended event is the New York City Marathon.

a. It is *more frequently* attended than other events.

b. The race is the *most frequently* attended event in New York.

1. Participants in the New York City Marathon run **quickly.**

   a. Some run _____ than others.

   b. The _____ runners win medals.

2. These medals are **highly** honored by participants.

   a. The silver medal is _____ honored than the bronze medal.

   b. Of the three medals, the gold medal is the _____ honored.

3. Frequent participants of this race are **widely** known.

   a. The best performers are _____ known.

   b. The winners are the _____ known.

4. It is difficult to keep a **good** pace throughout the race.

   a. The top finishers will have kept a _____ pace than others.

   b. The winner will have kept the _____ pace overall.

5. As runners cross the finish line, times are **carefully** checked.

   a. Times for close runners are _____ checked.

   b. Times for photo-finishers are the _____ checked.

Lesson 1-5: Prepositions

Prepositions are words that express relationships between nouns or pronouns and other words in the sentence. They do not stand on their own; they are part of prepositional phrases. These phrases are dependent and usually end with a noun or a pronoun. They are used to designate placement, time, or space. Consult the chart of common prepositions.

Common Prepositions				
about	behind	from	out	until
above	below	in	outside	up
across	beneath	inside	over	upon
after	beside	into	past	with
along	beyond	like	regarding	within
among	by	near	since	without
around	down	of	through	
as	during	off	since	
at	except	on	toward	
before	for	onto	under	

Examples

   The paper fell <u>behind</u> the desk.

The preposition *behind* shows the relationship of space for the paper.

We will meet <u>before</u> class.

Before shows the relationship of time in this example.

She completed her task <u>with</u> ease.

With shows a relationship between the independent clause and *ease.*

Sometimes **prepositions** are **compound.** They act as prepositions, but consist of more than one word. Some are *apart from, according to, as well as, because of, by way of, on top of, due to, instead of, next to,* and *in front of.*

Examples

He looked thinner <u>because of</u> his height.

Because of is the compound preposition that shows a relationship between the independent clause and *his height,* the object of the preposition.

The candle sits <u>on top of</u> the table.

The prepositional phrase *on top of* shows the relationship of space in this example.

There are two common errors with prepositions. These errors occur frequently, so be careful.

Never end a clause with a preposition. Place the preposition at the beginning of the phrase.

Example:

Incorrect: Which box did this cereal come <u>from</u>?

Correct: <u>From which</u> box did this cereal come?

Incorrect: Which theater do you want to go <u>to</u>?

Correct: <u>To which</u> theater do you want to go?

Use prepositions consistently in a series.

Example:

Incorrect: The bus stopped <u>at</u> New York, Boston, and <u>at</u> Portland.

Correct: The bus stopped <u>at</u> New York, <u>at</u> Boston, and <u>at</u> Portland.

Correct: The bus stopped <u>at</u> New York, Boston, and Portland. (one preposition for the list)

Exercise 1-16

For each of the following sentences, identify and underline all of the prepositions.

Example: Look <u>under</u> the bed <u>for</u> your socks.

1. Be careful as you step off the train.

2. The step moves from the platform.

3. Step onto the platform with care.

4. Take the stairs up to the second floor.

5. Walk across the level and down the hallway.

6. Instead of entering the first office, look for the red door.

7. Beneath the sign, there is a large lever.

8. Place the lever against the wall.

9. Walk carefully because of construction.

10. Go through the doorway and into the office.

Lesson 1-6: Conjunctions

Conjunctions join other words or groups of words. They are connectives, and there are four types: **coordinating conjunctions, correlative conjunctions, conjunctive adverbs,** and **subordinating conjunctions.**

Coordinating Conjunctions

Coordinating conjunctions are used to link parts of a sentence that are of equal, or coordinate, value. They include *and, but, or, for,* and *nor* and can be used to connect or contrast words, phrases, or independent clauses. Remember that they are used **in lieu of** a comma, not **in addition to,** unless they join two independent clauses.

Examples

Do you want tea <u>or</u> coffee?

Or is used as a conjunction to introduce an alternative.

We like skiing <u>but</u> prefer snowboarding.

But is used to contrast the two sports.

Our son trims the hedges, <u>and</u> our daughter mows the grass.

In this example, *and* connects two independent clauses. Remember: You must use a coordinating conjunction in this case; a comma alone would make the sentence a run-on. (We'll get into more detail about run-ons in the next chapter.)

There are several errors associated with coordinating conjunctions.

> **Do not forget to use a coordinating conjunction between two main clauses. Otherwise, you have a run-on sentence.**

Example:

Incorrect: There is a sale at the shoe store, I bought two pairs of shoes.

Correct: There is a sale at the shoe store, <u>and</u> I bought two pairs of shoes.

> **Do not use *so* as a coordinating conjunction in writing. Use *and so.***

Example:

Incorrect: I enjoy movies, <u>so</u> I go to the theater a lot.

Correct: I enjoy movies, <u>and so</u> I go to the theater a lot.

> **Do not use a comma before the coordinating conjunction that links the two parts of a compound verb.**

Example:

Incorrect: We showered, and changed after our workout.

Correct: We showered and changed after our workout.

Exercise 1-17

For each of the following sentences, identify and underline all of the coordinating conjunctions.

Example: We have a son <u>and</u> a daughter.

1. The twins are charming and witty.

2. They enjoy playing but do not like schoolwork.

3. Frequently, they can be found playing basketball or soccer.

4. They did not eat dinner, nor did they clean their rooms.

5. Will the party be indoors or outdoors?

6. Our school offers music and art as electives.

7. We couldn't stay for dinner, but we stayed for dessert.

8. He left the door open not once but twice.

9. She would eat the ice cream but she's on a diet.

10. Would you rather take a walk or go for a bike ride?

Correlative Conjunctions

As do coordinating conjunctions, correlative conjunctions also join words and groups of words, but they make the relationship between these words or groups of words a little clearer. They include *both...and, either...or, just as...so, neither...nor, though...yet,* and *whether...or.*

Examples

Both you and I need new sneakers.

Both...and connects the compound subject.

You may have either a dog or a cat.

In this example, the correlative conjunction *either...or* connects the compound direct objects.

Exercise 1-18

For each of the following sentences, identify and underline all of the correlative conjunctions.

Example: Neither lunch nor dinner with be provided.

1. Whether you are in a car or on foot, you need to know where you're going.

2. Both the restaurant and the inn provide excellent service.

3. In either hot or cold weather, you should avoid too much sun exposure.

4. Neither food nor drink is allowed in the classroom.

5. You can eat your dinner with either chopsticks or a fork.

6. Just as you spend, so must you earn.

7. Whether Alan brings Judy or Jennifer, he will definitely come to the party.

8. Both Spanish and Italian are popular language courses.

9. Neither German nor Portuguese is available.

10. Guests can be served either in the dining room or in the living room.

Conjunctive Adverbs

Conjunctive adverbs are used to clarify the relationship between main clauses. They can be used to replace *and,* to replace *but,* to state a result, or to state equality. Some examples include *however, also, besides, moreover, furthermore, nevertheless, consequently, therefore, likewise,* and *similarly.* Conjunctive adverbs always require punctuation between the main clauses. (For more on punctuation, see Chapter 4.)

Examples

Each of the students in the program is different. They all share a love of the subject area, <u>however</u>.

The conjunctive adverb *however* replaces *but* in this case.

The pair looked guilty; <u>furthermore</u>, there were several pieces of evidence to back up my suspicions.

The conjunctive adverb *furthermore* replaces *and* in this case.

Marcia would make a terrific candidate for Senior Class President. Sandra, <u>equally</u>, has leadership qualities.

In this sentence, the conjunctive adverb *equally* shows equality between the subjects of each main clause.

Exercise 1-19

For each of the following sentences, identify and underline all of the conjunctive adverbs.

Example: I am not hungry; <u>besides</u>, I had a late lunch.

1. Free membership to the gym is available. However, it is only good for one month.

2. My neighbor is a jogger; similarly, her daughter enjoys long-distance running.

3. I gave birth to a baby last year; consequently, I moved to a larger apartment.

4. My office assistant retired; therefore, I hired a replacement.

5. I injured my ankle during the race. I finished the competition, nevertheless.

6. It is raining out; moreover, my umbrella is broken.

7. Carol was asked to leave the club; furthermore, she was told never to return.

8. Eddie bought a new house. His sister, likewise, moved.

9. The car had a flat tire; also, the rim was bent.

10. Andrea did not have time to eat; besides, she was not really hungry.

Subordinating Conjunctions

Subordinating conjunctions are words or groups of words used to join subordinated clauses to main clauses in a sentence. They help to clarify the relationship of time, place, condition, or reason. Some common subordinating conjunctions are *after, as, because, before, if, since, than, though, until, when, whenever, where,* and *while.* Notice that many of these words can also be other parts of speech, such as prepositions. It all depends on how the word is used in the sentence.

Examples

Where once there was a simple field, there now stands a building.

Where is the subordinating conjunction that joins the two clauses.

Birds continue to build nests in the same place until their eggs are disturbed.

Until is the subordinating conjunction that joins the two clauses.

Some subordinating conjunctions are **compound.** In other words, they are made up of more than one word. Some examples include *as long as, as far as, as soon as, for fear that, in order that, supposing that,* and *so that.*

Examples

He bought a new umbrella <u>so that</u> he would stay dry.

So that is the compound subordinating conjunction that connects the two main clauses.

He closed his windows <u>for fear that</u> it would rain.

For fear that is the compound subordinating conjunction that connects the two main clauses.

Exercise 1-20

For each of the following sentences, identify and underline all of the subordinating conjunctions.

Example: We will finish math <u>before</u> we begin science.

1. Travelers frequently carry their passports wherever they go.

2. Since its formation, the band has played many venues.

3. I tore my room apart in the hope that I would find my keys.

4. Erin bought a guitar though she never plays it.

5. He cooked dinner while she watched television.

6. Patricia threw the ball as far as she could.

7. Until midnight, the doors remained open.

8. She threw out the milk for fear it expired.

9. Though she needed help, Suzy rode her own bike.

10. Kyle would not leave until the dishes were washed.

Answers to Exercises

Exercise 1-1

1.	His <u>speech</u> touched the <u>nation</u>.	*common*	*collective*
2.	<u>Ms. Peterson</u> eats <u>melons</u>.	*proper*	*common*
3.	Frequently the <u>group</u> travels to <u>San Pedro</u>.	*collective*	*proper*
4.	The <u>audience</u> enjoyed the <u>show</u>.	*collective*	*common*
5.	<u>Thanksgiving</u> is always on a <u>Thursday</u>.	*proper*	*proper*
6.	My <u>brother</u> spoke to his <u>class</u>.	*common*	*collective*

7. Meet the <u>committee</u> at the <u>school</u>.   *collective*   *common*

8. Our <u>school</u> hired a new <u>principal</u>.   *collective*   *common*

9. The <u>game</u> is scheduled for <u>May</u>.   *common*   *proper*

10. <u>Beth</u> sang with the <u>chorus</u>.   *proper*   *collective*

Exercise 1-2

1.	berry	*berries*	11.	zoo	*zoos*
2.	echo	*echoes*	12.	apartment	*apartments*
3.	person	*people*	13.	company	*companies*
4.	roof	*roofs*	14.	box	*boxes*
5.	knife	*knives*	15.	piano	*pianos*
6.	answer	*answers*	16.	plant	*plants*
7.	income	*incomes*	17.	crutch	*crutches*
8.	bush	*bushes*	18.	baby	*babies*
9.	loaf	*loaves*	19.	taboo	*taboos*
10.	life	*lives*	20.	tomato	*tomatoes*

Exercise 1-3

1. (<u>He</u> / Him) and Kate want to be married.

2. A puddle lay between my car and (I / <u>me</u>).

3. After work, John and (<u>she</u> / her) went to the movies.

4. Before eating, (<u>they</u> / them) set the table.

5. She is taller than (<u>I</u> / me).

6. To (he / <u>him</u>), the fence seemed too high.

7. The town gave (we / <u>us</u>) permission to build a deck.

8. Charlie and (<u>we</u> / us) carried the newspapers.

9. He gave (she / <u>her</u>) a box of chocolates.

10. (<u>They</u> / them) never visit their neighbors.

Exercise 1-4

1. The girls play in <u>their</u> backyard.   *the girls*

2. After dinner, Eric and I played cards in <u>our</u> room.   *Eric and I*

3. The committee adjourned <u>its</u> session.   *the committee*

4. My cousins like <u>their</u> new home.   *my cousins*

5. There is food for <u>whoever</u> wants <u>it</u>.   *food*

6.   The playground had <u>its</u> equipment painted.   *the playground*

7.   The team lost interest when <u>its</u> coach yelled.   *team*

8.   The bride and groom danced <u>their</u> first dance.   *the bride and groom*

9.   Later, the two people enjoyed <u>their</u> time alone.   *people*

10. Arnold gave <u>his</u> wife a ring.   *Arnold*

Exercise 1-5

1.   The young boy bathed *himself*.

2.   People who find *themselves* lost should get directions.

3.   I know you consider *yourself* an expert in mathematics.

4.   The team roused *itself* before the big game.

5.   We treated *ourselves* to a new dishwasher.

6.   She told the students, "Be good to *yourselves*."

7.   I bought *myself* a new car.

8.   Annie never lets *herself* feel gloomy.

9.   Tom's dog scratched *itself* on the ear.

10. The teacher frequently spoke to *himself/herself*.

Exercise 1-6

1.   Anyone can succeed if *he / she / he or she* tries.

2.   Everyone must clean *his / her / his or her* work area.

3.   No one needs to worry if *he / she / he or she* is prepared.

4.   The room was cold today so nobody took off *his / her / his or her* coat.

5.   Did the kids leave *their* socks on the floor?

6.   Anybody who leaves the room must wear *his / her / his or her* nametag.

7.   I need somebody to bring *his / her / his or her* copy of the documents.

8.   Nobody move from *his / her / his or her* seat!

9.   Can anyone feel *his / her / his or her* toes?

10. When one makes eggs, *he / she / he or she* should watch for shells.

Exercise 1-7

1.   To <u>whom</u> do you wish to speak?

2.   The story is about <u>a</u> boy who wants a puppy.

3.   <u>This</u> problem requires a solution.

4.   By the time we saw <u>that</u> traffic jam, we were already stuck.

5. <u>Whom</u> is Alison trying to find?

6. Patty was wearing <u>a</u> black dress.

7. Her child had <u>an</u> angelic face.

8. During <u>those</u> long classes, the students became tired.

9. For <u>whom</u> is this message?

10. If you wish to learn more about <u>that</u> event, consult the newspaper.

Exercise 1-8

1. One of the children lost *his / her / his or her* toys.

2. Firefighters and police officers frequently donate *their* time.

3. Chris is older than *I / you / she / he / we /they*.

4. Either of the parents can show *his / her / his or her* identification.

5. Neither can of peas is worth *its* cost.

6. The gift means more to Stephen than to *me / you / him / her / us / them*.

7. Ella and Patrick brought *their* suitcase.

8. We sometimes feel others are smarter than *we*.

9. She is just as funny as *I / you / she / he / we /they*.

10. After studying, every one of the girls closed *her* books.

Exercise 1-9

1. I <u>should clean</u> the house.

2. We <u>do need</u> a rug.

3. Margaret <u>does read</u> well.

4. Jerry <u>could have been</u> a rock star.

5. She <u>has been driving</u> for three hours.

6. He <u>will like</u> the movie.

7. Marcus <u>would</u> not <u>be happy</u>.

8. David <u>can dance</u>.

9. It <u>would be</u> fun.

10. Mark never <u>eats</u> dinner.

Exercise 1-10

1. Emily <u>is</u> an experienced chef.

2. She <u>seems</u> adept at many things.

3. Her food <u>smells</u> appealing.

4. The dishes <u>are</u> appetizing.

5. It all <u>looks</u> delicious.

6. Watching her cook <u>has become</u> impossible.

7. I <u>feel</u> ravenous.

8. Her friends <u>are</u> impressed with Emily's talents.

9. They <u>look</u> proud.

10. Emily <u>feels</u> satisfied.

Exercise 1-11

1.	The couple <u>enjoys</u> dancing.	*transitive verb*
2.	They never <u>tire</u>.	*intransitive verb*
3.	They <u>are</u> charming on the dance floor.	*linking verb*
4.	Dancing <u>is</u> fun.	*linking verb*
5.	After dinner, other couples <u>will dance</u>.	*intransitive verb*
6.	They <u>seem</u> youthful.	*linking verb*
7.	The music <u>sounds</u> beautiful.	*linking verb*
8.	The couple gracefully <u>crosses</u> the floor.	*transitive verb*
9.	The music <u>ends</u>.	*intransitive verb*
10.	The couple <u>opens</u> the door.	*transitive verb*

Exercise 1-12

1.	<u>Gardening</u> is Alice's favorite hobby.	*gerund*
2.	Every year, she looks forward to <u>planting</u> season.	*present participle*
3.	First, she likes <u>to weed</u> her vegetable garden.	*infinitive (noun)*
4.	She knows when the soil is ready <u>to produce</u>.	*infinitive (adverb)*
5.	She waits for the right time <u>to plant</u>.	*infinitive (adjective)*
6.	She can be found <u>sowing</u> seeds in her yard.	*gerund*
7.	<u>Dried</u> seeds are scattered.	*past participle*
8.	Birds like <u>to eat</u> the seeds.	*infinitive (noun)*
9.	<u>Tending</u> her garden keeps Alice happy.	*gerund*
10.	The <u>blossoming</u> produce provides nourishment.	*present participle*

Exercise 1-13

1. The <u>slender</u> child sat on a <u>large</u> precipice.

2. The <u>beautiful</u> sky became <u>cloudy</u>.

3. Inclement weather can be dangerous.

4. After several hours, his mother became worried.

5. She telephoned the local police to report the wayward child.

6. An alert officer noticed the helpless child.

7. Although they faced extreme danger, they took a calculated risk.

8. The daring officers rescued that child.

9. Fortunately, the child learned an invaluable lesson.

10. The remorseful child discovered a newfound appreciation for police officers.

Exercise 1-14

1. Very recently, I accepted a demanding job.

2. Realistically, I never should have taken this position.

3. The unusually stressful nature of the job left me completely exhausted.

4. This job quickly became tiring.

5. I very nearly collapsed one day.

6. I no longer felt well.

7. I reluctantly decided to respectfully resign.

8. Therefore, I needed more stimulating employment.

9. I happily entered the employment office.

10. Thankfully, they strategically solved my problem.

Exercise 1-15

1. Participants in the New York City Marathon run **quickly.**
    a. Some run *more quickly* than others.
    b. The *quickest* runners win medals.

2. These medals are **highly** honored by participants.
    a. The silver medal is *more highly* honored than the bronze medal.
    b. Of the three medals, the gold medal is the *highest* honored.

3. Frequent participants of this race are **widely** known.
    a. The best performers are *more widely* known.
    b. The winners are the *most widely* known.

4. It is difficult to keep a **good** pace throughout the race.
    a. The top finishers will have kept a *better* pace than others.
    b. The winner will have kept the *best* pace overall.

5. As runners cross the finish line, times are **carefully** checked.

    a. Times for close runners are *more carefully* checked.

    b. Times for photo-finishers are the *most carefully* checked.

Exercise 1-16

1. Be careful as you step <u>off</u> the train.
2. The step moves <u>from</u> the platform.
3. Step <u>onto</u> the platform <u>with</u> care.
4. Take the stairs <u>up to</u> the second floor.
5. Walk <u>across</u> the level and <u>down</u> the hallway.
6. <u>Instead of</u> entering the first office, look <u>for</u> the red door.
7. <u>Beneath</u> the sign, there is a large lever.
8. Place the lever <u>against</u> the wall.
9. Walk carefully <u>because of</u> construction.
10. Go <u>through</u> the doorway and <u>into</u> the office.

Exercise 1-17

1. The twins are charming <u>and</u> witty.
2. They enjoy playing <u>but</u> do not like schoolwork.
3. Frequently, they can be found playing basketball <u>or</u> soccer.
4. They did not eat dinner, <u>nor</u> did they clean their rooms.
5. Will the party be indoors <u>or</u> outdoors?
6. Our school offers music <u>and</u> art as electives.
7. We couldn't stay for dinner, <u>but</u> we stayed for dessert.
8. He left the door open not once <u>but</u> twice.
9. She would eat the ice cream <u>but</u> she's on a diet.
10. Would you rather take a walk <u>or</u> go for a bike ride?

Exercise 1-18

1. <u>Whether</u> you are in a car <u>or</u> on foot, you need to know where you're going.
2. <u>Both</u> the restaurant <u>and</u> the inn provide excellent service.
3. In <u>either</u> hot <u>or</u> cold weather, you should avoid too much sun exposure.
4. <u>Neither</u> food <u>nor</u> drink is allowed in the classroom.
5. You can eat your dinner with <u>either</u> chopsticks <u>or</u> a fork.
6. <u>Just</u> as you spend, <u>so</u> must you earn.

7. <u>Whether</u> Alan brings Judy <u>or</u> Jennifer, he will definitely come to the party.

8. <u>Both</u> Spanish <u>and</u> Italian are popular language courses.

9. <u>Neither</u> German <u>nor</u> Portuguese is available.

10. Guests can be served <u>either</u> in the dining room <u>or</u> in the living room.

Exercise 1-19

1. Free membership to the gym is available. <u>However</u>, it is only good for one month.

2. My neighbor is a jogger; <u>similarly</u>, her daughter enjoys long-distance running.

3. I gave birth to a baby last year; <u>consequently</u>, I moved to a larger apartment.

4. My office assistant retired; <u>therefore</u>, I hired a replacement.

5. I injured my ankle during the race. I finished the competition, <u>nevertheless</u>.

6. It is raining out; <u>moreover</u>, my umbrella is broken.

7. Carol was asked to leave the club; <u>furthermore</u>, she was told never to return.

8. Eddie bought a new house. His sister, <u>likewise</u>, moved.

9. The car had a flat tire; <u>also</u>, the rim was bent.

10. Andrea did not have time to eat; <u>besides</u>, she was not really hungry.

Exercise 1-20

1. Travelers frequently carry their passports <u>wherever</u> they go.

2. <u>Since</u> its formation, the band has played many venues.

3. I tore my room apart <u>in the hope that</u> I would find my keys.

4. Erin bought a guitar <u>though</u> she never plays it.

5. He cooked dinner <u>while</u> she watched television.

6. Patricia threw the ball <u>as far as</u> she could.

7. <u>Until</u> midnight, the doors remained open.

8. She threw out the milk <u>for fear</u> it expired.

9. <u>Though</u> she needed help, Suzy rode her own bike.

10. Kyle would not leave <u>until</u> the dishes were washed.

Phrases, Clauses, and Sentences

In language, we use words to express our thoughts and ideas. The words we use are clustered together in phrases, clauses, and sentences. A phrase is a group of words that does not contain a predicate. In other words, no action takes place. A clause contains a predicate and is sometimes a complete sentence; however, not all clauses are complete sentences. A sentence is a group of words that expresses a complete thought. In order to be complete, each sentence must contain at least one subject and one verb. Sentences vary in type, length, structure, and purpose, but they contain one thought or idea. This chapter examines the different forms of sentences and their purposes, highlights the types of phrases and clauses, and examines their roles in sentences.

Lesson 2-1: Types of Sentences

Sentences can differ in length and serve various purposes. Some are lengthy and contain many phrases and clauses, whereas others are simple and terse. Some sentences ask questions, and others answer questions. Although there seems to be many varieties in structure, there are only four basic types of sentences. The first kind of sentence is **declarative**. It makes a statement. This is the most common type of sentence. Notice that it ends in a period.

Example

The dog is asleep. The young puppy is sleeping soundly.

Both of these sentences are simple declarative sentences. Each sentence simply states a fact.

A sentence that asks a question has a different name. This is called an **interrogative** sentence. The interrogative sentence always ends in a question mark.

Example

Who ate the melon? Why does he seem unfriendly?

These two sentences are simple interrogative sentences. They both ask questions.

The third type of sentence is **imperative**. The imperative sentence gives a command or contains a sense of urgency. It usually ends with a period, but it can sometimes end with an exclamation mark. Because the imperative sentence frequently gives a command, the nominative pronoun, or subject of the sentence, is sometimes omitted. In those cases, the subject is implied.

Example

You are going to miss the bus. Never talk to strangers.

These two simple imperative sentences convey a feeling of importance and urgency. In the second sentence, the subject is omitted. The nominative pronoun *you* is understood.

The fourth and final type of sentence is the **exclamatory** sentence. This type of sentence expresses strong emotion, such as surprise or disbelief. The exclamatory sentence always ends in an exclamation mark. This variety of sentence also can have an understood subject. Therefore, the nominative pronoun is frequently omitted.

Example

You scared me! Watch out!

These two examples are both simple exclamatory sentences. In the second sentence, the nominative pronoun *you* is implied.

Exercise 2-1

For each of the following sentences, determine whether it is declarative, interrogative, exclamatory, or imperative, and write the answer in the space provided.

Example: Finish your homework. *declarative sentence*

1. Answer the phone. _____

2. Who is in the car? _____

3. My hand hurts! _____

4. The lunches are packed. _____

5. What did you say? _____

6. Stop it now! _____

7. The sun is shining. _____

8. Please clean your room. _____

9. Where are the documents? _____

10. The mail has arrived. _____

Lesson 2-2: The Simple Sentence

It is important to remember that a cluster of words is not necessarily a sentence. A sentence must express a complete thought and contain a subject and a predicate. The subject explains who or what the sentence is about. The predicate asks something about the subject or tells the subject to act and it must contain or be a verb.

The Simple Subject

The subject of a sentence can be a single word or a group of words. A subject made up of a group of words is called the complete subject. The complete subject always includes one key term. That important term is called the simple subject. Of course, a simple subject can occur by itself. The simple subject can be a common noun, a proper noun, a compound noun, a pronoun, a gerund, or an infinitive.

Examples

The <u>wind</u> blows.

In this sentence, *wind* is the simple subject. It stands alone and has no modifiers, other than the determiner (*the*).

The icy-cold <u>wind</u> from the North blows.

Wind is still the simple subject, although it is surrounded by modifiers.

The adjective (*icy-cold*) and the prepositional phrase (*from the North*) are part of the complete subject, but the simple subject remains the same. The simple subject never occurs within a prepositional phrase. Prepositional phrases can contain nouns, but they do not act as subjects.

Exercise 2-2

For each of the following sentences, underline the complete subject. Identify the simple subject and write it in the space provided.

Example: <u>New businesses</u> have opened recently.   *businesses*

1. Pet stores are booming._____

2. More and more locations are opening. _____

3. These new stores carry a variety of animals. _____

4. Several dog breeds can be found at these stores._____

5. Some people buy fish and birds. _____

6. Many types of pet toys are available for purchase. _____

7. A pet owner must choose carefully. _____

8. My personal favorites are the kittens._____

9. These playful creatures are adorable. _____

10. All pets are important to their owners._____

The Simple Predicate

The predicate tells what the subject does or is. The predicate must include either an action verb or a linking verb. The verb alone is called a simple predicate. The verb plus other objects or linking verbs is called a complete predicate. A predicate must always have a verb, not just a participle or an infinitive.

Examples

Students <u>learn</u>.

In this sentence, *learn* is the simple predicate. *Learn* is an intransitive verb and is a complete predicate on its own.

Students <u>learn</u> addition before multiplication.

In this sentence, *learn* is the simple predicate, but the phrase *learn addition before multiplication* is the complete predicate.

Exercise 2-3

For each of the following sentence, underline the complete predicate. Identify the simple predicate and write it in the space provided.

Example: I <u>love roses</u>.   *love*

1. Roses are beautiful flowers.   _____

2. There are so many varieties.   _____

3. Most roses bloom in the spring.   _____

4. The colors of roses are vibrant and deep.   _____

5. Their scent fills the room.   _____

6. My garden is filled with roses.   _____

7. Roses wither quickly.   _____

8. Their thorns protect them from nature's
    predators.   _____

9. Most varieties require full sunlight.   _____

10. Is there anything more lovely than a rose?   _____

If a group of words begins with a capital letter and finishes with end punctuation but does not have both a subject and a predicate, it is a **sentence fragment.** This means there might be a subject and a participle or infinitive, but it is still not complete.

Examples

Poorly made products.

This is a fragment. It contains a noun (*products*) and a participle (*made*), but there is no predicate.

<u>Poorly made products</u> are sold in this store.

Here, the subject is *poorly made products* and the complete predicate is *are sold in this store.*

To ski in the mountains.

This is also a fragment; it is an infinitive phrase. It contains the infinitive (*to ski*) but there is neither a subject nor a predicate.

Mark wants to ski in the mountains.

This is now a complete sentence. *Mark* is the subject and *wants* is the transitive verb. The infinitive phrase (*to ski in the mountains*) becomes the direct object of the verb.

Always use full sentences in writing. Here is one suggestion to avoid sentence fragments:

> **Be sure that each sentence contains an action verb or a linking verb, not just an infinitive or participle.**

Example:

Incorrect: People running.

Correct: People are running.

Incorrect: People to run.

Correct: People like to run.

Exercise 2-4

Determine whether each of the following numbered items is a complete sentence or a sentence fragment. Write *S* for a sentence or *F* for fragment in the space provided.

Example: *F*   Pilots flying in the air.

_____ 1. A new club has started at our school.

_____ 2. The Debate Club beginning.

_____ 3. To debate in the new club after school.

_____ 4. Many students have joined.

_____ 5. Interesting topics discussed.

_____ 6. Three matches have been won.

_____ 7. Meeting in the classroom near the main office.

_____ 8. The club's president is Walter Smith.

_____ 9. He running the debates in the auditorium.

_____ 10. Come join the club.

Objects and Complements

Simple sentences contain only one subject, which can be either simple or compound, and one predicate, which can be simple or complete; however, simple sentences can contain other elements. Sentences can be simple and still contain direct objects, indirect objects, subject complements, or object complements. Each of these elements serves different roles in sentences. A simple sentence may contain one or more of these elements.

▶ **Direct object.** This is a noun or pronoun that receives the action of a transitive verb. The direct object answers the question *what?* or *who?* in the sentence.

Example

The girl carried <u>a toy</u>.

In this sentence, *a toy* is the direct object. It answers the question of what the girl carried.

▶ **Indirect object.** This is a noun or pronoun that identifies to what or whom or for what or whom a transitive verb's action is performed.

Example

Ellen gave <u>Mark</u> a ride home.

In this sentence, *Mark* is the indirect object. It identifies to whom was give the ride.

▶ **Subject complement.** A complement is a word or group of words that completes the predicate in a sentence. A subject complement follows a linking verb and renames or describes the subject. It can be a predicate noun, a predicate adjective, and, in a few cases, a predicate adverb.

Example

Andrea was <u>unhappy</u>.

Unhappy is the subject complement (predicate adjective) that describes the subject.

▶ **Object complement.** An object complement renames or describes a direct object. It can be a noun or an adjective.

Example

I consider him a guest.

In this example, *a guest* (noun) renames the direct object (*him*).

Although simple sentences contain only one subject and one predicate, they can vary in length and style. In each of the following sentences, the subject remains the same, but the predicate changes. Remember that each of these examples is a simple sentence.

Examples

Trees bloom.
subject + verb

This small sentence is complete because is contains both a subject and a verb.

Trees grow fruit.
subject + verb + direct object

This sentence contains the subject, the transitive verb (*grow*), and the direct object (*fruit*).

Trees provide farmers income.
subject + verb + indirect object + direct object

In this sentence, there is both an indirect object (*farmers*) and a direct object (*income*). *Income* answers the question of what *trees provide* and is therefore the direct object of this sentence. *Farmers* answers the question of to whom the trees provide income and is therefore the indirect object.

Trees make yards attractive.
subject + verb + direct object + object complement
(adjective)

This sentence is an example of the direct object (*yards*) taking an object complement (*attractive*). *Attractive* is an adjective that modifies the direct object.

Trees make oxygen a reality.
subject + verb + direct object + object complement
(noun)

This sentence also contains an object complement, but it is a noun. *Reality* is the noun that modifies the direct object (*oxygen*).

> Trees are shrubbery.
> subject + linking verb + predicate noun

A linking verb must join a subject with a subject complement. In this example, there is a predicate noun (*providers*) complementing the subject (*trees*).

> Trees are beautiful.
> subject + linking verb + predicate adjective

In this example, there is a predicate adjective (*beautiful*) as a subject complement for *trees*.

> Trees are everywhere.
> subject + linking verb + predicate adverb

In this sentence, the predicate adverb (*everywhere*) is the subject complement for trees.

> Trees seem to flourish.
> subject + linking verb + infinitive

In this example, the infinitive (*to flourish*) acts as a subject complement for *trees*.

> Trees are in the fields.
> subject + linking verb + prepositional phrase

This sentence uses the prepositional phrase (*in the fields*) as a subject complement for *trees*.

> There are trees.
> subject + linking verb (inverted)

This is a simple inversion of the subject and the verb. A sentence such as this is grammatically correct; however, make sure it is not redundant. A simple sentence such as this, adding no specific information, can and should usually be eliminated from formal writing.

> Trees are planted by horticulturalists.
> passive voice

This sentence is written in the passive voice. Passive voice can be used for effect, but use it with caution. It is usually considered inaccurate. In most cases, the sentence should assert: Horticulturalists plant trees. *Horticulturalists* is the subject, and therefore should take the verb (*to plant*).

In some cases, such as technical writing, the passive voice is appropriate. However, in most cases it is not suitable. Therefore, double-check your sentences when you notice the preposition *by*. Make sure the subject takes the action of the sentence.

Exercise 2-5

For each of the following sentences, underline the complete predicate, and determine the subject, types of verbs, objects, and modifiers.

Example: The swimmers <u>are preparing</u> to race.

   subject + linking verb + infinitive

1. Swimming is fun.

2. Swimmers practice strokes.

3. Swimmers are in the water.

4. Swimming is healthy.

5. Swimmers seem to glide.

6. Swimmers make their strokes tight.

7. Swimmers are supported by their coaches.

8. Swimmers are muscular.

9. Practice gives swimmers an advantage.

10. Swimmers succeed.

The Compound Subject

Some sentences contain compound subjects. This means the sentence has two or more subjects joined by a coordinating conjunction (*and, but, or*) or a correlative conjunction (*both...and, either...or, neither...nor*). (For more about coordinating and correlative conjunctions, consult Lesson 1-6.) Both parts of the compound subject share the verb. The action verb or the linking verb of a sentence must agree in number with the subject. Not all compound subjects are plural, even though they have more than one part. To make the verb agree with a compound subject, you must pay attention to the conjunction joining the parts of the subject as well as the meaning of the subject.

Examples

Alice and Mary enjoy dancing.

This sentence contains a compound subject (*Alice, Mary*) with a coordinating conjunction (*and*). Note that the verb agrees in number with the plural subject.

Neither Alice nor Mary likes jogging.

This example has a compound subject with a correlative conjunction (*neither, nor*). The correlative conjunction in this case creates a third-person singular subject, and the verb shows agreement.

Alice, Mary, and Stephanie live together.

In this example, there are three parts to the compound subject. Notice the comma after the first two parts, but there is no comma after the last item in the series.

Exercise 2-6

For each of the following sentences, identify and underline the compound subjects.

Example: Regions and states are known for different attributes.

1. Florida and California are known for their citrus fruit.

2. Skiing and snowboarding are popular in Colorado.

3. Neither Alaska nor Washington is known for balmy weather.

4. Either New York or Illinois can provide big-city adventure.

5. Not California but Nevada has large gambling metropolises.

6. Delaware and New Jersey provide Atlantic beaches for swimmers.

7. Rodeos and horse shows are plentiful in Texas.

8. The badlands and Mount Rushmore can be found in South Dakota.

9. Residents and visitors enjoy the culture of Louisiana.

10. Mountains and valleys make scenic Tennessee so beautiful.

The Compound Predicate

Sentences can also contain **compound predicates.** This means the sentence has two or more verbs joined by a coordinating or correlative conjunction that share the same subject. Compound predicates can also consist of two or more linking verbs.

Examples

Mary also <u>walks</u>, <u>shops</u>, and <u>cycles</u>.

This sentence has a simple subject (*Mary*) and a compound predicate (*walks, shops, cycles*) with a coordinating conjunction (*and*).

Alice neither <u>walks</u> nor <u>cycles</u>.

This example contains a compound predicate (*walks, cycles*) with a correlative conjunction (*nor*).

Alice <u>is not and never will be</u> an athlete.

This example contains the linking verbs *is not* and *never will be*.

Exercise 2-7

For each of the following sentences, identify and underline the compound predicates.

Example: Cooks <u>chop and slice</u> their vegetables and meats.

1. Chefs sauté, simmer, and broil dishes.

2. The children do not eat nor drink in the living room.

3. Evan is and always will be a practical joker.

4. Students read, write, and edit their essays.

5. After lunch, the wait staff cleared and cleaned the tables.

6. She can be and should be the next president.

7. The disgruntled players criticized and challenged the umpire.

8. Her friends always disagree and argue over television shows.

9. John frequently travels and relocates for business.

10. Ella wants and deserves a raise from her employer.

Sentences with compound subjects and/or compound predicates can still be considered simple sentences. Coordinating conjunctions and correlative conjunctions link together the subjects or predicates. A sentence can have a compound subject or predicate and not be a compound or complex sentence. Compound and complex sentences will be covered in more detail later on in this chapter.

Exercise 2-8

For each of the following sentences, find and underline the conjunctions. In the space provided, write whether the sentence contains a compound subject or a compound predicate.

Example: Both children <u>and</u> adults need activities. *compound subject*

1. Parks, zoos, and museums are fun places to visit. _____

2. Families can either picnic or dine indoors. _____

3. Children are not only having fun but are learning. _____

4. Neither rain nor snow can prevent the fun. _____

5. Both adults and children enjoy the day. _____

6. The zebras eat and play. _____

7. The visitors are laughing and smiling. _____

8. Both animals and humans deserve a clean environment. _____

9. Do you see and hear the elephants? _____

10. Not people but animals live at the zoo. _____

Lesson 2-3: Phrases

A phrase is a group of words that lacks a subject, a predicate, or both. Phrases have different roles in sentences, but they cannot stand on their own as sentences. There are several types of phrases, including noun phrases, verb phrases, prepositional phrases, verbal phrases, absolute phrases, and appositive phrases. Theses phrases are used to add information to the sentence or to enhance the meaning of the sentence.

Example

The ravenous man will eat oatmeal in the morning.

This sentence contains a noun phrase as the subject, a verb phrase that is the participle, and a prepositional phrase as an adverb.

This chapter discusses the different types of phrases and how they are used in sentences.

Noun Phrases

A noun phrase consists of a noun and all its modifiers. Just as a noun alone can, it can function as a subject, an object, or a complement. (For more about nouns, see Lesson 1-1.)

Examples

Daring photographers take pictures.

In this example, a noun phase is the subject.

Photographers prefer cooperative subjects.

Here, the noun phrase is the object of the sentence.

Photographers are highly skilled.

In this sentence, the noun phrase is a subject complement.

Verb Phrases

A verb phrase consists of the main verb and all of its auxiliary verbs. It can only function as a predicate in the sentence. (For more about verbs and verb phrases, consult Lesson 1-3.)

Examples

Allison has been studying medicine.

This sentence contains a simple subject, a verb phrase, and a simple object.

She will become a doctor.

This example has a simple subject, a verb phrase, and a complement.

Prepositional Phrases

A prepositional phrase includes a preposition, a noun or pronoun as the object of the preposition, and any modifiers of the object. It begins with a preposition and usually ends with a noun or a pronoun. This type of phrase usually functions as an adjective or adverb. Occasionally, a prepositional phrase acts as a noun. Prepositional phrases can be used anywhere in a sentence. Sometimes a prepositional phrase is part of the subject, and sometimes it is part of the predicate. The prepositional phrase itself can be the subject of the sentence, but the subject can never occur within the prepositional phrase. (For more about prepositions, see Lesson 1-5 on page 46.)

Examples

Our neighbors <u>to the west</u> have a dog.

This phrase acts as an adjective; it modifies *neighbors.*

<u>In the evening</u>, you can hear the dog bark.

In this sentence, the prepositional phrase acts as an adverb.

The quietest time is <u>after dinner.</u>

The prepositional phrase in this example acts as a noun.

Exercise 2-9

For each of the following sentences, determine if the underlined phrase is a noun phrase, a verb phrase, or a prepositional phrase.

Example: <u>After lunch</u>, the mother rests.   *prepositional phrase*

1. The house is quiet <u>in the afternoon</u>.   _____

2. The children <u>are napping</u>.   _____

3. The <u>quiet house</u> is peaceful.   _____

4. I <u>will be entertaining</u> tonight.   _____

5. The people are gathering <u>near the door</u>.   _____

6. By tomorrow, the festival <u>will be over</u>.   _____

7. The <u>unobtrusive guest</u> slipped out the door.   _____

8. The couple <u>will have been married</u> two
   years in April.   _____

9. The garden is overrun <u>with weeds</u>.   _____

10. The <u>peevish child</u> ran into the yard.   _____

Verbal Phrases

Verbal phrases include a verbal and any modifiers, objects, or complements. They function as nouns, adjectives, or adverbs but not as the predicate of the sentence. The different types of verbal phrases are **participial, gerund,** and **infinitive.** (For more about verbals, see Lesson 1-3.)

Participial phrases consist of a present participle or a past participle and any modifiers, objects, or complements. They always function as adjectives.

Examples

A child <u>singing in the show</u> received applause.

This phrase contains a present participle and modifies *child.*

<u>Finished with the song</u>, the child left the stage.

The participial phrase in this sentence contains a past participle and also acts as an adjective.

Gerund phrases consist of a gerund and any modifiers, objects, or complements. This kind of phrase acts as a noun.

Examples

<u>A loud banging</u> came from my kitchen.

The gerund phrase in this sentence is the subject.

The workmen were found <u>hammering the floor</u>.

In this example, the gerund phrase acts as the direct object of the sentence.

Infinitive phrases consist of an infinitive and any modifiers, objects, or complements. These types of phrases can function as adjectives, adverbs, or nouns.

Examples

The instructor is a good person <u>to answer that question</u>.

The infinitive phrase here acts as an adjective, modifying *person.*

To answer a question, respond promptly.

This sentence contains an infinitive phrase as an adjective.

My job is to be a leader.

In this sentence the infinitive phrase is a noun acting as a subject complement.

Exercise 2-10

For each of the underlined verbal phrases, determine whether it is participial, gerund, or infinitive and write the answer in the space provided.

Example: She likes underline working in the sunshine.   *gerund phrase*

1. To become a lawyer takes years of schooling.   _____

2. He enjoys drinking hot cocoa in cold weather.   _____

3. The woman leading the discussion is charismatic.   _____

4. A puppy needs attentive nurturing.   _____

5. The flyer stapled to the light pole advertised
    a sale.   _____

6. The doctor needed to consult a colleague.   _____

7. Finished with college visits, Jay had time to relax.   _____

8. To enter the building, go to the side door.   _____

9. Questioning data is crucial for analysis.   _____

10. Return the book to the shelf labeled "Used."   _____

Absolute Phrases

An absolute phrase usually includes a noun or a pronoun in addition to a participle. This type of phrase modifies the entire sentence rather than a specific word. An absolute phrase is usually set apart from the rest of the sentence with commas.

Examples

The dinner ended, the guests leaving the table.

The absolute phrase here uses a present participle and modifies the rest of the sentence.

My training completed, I began my first assignment as an analyst.

This example uses a past participle in the absolute phrase.

Appositive Phrases

A noun that renames the noun or pronoun that immediately precedes it is called an **appositive.** Therefore, a noun phrase that restates the noun or pronoun it follows is called an appositive phrase.

Examples

My sister, a levelheaded woman, always weighs all of her options before making an important decision.

The appositive phrase here renames *my sister.*

Steve had only one option, to find a new job.

This example contains an appositive phrase that renames *option.*

Exercise 2-11

Expand each of the following sentences using either an absolute phrase or an appositive phrase.

Example: Jennifer is a scientist.   *Jennifer, my sister, is a scientist.*

1. Put on the coat. _____

2. Sheila frequently bakes. _____

3. The teacher went home. _____

4. My brother flies airplanes. _____

5. Angela listens to music. _____

6. Herbert walks. _____

7. I drained the tub. _____

8. Teresa traveled abroad. _____

9. Danny sees his brother. _____

10. Rose needed an iron. _____

Lesson 2-4: Clauses

A clause is a group of words that contains both a subject and a predicate. Clauses can be divided into two categories. First, there are independent clauses, also known as main clauses. Every sentence must contain at least one independent clause. Independent clauses are able stand on their own as complete sentences. They can also be connected to other independent clauses or dependent clauses, the second category of clauses.

Dependent clauses, or subordinate clauses, contain both a subject and a predicate, but they are fragments. They begin with either a subordinating conjunction (because, although, that, and so on) or a relative pronoun (who, which, whatever, and so forth). Subordinate clauses are unable to exist by themselves; they must be connected to an independent clause. These clauses function as nouns, adjectives, or adverbs.

Examples

The <u>boy cries</u>.

This clause is independent; it is a complete sentence. This clause contains both a subject (*boy*) and a predicate (*cries*).

After the <u>movie ends</u>.

This clause is dependent; it is an incomplete sentence. The clause contains a subject (*movie*) and a predicate (*ends*), but it cannot stand alone as a sentence because it begins with a subordinating conjunction.

Noun Clauses

Noun clauses are groups of words that act as nouns. They can function as subjects, direct objects, subject complements, or objects of prepositions. Noun clauses usually begin with *how, that, what, whatever, when, where, whether, which, whichever, who, whom, whomever,* or *whose.*

Examples

<u>How he supports himself</u> is important to her.

This noun clause is the subject of the sentence.

She asked <u>why he was crying</u>.

This subordinate noun clause is the direct object of the sentence.

His answer was that he felt betrayed.

This sentence has a noun clause for the subject complement.

He felt anxious about whatever came next.

The noun clause in this example is the object of the preposition.

Adjective Clauses

Adjective clauses are groups of words that act as adjectives in the sentence. They modify nouns and pronouns. In most cases they immediately follow the words that they modify. Adjective clauses usually begin with *that, when, where, which, who, whom, whose,* or *why.* Sometimes the subordinating word is omitted in these clauses.

Examples

The store manager, who is in charge of produce, inspected the apples.

This sentence contains an adjective clause that modifies *manager.*

The store where we bought the shoes closed recently.

In this example, the adjective clause modifies *store.*

There is one place (that) I intend to visit.

In this sentence, the subordinating word (*that*) can be omitted.

Adverb Clauses

Adverb are groups of words that act as adverbs. These clauses modify verbs, adjectives, or other adverbs. Adverb clauses begin with a subordinating conjunction.

Examples

We sat where we could find an empty table.

This adverb clause modifies the verb *sat.*

The test was easier than I'd ever seen.

This adverb clause modifies the adjective *easier.*

I adjusted as quickly as I could to my new home.

This adverb clause modifies the adverb *quickly.*

Exercise 2-12

For each of the underlined dependent clauses, determine whether it is a noun clause, an adjective clause, or an adverbial clause and write the answer in the space provided.

Example: I jumped <u>as I heard the siren</u>.　　　　*adverb clause*

1. We packed <u>when we heard the news</u>.　　　_____

2. The house <u>where I grew up</u> has been sold.　_____

3. She responded <u>when he addressed her</u>.　　_____

4. I opened the box as carefully <u>as I could</u>.　_____

5. The plane, <u>which had a damaged tailfin</u>, landed safely.　　　　　　　　　　　_____

6. The key was <u>where I had left it</u>.　　　　_____

7. <u>Whoever needs a place to stay</u> is welcome.　_____

8. He saved <u>in order to buy a boat</u>.　　　_____

9. They gave her <u>whatever she wanted</u>.　　_____

10. I fired the man <u>whom I considered incompetent</u>.　　　　　　　　　　　_____

Lesson 2-5: Sentence Structures

Writing should contain an interesting pace. It should change and vary to keep the reader interested. Therefore, writing must contain various sentence structures. These structures consist of the **simple sentence, the compound sentence, the complex sentence,** and **the compound-complex sentence.** The following sections examine the different sentence structures other than the simple sentence, which is covered in Lesson 2-2 on page 63.

Compound Sentences

A compound sentence consists of two or more independent clauses joined either by a comma and a coordinating conjunction, or by a semicolon. Each independent clause has its own subject and predicate. Compound sentences do not contain dependent clauses.

Examples

> The boat was loaded with passengers, and it was time for it to sail.

The two independent clauses in this compound sentence are connected with a comma followed by a coordinating conjunction.

> The passengers were on board; the boat was ready to sail.

These independent clauses are joined by a semicolon.

There are several punctuation errors associated with compound sentences. Be careful to avoid the following errors.

If a compound sentence has two main clauses joined by a coordinating conjunction, use a comma before the coordinating conjunction.

Example:

Incorrect: Zach is never late but Robert is more reliable.

Correct:　Zach is never late, but Robert is more reliable.

If a compound sentence has three or more main clauses joined by a coordinating conjunction, use a comma after each clause except the final clause.

Example:

Incorrect: Zach is never late, but Robert is more reliable and he never lets me down.

Correct:　Zach is never late, but Robert is more reliable, and he never lets me down.

If a sentence has two main clauses, do not only use a comma to separate the clauses. Otherwise, you have a comma splice.

Example:

Incorrect: Robert is more reliable, he never lets me down.

Correct:　Robert is more reliable, and he never lets me down.

Correct:　Robert is more reliable; he never lets me down.

For each of the following sentences, determine whether there are one or two main clauses. Write the answer in the space provided.

Example: Family, friends, and neighbors are visiting my house.
one main clause

1. Holidays are fun, but they are a lot of work. _____

2. The house must be cleaned and decorated. _____

3. The food is purchased and prepared. _____

4. My brother helps, and he is a great cook. _____

5. We sing, eat, and laugh during the holidays. _____

6. The children wake early, but they enjoy the excitement. _____

7. My sister makes desserts, and my aunt brings fresh bread. _____

8. After dinner, we relax by the fireplace. _____

9. The children play games, or they watch television. _____

10. After the excitement, we rest until the next year. _____

Complex Sentences

A complex sentence consists of one independent clause and at least one dependent clause. The order of clauses can differ. Some dependent clauses are separated by commas, while others are not. (For more about commas and dependent clauses, see Lesson 5-5 on page 193.)

Examples

I gave him money because he needed it.

This complex sentence contains one independent clause (*I gave him money*) and one dependent clause (*because he needed it*).

Although he needed help, he was reluctant to ask since he felt proud.

This complex sentence contains one independent clause (*he was reluctant to ask*) and two dependent clauses.

Compound-Complex Sentences

A compound-complex sentence contains two or more independent clauses and at least one dependent clause. In other words, it is both *compound* and *complex*.

Examples

I ran to the phone when it rang, but I was too late.

This sentence contains two independent clauses (*I ran to the phone* and *I was too late*) and one dependent clause (*when it rang*).

My sister is a woman who is successful, but she has doubts about what she wants to do next.

This sentence contains two independent clauses (*my sister is a woman* and *she has doubts*) and two dependent clauses (*who is successful* and *about what she want to do next*).

Exercise 2-14

For each of the following simple sentences, add another independent clause, a dependent clause, or both.

Example: She reads.
She reads while riding the train, and she naps.

1. John watches television.

_____

2. The book is interesting.

_____

3. The flowers bloom.

_____

4. The dog is running.

_____

5. The office building is closed.

_____

6. Marion and Rita are coming home.

_____

7. Susan likes musical theater.

   _____

8. The commuter bus fare has been raised.

   _____

9. The town board approved the zoning change.

   _____

10. Adam has been applying to colleges.

   _____

Answers to Exercises

Exercise 2-1

1.	Answer the phone.	*imperative sentence*
2.	Who is in the car?	*interrogative sentence*
3.	My hand hurts!	*exclamatory sentence*
4.	The lunches are packed.	*declarative sentence*
5.	What did you say?	*interrogative sentence*
6.	Stop it now!	*exclamatory sentence*
7.	The sun is shining.	*declarative sentence*
8.	Please clean your room.	*imperative sentence*
9.	Where are the documents?	*interrogative sentence*
10.	The mail has arrived.	*declarative sentence*

Exercise 2-2

1.	<u>Pet stores</u> are booming.	*stores*
2.	<u>More and more locations</u> are opening.	*locations*
3.	<u>These new stores</u> carry a variety of animals.	*stores*
4.	<u>Several dog breeds</u> can be found at these stores.	*breeds*
5.	<u>Some people</u> buy fish and birds.	*people*
6.	<u>Many types of pet toys</u> are available for purchase.	*toys*
7.	<u>A pet owner</u> must choose carefully.	*owner*
8.	<u>My personal favorites</u> are the kittens.	*favorites*
9.	<u>These playful creatures</u> are adorable.	*creatures*
10.	<u>All pets</u> are important to their owners.	*pets*

Exercise 2-3

1.	Roses <u>are beautiful flowers</u>.	*are*
2.	There <u>are so many varieties</u>.	*are*
3.	Most roses <u>bloom in the spring</u>.	*bloom*
4.	The colors of roses <u>are vibrant and deep</u>.	*are*
5.	Their scent <u>fills the room</u>.	*fills*
6.	My garden <u>is filled with roses</u>.	*is*
7.	Roses <u>wither quickly</u>.	*wither*
8.	Their thorns <u>protect them from nature's predators</u>.	*protect*
9.	Most varieties <u>require full sunlight</u>.	*require*
10.	<u>Is</u> there <u>anything more lovely than a rose</u>?	*is*

Exercise 2-4

_S_ 1. A new club has started at our school.

_F_ 2. The Debate Club beginning.

_F_ 3. To debate in the new club after school.

_S_ 4. Many students have joined.

_F_ 5. Interesting topics discussed.

_S_ 6. Three matches have been won.

_F_ 7. Meeting in the classroom near the main office.

_S_ 8. The club's president is Walter Smith.

_F_ 9. He running the debates in the auditorium.

_S_ 10. Come join the club.

Exercise 2-5

1. Swimming <u>is fun</u>.
   subject + linking verb + predicate nominative

2. Swimmers <u>practice strokes</u>.
   subject + verb + direct object

3. Swimmers <u>are in the water</u>.
   subject + linking verb + prepositional phrase

4. Swimming <u>is healthy</u>.
   subject + linking verb + predicate adverb

5. Swimmers <u>seem to glide</u>.
   subject + linking verb + infinitive

6. Swimmers <u>make their strokes tight</u>.
    subject + verb + direct object + object complement (adjective)

7. Swimmers <u>are supported</u> by their coaches.
    passive voice

8. Swimmers <u>are muscular</u>.
    subject + linking verb + predicate adjective

9. Practice <u>gives swimmers an advantage</u>.
    subject + verb + indirect object + direct object

10. Swimmers <u>succeed</u>.
    subject + verb

Exercise 2-6

1. <u>Florida</u> and <u>California</u> are known for their citrus fruit.
2. <u>Skiing</u> and <u>snowboarding</u> are popular in Colorado.
3. Neither <u>Alaska</u> nor <u>Washington</u> is known for balmy weather.
4. Either <u>New York</u> or <u>Illinois</u> can provide big-city adventure.
5. Not <u>California</u> but <u>Nevada</u> has large gambling metropolises.
6. <u>Delaware</u> and <u>New Jersey</u> provide Atlantic beaches for swimmers.
7. <u>Rodeos</u> and <u>horse shows</u> are plentiful in Texas.
8. The <u>badlands</u> and <u>Mount Rushmore</u> can be found in South Dakota.
9. <u>Residents</u> and <u>visitors</u> enjoy the culture of Louisiana.
10. <u>Mountains</u> and <u>valleys</u> make scenic Tennessee so beautiful.

Exercise 2-7

1. Chefs <u>sauté</u>, <u>simmer</u>, and <u>broil</u> dishes.
2. The children do not <u>eat</u> nor <u>drink</u> in the living room.
3. Evan <u>is</u> and always <u>will be</u> a practical joker.
4. Students <u>read</u>, <u>write</u>, and <u>edit</u> their essays.
5. After lunch, the wait staff <u>cleared</u> and <u>cleaned</u> the tables.
6. She <u>can be</u> and <u>should be</u> the next president.
7. The disgruntled players <u>criticized</u> and <u>challenged</u> the umpire.
8. Her friends always <u>disagree</u> and <u>argue</u> over television shows.
9. John frequently <u>travels</u> and <u>relocates</u> for business.
10. Ella <u>wants</u> and <u>deserves</u> a raise from her employer.

Exercise 2-8

1.	Parks, zoos, <u>and</u> museums are fun places to visit.	*compound subject*
2.	Families can <u>either</u> picnic <u>or</u> dine indoors.	*compound predicate*
3.	Children are <u>not only</u> having fun <u>but</u> are learning.	*compound predicate*
4.	<u>Neither</u> rain <u>nor</u> snow can prevent the fun!	*compound subject*
5.	<u>Both</u> adults <u>and</u> children enjoy the day.	*compound subject*
6.	The zebras eat <u>and</u> play.	*compound predicate*
7.	The visitors are laughing <u>and</u> smiling.	*compound predicate*
8.	<u>Both</u> animals <u>and</u> humans deserve a clean environment.	*compound subject*
9.	Do you see <u>and</u> hear the elephants?	*compound predicate*
10.	Not people <u>but</u> animals live at the zoo.	*compound subject*

Exercise 2-9

1.	The house is quiet <u>in the afternoon</u>.	*prepositional phrase*
2.	The children <u>are napping</u>.	*verb phrase*
3.	The <u>quiet house</u> is peaceful.	*noun phrase*
4.	I <u>will be entertaining</u> tonight.	*verb phrase*
5.	The people are gathering <u>near the door</u>.	*prepositional phrase*
6.	By tomorrow, the festival <u>will be over</u>.	*verb phrase*
7.	The <u>unobtrusive guest</u> slipped out the door.	*noun phrase*
8.	The couple <u>will have been married</u> two years in April.	*verb phrase*
9.	The garden is overrun <u>with weeds</u>.	*prepositional phrase*
10.	The <u>peevish child</u> ran into the yard.	*noun phrase*

Exercise 2-10

1.	<u>To become a lawyer</u> takes years of schooling.	*infinitive phrase*
2.	He enjoys <u>drinking hot cocoa</u> in cold weather.	*gerund phrase*
3.	The woman <u>leading the discussion</u> is charismatic.	*participial phrase*
4.	A puppy needs <u>attentive nurturing</u>.	*gerund phrase*
5.	The flyer <u>stapled to the light pole</u> advertised a sale.	*participial phrase*
6.	The doctor needed <u>to consult a colleague</u>.	*infinitive phrase*
7.	<u>Finished with college visits</u>, Jay had time to relax.	*participial phrase*
8.	<u>To enter the building</u>, go to the side door.	*infinitive phrase*
9.	<u>Questioning data</u> is crucial for analysis.	*gerund phrase*
10.	Return the book to the shelf <u>labeled "Used."</u>	*participial phrase*

Exercise 2-11

Possible Answers

1.	Put on the coat.	*Put on the coat, the one with the blue buttons.*
2.	Sheila frequently bakes.	*Having the time, Sheila frequently bakes.*
3.	The teacher went home.	*The teacher, Anne, went home.*
4.	My brother flies airplanes.	*My brother, being retired, flies airplanes.*
5.	Angela listens to music.	*Needing relaxation, Angela listens to music.*
6.	Herbert walks.	*Herbert, our friend from the neighborhood, walks.*
7.	I drained the tub.	*Finishing my bath, I drained the tub.*
8.	Teresa traveled abroad.	*Teresa, my niece, traveled abroad.*
9.	Danny sees his brother.	*Danny sees his brother, Billy.*
10.	Rose needed an iron.	*Doing laundry, Rose needed an iron.*

Exercise 2-12

1.	We packed <u>when we heard the news</u>	*adverb clause*
2.	The house <u>where I grew up</u> has been sold.	*adjective clause*
3.	She responded <u>when he addressed her</u>.	*adverb clause*
4.	I opened the box as carefully <u>as I could</u>.	*adverb clause*
5.	The plane, <u>which had a damaged tailfin</u>, landed safely.	*adjective clause*
6.	The key was <u>where I had left it</u>.	*noun clause*
7.	<u>Whoever needs a place to stay</u> is welcome.	*noun clause*
8.	He saved <u>in order to buy a boat</u>.	*adverb clause*
9.	They gave her <u>whatever she wanted</u>.	*noun clause*
10.	I fired the man <u>whom I considered incompetent</u>.	*adjective clause*

Exercise 2-13

1.	Holidays are fun, but they are a lot of work.	*two main clauses*
2.	The house must be cleaned and decorated.	*one main clause*
3.	The food is purchased and prepared.	*one main clause*
4.	My brother helps, and he is a great cook.	*two main clauses*
5.	We sing, eat, and laugh during the holidays.	*one main clause*
6.	The children wake early, but they enjoy the excitement.	*two main clauses*
7.	My sister makes desserts, and my aunt brings fresh bread.	*two main clauses*
8.	After dinner, we relax by the fireplace.	*one main clause*
9.	The children play games, or they watch television.	*two main clauses*
10.	After the excitement, we rest until the next year.	*one main clause*

Exercise 2-14

Possible answers

1. John watches television.

   John watches television while he finishes paperwork.

2. The book is interesting.

   The book is interesting, but the plot is complicated.

3. The flowers bloom.

   As the sun comes out, the flowers bloom.

4. The dog is running.

   The dog is running, and the owner is frustrated.

5. The office building is closed.

   While it is being constructed, the office building is closed.

6. Marion and Rita are coming home.

   When they are tired, Marion and Rita are coming home.

7. Susan likes musical theater.

   Susan likes musical theater, but her husband prefers drama.

8. The commuter bus fare has been raised.

   Taxes have been increased, and the commuter bus fare has been raised.

9. The town board approved the zoning change.

   After it heard the presentation, the town board approved the zoning change.

10. Adam has been applying to colleges.

    Adam has been applying to colleges while his parents have been saving.

Tense Review

Verbs can be confusing. They show action, but they also express the time in which the action occurs. Some actions take place in the present, some in the past, and some in the future. Certain events are limited to a certain time period, whereas others are ongoing or continual. They must also agree in number with the subject. Changing the verb to the correct form is called conjugation. When conjugating verbs, we change the verb form and sometimes add auxiliary verbs. (For more on verbs and auxiliary verbs, see Lesson 1-3 on page 32.) There are several ways to conjugate verbs, and each verb form signifies a different tense. For instance, compare *you walked* to *you have walked.* These two clauses are similar, but they differ in tense. We must be aware of meaning in what we write. Therefore, it is crucial to be cognizant of each tense. This chapter examines the different tenses and verb forms, as well as ways in which meaning and tone can change with each tense.

Lesson 3-1: Verb Forms

Verbs have different forms. The verb form used to indicate the time of an event is called **tense.** These structures include the base form and the modifications the verb undergoes for each tense. The different forms a verb can take include the base form, the way it is listed in the dictionary; the form for past tense, used alone for simple past tense; the past participle, used with auxiliary verbs and modals for different tenses; the present participle, used for progressive and perfect tenses; and the –s form, used for the third-person singular pronoun case. These can also be used for verbals. (For more about verbals, see Lesson 1-3.) Here is a chart of the different forms for some common verbs. Notice that some are **regular,** and therefore follow rules, whereas others are **irregular,** and their conjugations do not follow a set pattern.

Base Form	Past Tense	Past Participle	Present Participle	–s Form
talk	talked	talked	talking	talks
have	had	had	having	has
listen	listened	listened	listening	listens
engage	engaged	engaged	engaging	engages
speak	spoke	spoken	speaking	speaks
rise	rose	risen	rising	rises
run	ran	ran	running	runs
eat	ate	eaten	eating	eats

We use many tenses on a daily basis, and each one has a different meaning. The base form of the verb is conjugated in each tense, according to the pronoun. In some tenses, the verb stands alone; in other instances, the verb takes auxiliary verbs. By adding an auxiliary verb, you change the tense, and thus the meaning of the entire sentence changes. Each pronoun has its own form for each tense. Therefore, there is a multitude of ways to conjugate each verb. One common verb is *to walk.* The following chart shows a variety of forms this verb can take in the first-person singular pronoun case.

I walk.	I walked.	I will walk.
I am walking.	I was walking.	I will/shall be walking.
I have walked.	I had walked.	I will/shall have walked.
I have been walking.	I had been walking.	I will/shall have been walking.

All of these examples are in **first-person singular.** Imagine all of the ways to conjugate *to walk* using the other pronoun cases. There are numerous conjugations for each verb. However, with regular verbs there are certain rules we can follow to make choosing the correct verb easier.

Lesson 3-2: Simple Tenses

The simple tenses are **present, past,** and **future.** They represent general periods of time when actions take place.

Present Tense

The present tense signals that the action is currently taking place. It is also used to express a general truth or something that happens habitually. There is no specific time frame other than the present.

Examples

He exercises.

This tense shows that the statement is current. It also implies an ongoing activity. This statement can be made clearer with modifiers.

He exercises regularly.

By adding the adverb *regularly*, the idea of habit is reinforced.

He rarely exercises.

With the addition of the adverb *rarely,* the meaning of the sentence completely changes. However, all three of these sentences take place during this present time. Therefore, they are all the same tense.

To form the present tense of most verbs, use the base form for pronouns except the third-person singular. For that case, use the –*s* form of the verb. The following chart shows all the pronoun cases for the present tense of the verb *to exercise.*

Remember that *exercise* is a regular verb, and therefore it follows a pattern. If you learn how to conjugate one regular verb, you can conjugate them all.

Pronoun Case	Singular	Plural
1st Person	I exercise	we exercise
2nd Person	you exercise	you exercise
3rd Person	he/she/it exercises	they exercise

Exercise 3-1

For each of the following sentences, underline the correct form of the verb for the *present tense.*

Example: My car (require, <u>requires</u>) new tires.

1. I (need, needs) a haircut.

2. John (prefer, prefers) chocolate more than vanilla.

3. Some people (write, writes) letters on the computer.

4. Reading (enhance, enhances) our vocabulary.

5. He (like, likes) to awaken early on Sundays.

6. We frequently (walk, walks) to work.

7. You never (speak, speaks) in front of crowds.

8. I always (add, adds) oregano to that chicken recipe.

9. The class (work, works) on mathematics.

10. Erica (listen, listens) to music with her headphones.

There are a few simple spelling rules for regular present tense verbs. They deal with the third-person singular.

To form the third-person singular, generally add –s to the basic verb.

Example:

I run.   She runs.

If the verb ends in s, o, x, zz, ch, or sh, add –es.

Examples:

I relax.	He relaxes.	We catch.	He catches.
They buzz.	It buzzes.	They confess.	She confesses.
I fish.	He fishes.	They do.	She does.

If the verb ends in a consonant + y, change the y to I and add –es.

Example:

I study.   He studies.

Exercise 3-2

For each of the present tense verbs here, change the spelling to third-person singular.

Example: I watch. She *watches.*

1. They dance. He _____.

2. I wish. She _____.

3. We dry. He _____.

4. They complain. She _____.

5. We rinse. He _____.

6. We smash. She _____.

7. I try. He _____.

8. We intercede. She _____.

9. They fly. It _____.

10. I exercise. He _____.

Past Tense

The past tense tells what has already happened. It signals that the action is over; it was completed in the past. Other than the general term of the past, there is no explicit time frame.

Examples

I <u>witnessed</u> an accident.

This action (*witnessed*) was completed in the past. It does not spill into the present. You could make the statement clearer with modifiers.

<u>Yesterday</u>, I <u>witnessed</u> an accident.

The addition of the adverb *yesterday* makes the timeframe more specific, but the total action still takes place in the past.

To form the past tense of a regular verb, add –*ed* to the base regardless of pronoun case. If the verb ends in *e*, simply add –*d* to the base to make it past tense. The following chart shows all the pronoun cases for the past tense of the verb *to witness.*

Pronoun Case	Singular	Plural
1st Person	I witnessed	we witnessed
2nd Person	you witnessed	you witnessed
3rd Person	he/she/it witnessed	they witnessed

Once again, witness is a regular verb, and all of the past tense cases are the same. Remember that irregular verbs are not as consistent in their conjugations. (For more about irregular verbs, see Lesson 3-8.)

Future Tense

The future tense tells what will happen in the future. It signals that no part of the action has yet begun. The verb in the future tense, without modifiers, shows no specific time frame other than the future.

Examples

I will call Margaret.

The action of this sentence (*to call*) has not begun; it will take place sometime in the future. The time frame in the future can be modified by adverbs, but the tense does not change. Here is the same sentence with modifiers.

I will call Margaret in a few days.

The action of this sentence will still take place in the future, but the modifier makes the future more specific. *In a few days* is a prepositional phrase acting as an adverb. It signifies a more detailed time frame in the future.

I will call Margaret immediately.

The adverb *immediately* changes the time frame of the action, but the entire action of the sentence will still take place in the future.

To conjugate the future tense of a regular verb, add the modal auxiliary *will* to the base form of the verb for all pronoun cases. Here is an example of all the pronoun cases for the future tense of the verb *call*.

Pronoun Case	Singular	Plural
1st Person	I will/shall call	we will/shall call
2nd Person	you will/shall call	you will/shall call
3rd Person	he/she/it will/shall call	they will/shall call

The modal auxiliary, or helping verb, *will* is used in all of the pronoun cases in this example. However, in some cases *shall* is appropriate. The auxiliary *shall* is used less and less frequently; it is becoming obsolete. *Shall* is not heard often anymore, but it is correct with use of first-person singular and plural pronouns. Examine the differences in the following chart.

Pronoun Case	Singular	Plural
1st Person	I will/shall call	we will/shall call
2nd Person	you will/shall call	you will/shall call
3rd Person	he/she/it will/shall call	they will/shall call

Exercise 3-3

For each of the following sentences, take the *present* tense verb and change it to both *past* tense and *future* tense.

	past tense	future tense
Example: Peter <u>enjoys</u> hiking.	*enjoyed*	*will enjoy*

1. Dominic <u>lives</u> in Vancouver. _____ _____

2. He <u>loves</u> gardening. _____ _____

3. Her sisters <u>play</u> outside. _____ _____

4. I <u>wish</u> her happiness. _____ _____

5. Peter <u>remembers</u> his appointment. _____ _____

6. The team <u>practices</u>. _____ _____

7. Eddie <u>cleans</u> out his locker. _____ _____

8. We <u>dress</u> for dinner. _____ _____

9. You <u>smile</u> frequently. _____ _____

10. They <u>add</u> tax to the bill. _____ _____

Lesson 3-3: Perfect Tenses

Perfect tenses designate a continuing action or a completed action that spills from one frame of time into the next. These tenses require auxiliary verbs to show when the action occurs. Each perfect tense specifies different periods of time, but they all require the use *to have* as an auxiliary verb.

Present Perfect

The present perfect tense shows something that started in the past and was completed at some unspecified time in the past, or still continues into the present. It always involves more than one period of time.

Examples

I <u>have reviewed</u> the material.

With the use of the verb *to have,* the action started in the past and was completed at another undetermined time in the past. This sentence in the simple past tense has a different meaning.

I <u>reviewed</u> the material.

In this case, all of the action is completed in the past. There is only one period of time here.

The men <u>have worked</u> for a long time.

With this example, the action started in the past and is still continuing in the present. The men started working in the past and are still working. This sentence in the present tense means something else.

The men <u>work</u> for a long time.

Here, the action is limited to the present. The action did not begin in the past.

To form the present perfect tense of all verbs, use the base form of the verb *to have* before the past participle of the main verb. Here is an example of all the pronoun cases for the present perfect tense of the verb to work.

Pronoun Case	Singular	Plural
1st Person	I have worked	we have worked
2nd Person	you have worked	you have worked
3rd Person	he/she/it has worked	they have worked

Notice that the verb *to have* is also conjugated according to the pronoun case. Use *has* with third-person singular. With all other singular and plural cases, use *have*. Remember to look out for irregular verbs. They also use the present tense of *to have* followed by the past participle, but their past participles do not follow the same pattern as regular verbs.

Exercise 3-4

For each of the following sentences, take the *present* tense verb and change it to *present perfect* tense.

present perfect

Example: She <u>eats</u> peaches.   *has eaten*

1. Bill and I <u>walk</u> to the store.   _____

2. The mother and father <u>watch</u> their child.   _____

3. Our friends <u>purchase</u> concert tickets.   _____

4. Robert <u>dreams</u> of winning an award.   _____

5. Kristina's cousin <u>finishes</u> projects.   _____

6. She <u>gives</u> her manager an answer.   _____

7. The girl <u>has</u> a cold.   _____

8. In the dark, you <u>see</u> a shadow.   _____

9. We <u>complete</u> our work.   _____

10. Melissa and Jennifer <u>play</u> checkers.   _____

Past Perfect

The past perfect tense shows something that started in the *past* and was completed at another time in the past. It signals two periods of time in the past. None of the action takes place in the present.

Examples

I <u>had tried</u> on the coat earlier.

With the use of the verb *to have,* the action started in the past and was completed before a certain time in the past. There are two periods of time implied here. This sentence in the past tense has a different meaning.

I <u>tried</u> on the coat earlier.

In this case, all of the action is completed during the same time in the past. There is only one period of time. In both cases, the adverb *earlier* makes the time in the past more specific, but it does not create a separate time period.

Ryan <u>had walked</u> home when he noticed the rain.

With the past perfect tense, Ryan started walking in the past and finished walking at another time in the past. This sentence in the past tense means something else.

Ryan <u>walked</u> home when he noticed the rain.

Here, the action is limited to one instance in the past. The action does not continue to another time in the past. The adverb clause (*when he noticed the rain*) limits the time in the past, but it does not create a separate time period. The entire action takes place in the past.

To form the past perfect tense of all verbs, use the past participle of the verb *to have* before the past participle of the main verb. Here is an example of all the pronoun cases for the past perfect tense of the verb *to walk.*

Notice that in all pronoun cases, the past tense of the verb *to have* is *had.* Remember

Pronoun Case	Singular	Plural
1st Person	I had walked	we had walked
2nd Person	you had walked	you had walked
3rd Person	he/she/it had walked	they had walked

that adding *had* before the past participle changes the tense to past perfect. Do not use *had* before the verb unless your intent is to show two time periods within the past tense.

One common error in writing is the incorrect use of the past perfect tense. The simple past tense should be used with more frequency. The perfect tense has a specific meaning; be aware of the difference. Do not use past perfect when past tense is appropriate.

Example:

Incorrect: Paul <u>had lost his wallet</u> yesterday.

Correct: Paul <u>lost his wallet</u> yesterday.

Incorrect: On Saturday they <u>had painted their home.</u>

Correct: On Saturday they <u>painted their home.</u>

Exercise 3-5

For each of the following sentences, take the present tense verb and change it to *past perfect* tense.

past perfect

Example: They <u>see</u> the yellow car.   *had seen*

1. Tom <u>reaches</u> the stairs.   _____

2. We <u>watch</u> television.   _____

3. No one <u>sees</u> the dog.   _____

4. I <u>laugh</u> at the funny comedian.   _____

5. Patrick <u>paints</u> his ceiling.   _____

6. Steve and Patty <u>give</u> to charity.   _____

7. You <u>need</u> a ticket for the movie.   _____

8. They <u>send</u> a card to their neighbor.   _____

9. Mary and I <u>answer</u> the telephone.   _____

10. You <u>look</u> beautiful.   _____

Future Perfect

The future perfect tense is used when the action will be completed before some definite time in the future. It contrasts two periods of time in the future.

Examples

If they win, they <u>will have succeeded</u> for the third time.

With the use of the future perfect tense, the action will be completed at a specific time in the future. This sentence in the present perfect tense has a different meaning.

If they win, they <u>have succeeded</u> for the third time.

In this case, the action started in the past and is still continuing.

We <u>will have asked</u> for three extensions to the deadline.

With the future perfect tense, the action has begun and will be completed before a specific time. This sentence in the future tense means something else.

We <u>will ask</u> for three extensions to the deadline.
Here, the entire action will take place in the future.

Conjugate the future perfect tense of all verbs by using the two auxiliaries, *will* and the base form of the verb *to have*, before the past participle of the main verb. Here is an example of all the pronoun cases for the future perfect tense of the verb *ask*.

Pronoun Case	Singular	Plural
1st Person	I will/shall have asked	we will/shall have asked
2nd Person	you will/shall have asked	you will/shall have asked
3rd Person	he/she/it will/shall have asked	they will/shall have asked

Notice that in all pronoun cases, the future perfect tense is formed by using the auxiliaries *will* and the present form of the verb *to have*. Remember that the use of *shall* instead of will is also correct, although antiquated, for the first-person singular and first-person plural pronoun cases.

Pronoun Case	Singular	Plural
1st Person	I will/shall have asked	we will/shall have asked
2nd Person	you will/shall have asked	you will/shall have asked
3rd Person	he/she/it will/shall have asked	they will/shall have asked

Exercise 3-6

For each of the following sentences, take the present tense verb and change it to *future perfect* tense.

future perfect

Example: Everyone <u>finds</u> the new teacher pleasant. *will have found*

1. I <u>work</u> in the office. _____

2. We <u>walk</u> before lunch. _____

3. Elizabeth <u>goes</u> to the beach. _____

4. The daring players <u>win</u> the match. _____

5. Andrea <u>eats</u> apples after breakfast. _____

6. My friends <u>miss</u> their train. _____

7. You <u>hope</u> for a high paying job. _____

8. They <u>line</u> up in formation. _____

9. Bruce and I <u>reach</u> the end of the bike path. _____

10. He <u>uses</u> his new tools. _____

Lesson 3-4: Progressive Tenses

The progressive tenses signify actions or conditions that are ongoing. They all use the present participle, but some require auxiliary verbs.

Present Progressive

The present progressive indicates an action that is ongoing in the present. In other words, it is currently happening.

Examples

We <u>are running</u> quickly.

This action is taking place, or progressing, in the present time. Notice how the sentence is different in the present tense.

We <u>run</u> quickly.

With the simple present tense, the time period is current, but the action is not necessarily happening right now.

He <u>is driving</u> to the shopping center.

With the present progressive tense, the driving is currently taking place. This sentence in the present tense means something else.

He <u>drives</u> to the shopping center.

In this example he drives, but the action is not progressing at this time.

To form the present progressive tense of all verbs, use the present tense of the verb *to be* before the present participle of the main verb. Here is an example of all the pronoun cases for the present progressive tense of the verb *to drive*.

Pronoun Case	Singular	Plural
1st Person	I am driving	we are driving
2nd Person	you are driving	you are driving
3rd Person	he/she/it is driving	they are driving

In the first-person singular pronoun case, the present tense of the verb *to be* is *am*. The conjugation of *to be* in third-person singular is *is*. For all other cases, use *are*. (For more about irregular verbs, see Lesson 3-8.)

Exercise 3-7

For each of the following sentences, take the *present* tense verb and change it to *present progressive* tense.

                                                            present progressive

Example: Richard <u>asks</u> for help.   *is asking*

1. They <u>look</u> at the stars.   _____

2. We <u>notice</u> the new street sign.   _____

3. No one <u>answers</u> the telephone.   _____

4. I <u>check</u> my e-mail first thing in the morning.   _____

5. Grant <u>needs</u> new clothes.   _____

6. Barry <u>gives</u> advice to his younger sister.   _____

7. I <u>look</u> tired.   _____

8. David and Susan <u>teach</u> a class together.   _____

9. We <u>return</u> the movie rentals on time.   _____

10. She <u>feels</u> better.   _____

Past Progressive

The past progressive tense indicates an action that was ongoing in the past, but it is now over. It implies another time when the action *was* ongoing.

Examples

We <u>were living</u> in Santa Fe.

This action was taking place, or progressing, in the past, but now it has stopped. Notice how the sentence is different in the simple past tense.

We <u>lived</u> in Santa Fe.

With the past tense, the action is completed in the past, but there is no contrast to another time period.

They <u>were eating</u> dinner.

With the past progressive tense, the eating was happening, but now it is not. This sentence in the present tense means something else.

They <u>ate</u> dinner.

In this example, they ate, but there is no hint of another time.

To form the past progressive tense of all verbs, use the past tense of the verb *to be* before the present participle of the main verb. Here is an example of all the pronoun cases for the present progressive tense of the verb *to eat.*

Pronoun Case	Singular	Plural
1st Person	I was eating	we were eating
2nd Person	you were eating	you were eating
3rd Person	he/she/it was eating	they were eating

Notice the irregularity of the verb *to be*. It must be conjugated in the past tense, according to the pronoun case. In the first-person singular and third-person singular pronoun cases, the past tense of the verb *to be* is *was*. For all other cases, use *were*.

Exercise 3-8

For each of the following sentences, take the *present* tense verb and change it to *past progressive* tense.

                                           past progressive

Example: Anthony <u>studies</u> French.   *was studying*

1. John <u>navigates</u> the boat.   _____

2. She <u>labors</u> over difficult choices.   _____

3. Emily and her dog <u>lag</u> behind.   _____

4. My friends and I <u>buy</u> furniture at the outlet store.   _____

5. Sandy's impulsive decision <u>haunts</u> her.   _____

6. The school <u>prohibits</u> smoking.   _____

7. You <u>remodel</u> your out-of-date kitchen.   _____

8. They <u>retouch</u> the actresses' makeup.   _____

9. Ella and I <u>deliver</u> newspapers.   _____

10. The class <u>raises</u> money for the homeless.   _____

Future Progressive

The future progressive indicates continuing actions that will take place in the future. The action has not yet begun, but in the future it will continue for a set period of time.

Examples

They <u>will be dancing</u> at the party.

This action will progress in the future for a period of time. Notice how the sentence is different in the simple future tense.

They <u>will dance</u> at the party.

With the future tense, the action has also not yet begun, but there is no hint that it will progress for any length of time.

He <u>will be choosing</u> a repairman.

With the future progressive tense, the choosing will take place and continue in the future for a period of time. This sentence in the future tense means something else.

He <u>will choose</u> a repairman.

In this example, he will choose, but it will not be a continuous action.

To form the future progressive tense of all verbs, use the two auxiliaries, *will* and *be,* before the present participle of the main verb. Here is an example of all the pronoun cases for the future progressive tense of the verb *to choose.*

Pronoun Case	Singular	Plural
1st Person	I will/shall be choosing	we will/shall be choosing
2nd Person	you will be choosing	you will be choosing
3rd Person	he/she/it will be choosing	they will be choosing

Notice that the auxiliary verbs are the same for all pronoun cases. However, you can substitute *shall* for *will* in the first-person singular and first-person plural cases.

Exercise 3-9

For each of the following sentences, take the present tense verb and change it to *future progressive* tense.

future progressive
will be enjoying

Example: Catlin <u>enjoys</u> her lunch.

1. Marie <u>sets</u> the table.   _____

2. We <u>create</u> artwork.   _____

3. My brother <u>reads</u> the owner's manual.   _____

4. I <u>count</u> the remaining cans of coffee.   _____

5. He <u>rubs</u> the paste off his fingers.   _____

6. They <u>enjoy</u> ice cream in the summer.   _____

7. You <u>pinch</u> the ends to seal the bag.   _____

8. Donna and Lisa <u>slice</u> the watermelon.   _____

9. We <u>contribute</u> to the pension fund.   _____

10. You <u>require</u> extra time to prepare for guests. _____

Lesson 3-5: Perfect Progressive Tenses

The perfect progressive tenses are the most complex. They designate continuing actions that are related to more than one period of time. They require the auxiliary verbs *to have* and *to be,* along with the present participle of the main verb. In the future perfect progressive, *will* or *shall* is also needed.

Present Perfect Progressive

The present perfect progressive tense indicates continuing actions begun in the past and still continuing into the present.

Examples

Michael <u>has been dating</u> a young woman.

The action here began in the past and is continuing into the present. Notice how the meaning changes when the sentence is in present progressive tense.

Michael <u>is dating</u> a young woman.

In this example, all of the action continues in the present tense. There is no hint of the past here.

They <u>have been trying</u> to settle the disagreement.

This sentence demonstrates that the action started in the past and is ongoing. The sentence has a different meaning in the present perfect tense.

They <u>have tried</u> to settle the disagreement.

In this example, all of the action takes place in the past. The action began in the past and ended at an unspecified time in the past.

To form the present perfect progressive tense of all verbs, you need two auxiliaries followed by the main verb. Use the base form of the verb *to have,* the past tense of the verb *to be,* and the present participle of the main verb. You must adhere to this specific order of verbs. Here is an example of all the pronoun cases for the present perfect progressive tense of the verb *to try.*

Pronoun Case	Singular	Plural
1st Person	I have been trying	we have been trying
2nd Person	you have been trying	you have been trying
3rd Person	he/she/it has been trying	they have been trying

Notice the irregularity of the verb *to have.* It must be conjugated in the present tense, according to the pronoun case. In the third-person singular, the present tense of the verb *to have* is *has.* For all other cases, use *have.* All of the pronoun cases take the past participle of *to be* and the present participle of the main verb.

Exercise 3-10

For each of the following sentences, take the *present* tense verb and change it to *present perfect progressive* tense. Look out for irregular verbs.

present perfect progressive

Example: Vanessa <u>drives</u> to school.   *has been driving*

1. Jennifer <u>comes</u> to the gym.   _____

2. We <u>enjoy</u> the party.   _____

3. They <u>visit</u> her sister.   _____

4. My friends and I <u>follow</u> sports.   _____

5. Isaac <u>auctions</u> rare artwork.   _____

6. The company <u>incurs</u> the cost of the damage. _____

7. The attorney and the accountant <u>certify</u>
   their work.   _____

8. We <u>reach</u> a mutual agreement.   _____

9. Aaron <u>delivers</u> beverages for the distributor. _____

10. The theater group <u>creates</u> superb drama.   _____

Past Perfect Progressive

The past perfect progressive demonstrates progressive actions that began in the past before a specific time or event. In other words, there was a continuing action in a separate time in the past.

Examples

Mark <u>had been planning</u> a huge wedding.

In this sentence, the action began, progressed, and was completed before another time. The tense can be made clearer with modifiers.

<u>Until he was fired,</u> Mark <u>had been planning</u> a huge wedding.

By highlighting the specific point in time when the continuing action ended, the use of the past perfect progressive tense is easier to understand. Note how the sentence is different in the past perfect tense.

Mark <u>had planned</u> a huge wedding.

In this case, the action began in the past and ended at a separate time in the past, but there was no continuing action.

We <u>had been saving</u> to buy a house before purchasing this apartment.

This example shows a continuing action that started in the past, continued, and ended at a specific time, with the purchase of the apartment. The sentence changes meaning in the past progressive tense.

We <u>were saving</u> to buy a house before purchasing this apartment.

In this sentence, all of the action was ongoing in the past and has ended, but not necessarily before any specific time.

To form the past perfect progressive tense of all verbs, you need two auxiliaries followed by the main verb. Use the past participles of the verbs *to have* and *to be,* followed by the present participle of the main verb. You must adhere to this specific order of verbs. Here is an example of all the pronoun cases for the past perfect progressive tense of the verb *to save.*

Pronoun Case	Singular	Plural
1st Person	I had been saving	we had been saving
2nd Person	you had been saving	you had been saving
3rd Person	he/she/it had been saving	they had been saving

Notice that the auxiliary verbs are the same for all pronoun cases. Each case also takes the present participle of the main verb.

Exercise 3-11

For each of the following sentences, take the present tense verb and change it to *past perfect progressive* tense. Look out for irregular verbs.

past perfect progressive

Example: The scientist <u>researches</u> abnormal
cells.   *had been researching*

1. My mechanic <u>repairs</u> my car.   _____

2. We <u>dine</u> at the expensive restaurant.   _____

3. They <u>relax</u> after a late dinner.   _____

4. My friends and I <u>play</u> hockey.   _____

5. Anthony <u>participates</u> in charity events.   _____

6. The ship <u>moors</u> at the south pier.   _____

7. Our aunt <u>bakes</u> delicious cinnamon rolls.   _____

8. We <u>consider</u> Laura a good friend.   _____

9. His employer <u>arrives</u> in a blue limousine. _____

10. The environmental group <u>distributes</u> literature. _____

Future Perfect Progressive

The future perfect progressive tense shows continuing actions that have already begun, but will be completed at some point in the future.

Examples

They <u>will have been driving</u> for several hours.

The action is progressing and will be completed at some time in the future. Notice how the meaning of the sentence changes when it is in the future progressive tense.

By four o'clock, <u>we will have been watching</u> television for three hours.

The action in this sentence has already begun, and it will continue progressing until a later point in time. This sentence is different in the future perfect tense.

By four o'clock, <u>we will have watched</u> television for three hours.

In this example, the action began in the past and will be completed at a specific point in the future, but the action will not continue progressing.

To form the future perfect progressive tense of all verbs, you need two auxiliaries, *will* and the base form of *to have,* followed by the present participle of the main verb. Here is an example of all the pronoun cases for the past perfect progressive tense of the verb *to watch.*

Pronoun Case	Singular	Plural
1st Person	I will have been watching	we will have been watching
2nd Person	you will have been watching	you will have been watching
3rd Person	he/she/it will have been watching	they will have been watching

Notice that the auxiliary verbs are the same for all pronoun cases. However, you can substitute *shall* for *will* in the first-person singular and first-person plural cases.

Pronoun Case	Singular	Plural
1st Person	I shall have been watching	we shall have been watching
2nd Person	you will have been watching	you will have been watching
3rd Person	he/she/it will have been watching	they will have been watching

Exercise 3-12

For each of the following sentences, take the *present* tense verb and change it to *future perfect progressive* tense.

Example: Stella <u>writes</u> poetry.

future perfect progressive
will have been writing

1. My mother <u>finds</u> movies enjoyable.   _____

2. We <u>refuse</u> to pay the exorbitant rental fees.   _____

3. They <u>answer</u> a series of questions.   _____

4. My friends and I <u>shop</u> for luggage.   _____

5. He <u>drives</u> on the major highways.   _____

6. The woman <u>practices</u> her golf swing.   _____

7. Judith <u>teaches</u> a variety of subjects.   _____

8. The energetic cat <u>chases</u> the mouse.   _____

9. They <u>offer</u> several payment options.   _____

10. Citizens <u>vote</u> for the candidate of
    their choice.   _____

Lesson 3-6: The Passive Voice

The voice of a sentence indicates whether someone or something actually performs the action of the verb or is instead acted upon. Sentences can be in either the **active** or the **passive voice.** The active voice is appropriate in most cases; it is structured so that the subject takes the action of the verb. Sometimes however, you may need to use the passive voice. The passive voice is formed by using the appropriate form of the verb *to be* followed by the past participle of the main verb. The following examples highlight the differences between these two voices.

Examples

The <u>baseball</u> was caught by Alex.

This sentence is in the passive voice. The subject of this sentence is *baseball*, but the object of the preposition (*Alex*) takes the action. Here is the same sentence in the active voice.

<u>Alex</u> caught the baseball.

Removing the verb *to be* makes the sentence is more precise. The subject (*Alex*) takes the action.

The young <u>child</u> flew her kite.

Child is the subject of the sentence, and *flew* is the verb. This sentence is active. Look at the same sentence in the passive voice.

The <u>kite</u> was flown by the young child.

In this example, *kite* is the subject and *child* is the object. The *kite* completes the action, and *child* is the object of the preposition. There is little difference in meaning between these sentences, but the first example is correct; it is more concise.

Although the differences seem marginal, it is important to recognize the subject of the sentence and make it the center of the action. The way to accomplish this is with the active voice. The passive voice has a different effect. It is sometimes used, but unless there is a specific reason, such as with technical writing, the active voice should be used. A general rule is to avoid overuse of the verb *to be*.

Exercise 3-13

Determine whether or not each of the following sentences in the passive voice can be changed to the *active voice*. When possible, convert to the *active voice*.

Example: The car is driven by Sam.   *Sam drives the car.*

1. The dish was broken by my mother.

    _____

2. I was taken to the cleaners.

    _____

3. Melissa is tutored by Margaret.

    _____

4. The group was brought up to the stage.

_____

5. Rain can be indicated by clouds.

_____

6. The test was given by my math teacher.

_____

7. The leaves are raked by the gardener.

_____

8. The cranky child was put to bed.

_____

9. The boat is navigated by Donna.

_____

10. The questions were answered by Tom.

_____

Lesson 3-7: Mood and the Subjunctive

Mood is used to indicate the attitude of the writer toward what he or she is writing. There are three moods in English, and each mood has its own purpose.

▶ The **indicative mood** is used to express a fact, an opinion, or an inquiry. This is the most common mood. It is used for most declarative sentences and some interrogative sentences.

Examples:

I made the right decision.

I bought the right car.

▶ The **imperative mood** is used to express a command or request. It is used with some interrogative sentences and most exclamatory sentences.

Examples:

Choose a dress for the party.

Can you please turn off the music?

▶ The **subjunctive mood** is used to indirectly express a demand, a requirement, a recommendation, a wish, or a condition that is contrary to fact. It is rarely used, and the situations in which the subjunctive is used are frequently formal. The subjunctive mood is formed by using the base form of the verb.

Examples:

We insist that he pay his own way through school.

This sentence expresses a demand in the subjunctive. Notice the use of the base form of the verb *to pay*. In present tense for third-person singular, this verb would be conjugated *he pays*.

May the better player win.

This sentence expresses a wish in the subjunctive. Again, the base form of the verb is used, even in third-person singular.

If she were responsible, I would lend her my new earrings.

This statement expresses a condition contrary to what is fact. With this type of subjunctive clause, the past tense of the verb *to be* is used. However, it is conjugated as *were* in all pronoun cases; you do not use *was* for first-person singular or third-person singular.

Lesson 3-8: Irregular Verbs

Irregular verbs do not follow normal patterns of conjugation. Instead of adding an *–ed* to the base verb, an irregular verb requires some other spelling change or takes no change at all. We must simply learn and memorize the frequently used irregular verbs.

The most common irregular verb is *to be*. It has an unusual conjugation for all of the pronoun cases. In most situations, *to be* is a helping verb in the present, past, and future tenses. It rarely stands on its own, and when it does it is most likely an abbreviated response.

To Be		
Pronoun Case	**Singular**	**Plural**
1st Person	I am	we are
2nd Person	you are	you are
3rd person	he/she/it is	they are

However, *to be* is a common helping verb and should be memorized. Here is a chart of the present tense of the verb *to be* for the different pronoun cases.

There are many other common irregular verbs; these are also important to know. The following chart contains the most common irregular verbs, the past tense conjugation, and the past participle.

Common Irregular Verbs		
Base Form	**Past Tense**	**Past Participle**
be	was/were	been
bear	bore	borne
beat	beat	beaten
become	became	become
begin	began	begun
bite	bit	bitten
blow	blew	blown
break	broke	broken
bring	brought	brought
catch	caught	caught
choose	chose	chosen
come	came	come
creep	crept	crept
dive	dived or dove	dived
do	did	done
draw	drew	drawn
drink	drank	drunk
drive	drove	driven
eat	ate	eaten
fall	fell	fallen
feel	felt	felt
fling	flung	flung
fly	flew	flown
freeze	froze	frozen
get	got	gotten
give	gave	given
go	went	gone
grow	grew	grown
hang	hanged or hung	hanged or hung

Common Irregular Verbs		
Base Form	**Past Tense**	**Past Participle**
have	had	had
know	knew	known
lay	laid	laid
lead	led	led
lend	lent	lent
lie	lay	lain
lose	lost	lost
put	put	put
ride	rode	ridden
ring	rang	rung
rise	rose	risen
run	ran	run
say	said	said
see	saw	seen
shake	shook	set
shine	shined or shone	shined or shone
sing	sang	sung
sink	sank or sunk	sunk
sit	sat	sat
speak	spoke	spoken
spring	sprang or sprung	sprung
steal	stole	stolen
swim	swam	sworn
swing	swung	swum
take	took	taken
tear	tore	torn
think	thought	thought
throw	threw	thrown
try	tried	tried
wear	wore	worn
win	won	won
write	wrote	written

Answers to Exercises

Exercise 3-1

1. I (<u>need</u>, needs) a haircut.

2. John (prefer, <u>prefers</u>) chocolate more than vanilla.

3. Some people (<u>write</u>, writes) letters on the computer.

4. Reading (enhance, <u>enhances</u>) our vocabulary.

5. He (like, <u>likes</u>) to awaken early on Sundays.

6. We frequently (<u>walk</u>, walks) to work.

7. You never (<u>speak</u>, speaks) in front of crowds.

8. I always (<u>add</u>, adds) oregano to that chicken recipe.

9. The class (work, <u>works</u>) on mathematics.

10. Erica (listen, <u>listens</u>) to music with her headphones.

Exercise 3-2

1. They dance.   He *dances*.

2. I wish.   She *wishes*.

3. We dry.   He *dries*.

4. They complain.   She *complains*.

5. We rinse.   He *rinses*.

6. We smash.   She *smashes*.

7. I try.   He *tries*.

8. We intercede.   She *intercedes*.

9. They fly.   It *flies*.

10. I exercise.   He *exercises*.

Exercise 3-3

	past tense	future tense
1. Dominic <u>lives</u> in Vancouver.	*lived*	*will live*
2. He <u>loves</u> gardening.	*loved*	*will love*
3. Her sisters <u>play</u> outside.	*played*	*will play*
4. I <u>wish</u> her happiness.	*wished*	*will/shall wish*
5. Peter <u>remembers</u> his appointment.	*remembered*	*will remember*
6. The team <u>practices</u>.	*practiced*	*will practice*
7. Eddie <u>cleans</u> out his locker.	*cleaned*	*will clean*

8. We <u>dress</u> for dinner.   *dressed*   *will/shall dress*

9. You <u>smile</u> frequently.   *smiled*   *will smile*

10. They <u>add</u> tax to the bill.   *added*   *will add*

Exercise 3-4

             present perfect

1. Bill and I <u>walk</u> to the store.   *have walked*

2. The mother and father <u>watch</u> their child.   *have watched*

3. Our friends <u>purchase</u> concert tickets.   *have purchased*

4. Robert <u>dreams</u> of winning an award.   *has dreamed*

5. Kristina's cousin <u>finishes</u> projects.   *has finished*

6. She <u>gives</u> her manager an answer.   *has given*

7. The girl <u>has</u> a cold.   *has had*

8. In the dark, you <u>see</u> a shadow.   *have seen*

9. We <u>complete</u> our work.   *have completed*

10. Melissa and Jennifer <u>play</u> checkers.   *have played*

Exercise 3-5

             past perfect

1. Tom <u>reaches</u> the stairs.   *had reached*

2. We <u>watch</u> television.   *had watched*

3. No one <u>sees</u> the dog.   *had seen*

4. I <u>laugh</u> at the funny comedian.   *had laughed*

5. Patrick <u>paints</u> his ceiling.   *had painted*

6. Steve and Patty <u>give</u> to charity.   *had given*

7. You <u>need</u> a ticket for the movie.   *had needed*

8. They <u>send</u> a card to their neighbor.   *had sent*

9. Mary and I <u>answer</u> the telephone.   *had answered*

10. You <u>look</u> beautiful.   *had looked*

Exercise 3-6

             future perfect

1. I <u>work</u> in the office.   *will/shall have worked*

2. We <u>walk</u> before lunch.   *will /shall have walked*

3. Elizabeth <u>goes</u> to the beach.   *will have gone*

4. The daring players <u>win</u> the match.   *will have won*

5. Andrea <u>eats</u> apples after breakfast.   *will have eaten*

6. My friends <u>miss</u> their train.   *will have missed*

7. You <u>hope</u> for a high paying job.   *will have hoped*

8. They <u>line</u> up in formation.   *will have lined*

9. Bruce and I <u>reach</u> the end of the bike path.   *will /shall have reached*

10. He <u>uses</u> his new tools.   *will have used*

Exercise 3-7

present progressive

1. They <u>look</u> at the stars.   *are looking*

2. We <u>notice</u> the new street sign.   *are noticing*

3. No one <u>answers</u> the telephone.   *is answering*

4. I <u>check</u> my e-mail first thing in the morning.   *am checking*

5. Grant <u>needs</u> new clothes.   *is needing*

6. Barry <u>gives</u> advice to his younger sister.   *is giving*

7. I <u>look</u> tired.   *am looking*

8. David and Susan <u>teach</u> a class together.   *are teaching*

9. We <u>return</u> the movie rentals on time.   *are returning*

10. She <u>feels</u> better.   *is feeling*

Exercise 3-8

past progressive

1. John <u>navigates</u> the boat.   *was navigating*

2. She <u>labors</u> over difficult choices.   *was laboring*

3. Emily and her dog <u>lag</u> behind.   *were lagging*

4. My friends and I <u>buy</u> furniture at the outlet store.   *were buying*

5. Sandy's impulsive decision <u>haunts</u> her.   *was haunting*

6. The school <u>prohibits</u> smoking.   *was prohibiting*

7. You <u>remodel</u> your out-of-date kitchen.   *were remodeling*

8. They <u>retouch</u> the actresses' makeup.   *were retouching*

9. Ella and I <u>deliver</u> newspapers.   *were delivering*

10. The class <u>raises</u> money for the homeless.   *was raising*

Exercise 3-9

future progressive

1. Marie <u>sets</u> the table. — *will be setting*
2. We <u>create</u> artwork. — *shall/will be creating*
3. My brother <u>reads</u> the owner's manual. — *will be reading*
4. I <u>count</u> the remaining cans of coffee. — *shall/will be counting*
5. He <u>rubs</u> the paste off his fingers. — *will be rubbing*
6. They <u>enjoy</u> ice cream in the summer. — *will be enjoying*
7. You <u>pinch</u> the ends to seal the bag. — *will be pinching*
8. Donna and Lisa <u>slice</u> the watermelon. — *will be slicing*
9. We <u>contribute</u> to the pension fund. — *shall /will be contributing*
10. You <u>require</u> extra time to prepare for guests. — *will be requiring*

Exercise 3-10

present perfect progressive

1. Jennifer <u>comes</u> to the gym. — *has been coming*
2. We <u>enjoy</u> the party. — *have been enjoying*
3. They <u>visit</u> her sister. — *have been visiting*
4. My friends and I <u>follow</u> sports. — *have been following*
5. Isaac <u>auctions</u> rare artwork. — *has been auctioning*
6. The company <u>incurs</u> the cost of the damage. — *has been incurring*
7. The attorney and the accountant <u>certify</u> their work. — *have been certifying*
8. We <u>reach</u> a mutual agreement. — *have been reaching*
9. Aaron <u>delivers</u> beverages for the distributor. — *has been delivering*
10. The theater group <u>creates</u> superb drama. — *has been creating*

Exercise 3-11

past perfect progressive

1. My mechanic <u>repairs</u> my car. — *had been repairing*
2. We <u>dine</u> at the expensive restaurant. — *had been dining*
3. They <u>relax</u> after a late dinner. — *had been relaxing*
4. My friends and I <u>play</u> hockey. — *had been playing*
5. Anthony <u>participates</u> in charity events. — *had been participating*
6. The ship <u>moors</u> at the south pier. — *had been mooring*
7. Our aunt <u>bakes</u> delicious cinnamon rolls. — *had been baking*

8. We <u>consider</u> Laura a good friend.   *had been considering*

9. His employer <u>arrives</u> in a blue limousine.   *had been arriving*

10. The environmental group <u>distributes</u> literature. *had been distributing*

Exercise 3-12

                                                    future perfect progressive

1. My mother <u>finds</u> movies enjoyable.   *will have been finding*

2. We <u>refuse</u> to pay the exorbitant rental fees.   *will have been refusing*

3. They <u>answer</u> a series of questions.   *will have been answering*

4. My friends and I <u>shop</u> for luggage.   *will have been shopping*

5. He <u>drives</u> on the major highways.   *will have been driving*

6. The woman <u>practices</u> her golf swing.   *will have been practicing*

7. Judith <u>teaches</u> a variety of subjects.   *will have been teaching*

8. The energetic cat <u>chases</u> the mouse.   *will have been chasing*

9. They <u>offer</u> several payment options.   *will have been offering*

10. Citizens <u>vote</u> for the candidate of their choice. *will have been voting*

Exercise 3-13

1. The dish was broken by my mother.   *My mother broke the dish.*

2. I was taken to the cleaners.   no change

3. Melissa is tutored by Margaret.   *Margaret tutors Melissa.*

4. The group was brought up to the stage.   no change

5. Rain can be indicated by clouds.   *Clouds can indicate rain.*

6. The test was given by my math teacher.   *My math teacher gave the test.*

7. The leaves are raked by the gardener.   *The gardener rakes the leaves.*

8. The cranky child was put to bed.   no change

9. The boat is navigated by Donna.   *Donna navigates the boat.*

10. The questions were answered by Tom.   *Tom answered the questions.*

Selecting Effective Words

In the English language, there are so many words from which we can choose. There is no limit to the varieties of ways to say the same, or almost the same, thing. Diversity in writing is important; so is avoiding redundancy. With so many different ways to say something, how do you know which words are best? Concise and precise writing is also necessary. To be precise, we must use a word with exactly the intended meaning. To be concise, we must write clearly and with as few words are possible. This chapter examines the many ways to state ideas. It also looks at errors to avoid when choosing words.

Lesson 4-1: Choosing the Correct Word

Because of the inconsistencies in this language, we have words that are close in spelling but differ in pronunciation. We have words that are spelled the same but do not the same meaning or are even the same part of speech. For example, examine the following statement: *The dump was so full that it had to refuse more refuse.* When used the first time, *refuse* is the verb meaning to *turn away.* In its second appearance, the same letters form the word *refuse,* meaning *garbage.* Another example is the word *read.* It can be the past participle or the base form of the verb *to read,* but each has a different pronunciation. The past participle is a homonym for the color red. The base form is a homonym for reed, a stalk of grass. Some words are spelled identically, have similar pronunciations, but are dissimilar parts of speech with unlike meanings. This is exemplified in the sentence: *The farm was used to produce produce.* These are just a few of the many irregularities that can lead to special problems when choosing the right word.

Spelling

Even with today's technology, students are still expected to write by hand in some situations. Many state and standardized exams must be hand-written. In class, students must write essays or lengthy test answers. Here is a list of 50 words that are frequently spelled incorrectly. Look at this list to check which ones you frequently spell incorrectly.

The Most Common Misspelled Words

1. their/there/they're	18. through	35. business/–es
2. to/too/two	19. until	36. dependent
3. a lot	20. where	37. every day
4. noticeable	21. successful/–ly	38. may be
5. receive/–d/–s	22. truly	39. occasion/–s
6. lose	23. argument/–s	40. occurrences
7. you're/your	24. experience/–s	41. woman
8. an/and	25. environment	42. all right
9. develop/–s	26. exercise/–s/–ing	43. apparent/–ly
10. definitely	27. necessary	44. categories
11. than/then	28. sense	45. final/–ly
12. believe/–d/–s	29. therefore	46. immediate/–ly
13. occurred	30. accept/–ed	47. roommate/–s
14. affect/–s	31. heroes	48. against
15. cannot	32. professor	49. before
16. separate	33. whether	50. beginning
17. success	34. without	

Exercise 4-1

For each of the following sentences, choose and underline the correct spelling of the word in parentheses.

Example: The event (occured / <u>occurred</u>) at a (<u>separate</u>/ seperate) location.

1. (Their / There / They're) going to build (their / there / they're) new home over (their / there / they're) near the water.

2. Melissa likes (to / too) eat marshmallows (to / too).

3. The (begining / beginning) of this play is (definately / definitely) similar to the last play we saw.

4. The local (bussiness / business) (received / recieved) (a lot / alot) of coverage in the newspaper.

5. (Wheather / Whether) or not you (believe / beleive) her story, you must (immediately / immedietly) investigate the situation.

6. Some couples (develaop / develop) (seperate / separate) identities as they grow older.

7. The (heroes / heros) (acepted / accepted) (their / there / they're) award for "valor under (truly / truley) difficult circumstances."

8. She (cannot / canot) remove the (noticable / noticeable) stain from her carpet.

9. They (sucessfully / successfully) (experienced / expirienced) a peaceful holiday in a harmonious (enviroment / environment).

10. My (professor / proffesor) has an (arguement / argument) with a student (everyday / every day).

Homonyms

Homonyms are words that sound alike but mean different things. They are a common problem for students. This can cause difficulty with both the handwritten response and the typed response because computers might not catch the use of a homonym. Following is a list of common homonyms and their meanings.

Homonyms Chart

accept: to take or receive	except: to leave out
advice: suggestion	advise: to suggest
affect: an emotion; to influence	effect: a result; to cause to happen
allude: to refer	elude: to evade or escape
allusion: reference	illusion: false appearance
altar: place of worship	alter: to change
are: form of to be	our: belonging to us
bare: uncovered	bear: animal; to endure
board: piece of lumber	bored: disinterested
brake: to stop; device for stopping	break: hiatus; to shatter
buy: to purchase	by: near; beside
capital: headquarters or principal city	capitol: legislators' building
cite: to refer to	site: location
coarse: rough	course: path; plan of study
complement: to make complete	compliment: praise; to praise
conscience: scruples	conscious: mentally aware
council: ruling body	counsel: advice; to advise
desert: dry land; to abandon	dessert: sweet treat
device: gadget; something invented	devise: to plan or invent
die: to expire	dye: to color; color
elicit: to draw forth	illicit: illegal
eminent: distinguished	imminent: impending
fair: just; light in complexion	fare: fee for transportation; to experience
forth: forward	fourth: follows third
hear: to perceive sound	here: in this place
heard: past tense of hear	herd: group of animals
hoarse: sounding rough or harsh	horse: animal
its: possessive form of it	it's: contraction of *it is*

Homonyms Chart

know: to understand	no: opposite of yes
lead: a metal; to go before	led: past tense of *lead*
loose: not confined	lose: to misplace; to not win
meat: food	meet: to encounter
passed: went by	past: beyond; previous events
patience: endurance	patients: people under medical care
peace: tranquility	piece: part
personal: private	personnel: employees
plain: simple; flat land	plane: airplane; tool; level surface
presence: attendance; poise	presents: gifts; gives
principal: most important; head of school	principle: fundamental rule
rein: strap to control a horse	reign: period of rule; to rule
right: correct; direction opposite of left	rite: ceremony
road: street or highway	rode: past tense of *ride*
scene: setting; view	seen: past participle of *see*
stationary: unmoving	stationery: writing paper
than: as compared to	then: at that time; therefore
their: possessive form of they	there: that place
threw: past tense of *throw*	through: from beginning to end; throughout
too: also	two: number following one
waist: middle section of the body	waste: to squander
weak: feeble	week: seven days
wear: to be dressed in; deterioration	where: in what place
whether: if	weather: atmospheric conditions
which: what; that	witch: woman with supernatural powers
who's: contraction of *who is*	whose: possessive form of *who*
your: possessive form of *you*	you're: contraction of *you are*

Exercise 4-2

For each of the following sentences, choose and underline the correct form of the word in parentheses.

Example: To stop the (hoarse / <u>horse</u>), I grabbed the (reign / <u>rein</u>).

1. The (personal / personnel) (hear / here) at this company are (scene / seen) as quite competent.

2. (Are / Our) (principal / principle) (through / threw) a holiday party for the faculty.

3. I (council / counsel) you to (cite / site) sources used on (your /you're) research paper.

4. In one (weak / week) we will (buy / by) (presence / presents) for the children.

5. The bus (fair / fare) went up for the (forth / fourth) time this year.

6. It is difficult to (elicit / illicit) responses from (board / bored) students.

7. Julia required (plain / plane) (stationary / stationery) on (which / witch) to write her letters.

8. We (heard / herd) the doctor (compliment / complement) the nurses' care of (patience / patients).

9. The (eminent / imminent) activist (led / lead) a march (threw / through) the streets.

10. We must (altar / alter) our (coarse / course) to get back on the (right / rite) track.

Lesson 4-2: Spelling Rules

There are many homonyms, and these words are cause for many spelling errors. In addition, we have inconsistencies in pronunciation that also lead us astray. Because of these quirks in the English language, spelling can be difficult. However, this task can be easier if certain rules are followed. This section reviews the rules related to the most common spelling errors.

Put *I* Before *E*

Do you remember this rule from elementary school? "Put *i* before *e* except after *c* or when pronounced *ay* as in *neighbor* and *weigh*." This rhyme is a good start, but keep in mind that there are also exceptions.

Examples

achieve, brief, friend

These words demonstrate the rule of putting *i* before *e*.

ceiling, conceive, receive

These words demonstrate the exceptions for after *c*.

eighth, neighbor, reign

These words show the exceptions for the *ay* sound.

In addition, there is a list of words that do not fit the rule. These include *ancient, caffeine, conscience, either, foreign, height, leisure, neither, science, seize, species,* and *weird*.

Exercise 4-3

For each of the following words, insert either *ei* or *ie* into the space provided.

Example: rec *ei* ve

1. sl____gh

2. h____ght

3. fr____nd

4. ach____ve

5. w____rd

6. consc____nce

7. for____gn

8. p____rce

9. br____f

10. s____ze

Adding Prefixes

Prefixes are elements placed at the beginning of words to enhance or qualify their meaning. By adding a few letters to the beginning of words, you can modify the meaning of the word. Prefixes each have different meanings; through comprehension of prefixes and their definitions, you can decipher the meaning of the entire word. For example, *un–* is a prefix that means *opposite*. When added to a word, the denotation of the word becomes opposite. (For more about prefixes and their meanings, see Lesson 4-3.) Prefixes do not change the spelling of the words they are added to, even when the last letter of the prefix is the same as the first letter of the word.

Examples

mal + nourished = malnourished

Adding the prefix *mal–* to *nourished* changes the meaning of the word but not the spelling. The prefix *mal–* is bad, so malnourished means *badly nourished.*

un + necessary = unnecessary

When the prefix *un–* is added to *necessary,* the word changes to the opposite meaning. Notice that both *n*'s remain when the prefix is added.

dis + service = disservice

The prefix *dis–* means *separate* or *not.* Therefore, the meaning changes to *not a service.* In this example, the prefix ends with *s* and the word begins with *s,* and both remain in the joined word.

Exercise 4-4

Add prefixes to each of the following words. Note the spelling for each of the combined words.

Example: Add *in–* to these words. *In–* can mean *in* or *not.*

applicable	*inapplicable*	definable	*indefinable*
capable	*incapable*	edible	*inedible*
considerate	*inconsiderate*	sensitive	*insensitive*

1. Add *dis–* to these words. *Dis–* can mean *separate* or *not.*

accord	_____	honest	_____
believe	_____	service	_____
establish	_____	similar	_____

2. Add *mal–* to these words. *Mal–* means *bad* or *imperfect.*

adjusted	_____	odorous	_____
adroit	_____	practice	_____
content	_____	treat	_____

3. Add *non–* to these words. *Non–* means *not.* It is not as emphatic as *un–* or *in–*.

essential	_____	support	_____
fiction	_____	union	_____
stop	_____	violence	_____

4. Add *pre–* to these words. *Pre–* means *before in time or place.*

amble	_____	determine	_____
conceive	_____	dispose	_____
condition	_____	eminent	_____

5. Add *trans–* to these words. *Trans–* means *across* or *beyond.*

continental	_____	fuse	_____
figure	_____	plant	_____
form	_____	pose	_____

Adding Suffixes

Suffixes are elements placed at the end of words to form related words. For instance, they are used to change verb forms. To change the verb *talk* from the base form to the present participle *talking,* the suffix *–ing* is needed. To change the same verb to the past participle *talked,* the suffix *–ed* is needed. Certain rules exist for suffixes, but they are not always consistent. Here are some rules for suffixes. (For more about suffixes, see Lesson 4-3.)

Words ending in silent e

There is no one rule for words ending in an unpronounced *e* (receive, lose, exercise). You must decide whether or not to drop the *e* when adding a suffix. As a guideline, if the suffix starts with a **vowel**, drop the *e*.

Examples

explore + –ation = exploration

The suffix *–ation* begins with a vowel. Therefore, drop the *e* when adding it to *explore*.

imagine + –able = imaginable

The suffix *–able* begins with a vowel. Therefore, drop the *e* when adding it to *imagine*.

recite + –ing = reciting

The suffix *–ing* also begins with a vowel. Again, drop the *e* when adding it to *recite.*

continue + –ous = continuous

Because the suffix *–ous* begins with a vowel, the *e* is dropped when adding it to *continue.*

state + –ed = stated

Although the word ends with an *e,* if you remember to drop the vowel and add the suffix *–ed,* it is easier to stay consistent.

However, not all words fit this guideline. There are words that retain the *e* even when the suffix begins with a vowel. These words include:

dye + –ing = dyeing   marriage + –able = marriageable

notice + –able = noticeable   courage + –ous = courageous

The second guideline for adding suffixes when the word ends in *e* is that if the suffix starts with a **consonant,** keep the *e.*

Examples

force + –ful = forceful

The word ends in *e,* and the suffix begins with a consonant. Therefore, keep the *e.*

lone + –ly = lonely

The suffix *–ly* starts with a consonant and the word ends in an *e,* and so the *e* remains.

excite + –ment = excitement

This suffix *–ment* also begins with a consonant. Therefore, the *e* remains.

forgive + –ness = forgiveness

The word *forgive* ends in an e and the suffix begins with a consonant. In this example, the *e* remains.

There is also a list of words that do not fit this guideline. They drop the *e* even when the suffix begins with a vowel. These words include:

argue + –ment = argument   true + –ly = truly

judge + –ment = judgment   nine + –th = ninth

Exercise 4-5

Add suffixes to each of the following words. Drop the *e* when necessary.

Example: imagine + –ation   *imagination*

1. notice + –able _____

2. separate + –ness _____

3. implore + –ing _____

4. acute + –ly _____

5. bereave + –ment _____

6. gape + –ing _____

7. shake + –en _____

8. outrage + –ous _____

9. procure + –ment _____

10. note + –ed _____

The suffixes *–ally* and *–ly*

The guideline for choosing either *–ally* or *–ly* depends on how the root word ends. If the word ends in *ic,* use *–ally*. If the word does not end in *ic,* use *–ly*.

Examples

       drastic + –ally = drastically

Drastic ends in *ic*. Therefore, the suffix *–ally* is used here.

       magic + –ally = magically

The root word ends in *ic,* and so the suffix *–ally* is added.

       obvious + –ly = obviously

In this example, the root word does not end in *ic*. Therefore, the suffix *–ly* is used.

       usual + –ly = usually

Again, this root word does not end in *ic,* and so the suffix *–ly* is used here.

There is an exception to this rule: public + –ly = publicly.

The suffixes *–cede, –ceed,* and *–sede*

The guideline for choosing a suffix, either *–cede, –ceed,* or *–sede* is relatively easy. Almost all words ending with the sound *seed* use the suffix *–cede*. Only one word takes *–sede*: supersede. Only three words use the suffix *–ceed*: exceed, proceed, and succeed. Use the suffix *–cede* with all other words.

Examples

super + –sede = supersede   pro + –ceed = proceed

inter + –cede = intercede   pre + –cede = precede

con + –cede = concede   re + –cede = recede

Words ending in *y*

There are two general guidelines for adding suffixes to words ending in *y*. The first general rule is that if the *y* is preceded by a **consonant**, change the *y* to *i* when adding the suffix.

Examples

bounty + –ful = bountiful

In this example, the *y* is preceded by a consonant. Therefore, the *y* changes to *i* when the suffix *–ful* is added.

lazy + –ness = laziness

When the suffix *–ness* is added, the *y* changes to *i* because it is preceded by a consonant.

try + –ed = tried

The *y* is preceded by a consonant, and so it changes to *i* when the suffix *–ed* is added.

silly + –er = sillier

Here, the *y* is preceded by a consonant. Therefore, the *y* changes to *i* when the suffix *–er* is added.

crazy + –ly = crazily

The *y* is preceded by a consonant, and so it changes to *i* when the suffix *–ly* is added.

However, there is a list of words that do not fit this guideline; they retain the *y* even when the *y* is preceded by a consonant. These words include:

shy + –er = shyer   dry + –ly = dryly   wry + –ness = wryness

The second guideline for adding suffixes to words that end in *y* is that if the *y* is preceded by a **vowel,** if the word is a proper name, or if the suffix begins with an *i,* keep the *y.*

Examples

joy + –ous = joyous

In this example, the *y* is preceded by a vowel. Therefore, the *y* is retained.

Hardy + –esque = Hardyesque

This example retains the *y* because *Hardy* is a proper name. This example would be used for an allusion made to the author, Thomas Hardy, or another proper name ending in a *y* and preceded by a consonant.

dry + –ing = drying

The suffix *–ing* begins with a vowel, and so the *y* is retained in this example.

There are also words that do not fit this guideline. These words change the *y* to *i* even when the *y* is preceded by a vowel. These words include:

day + –ly = daily   gay + –ly = gaily

Exercise 4-6

Add suffixes to each of the following words. Change the *y* to *i* when necessary.

Example: carry + –ed = *carried*

1. busy + –er   _____

2. cry + –ing   _____

3. play + –ful   _____

4. breezy + –ness   _____

5. boy + –ish   _____

6. happy + –ness   _____

7. zany + –er   _____

8. defy + –ance _____

9. duty + –ful _____

10. likely + –hood _____

Words ending in a consonant

When a suffix beginning with a vowel is added to a word ending in a consonant, the consonant is sometimes doubled. There are two guidelines for adding suffixes to words ending in a consonant. The first rule is to double the final consonant if the word ends in consonant + vowel + consonant, and the word contains only one syllable or if it ends in the accented syllable.

Examples

stop + –ing = stopping

The ending consonant is doubled here because the suffix *–ing* begins in a vowel and the one-syllable word to which it is added ends in consonant + vowel + consonant.

slap + –ed = slapped

This ending consonant is doubled because this suffix also begins in a vowel and the one-syllable word to which it is added ends in consonant + vowel + consonant.

begin + –ing = beginning

Although the word *begin* is two syllables, it ends in the accented syllable. Therefore, because it ends in consonant + vowel + consonant, the final consonant is doubled.

occur + –ence = occurrence

Occur also has two syllables and ends in the accented syllable. Again, because it ends in consonant + vowel + consonant, the final consonant is doubled.

_____

The second general rule is that you do not double the consonant if it is preceded by more than one vowel or by another consonant, if the suffix begins with a consonant, if the word is not accented on the last syllable, or if the accent shifts from the last to the first syllable when the suffix is added.

Examples

> sleep + –ing = sleeping

The final consonant is not doubled in this case because it is preceded by more than one vowel.

> dart + –ed = darted

In this example, the final consonant is not doubled because it is preceded by another consonant.

> ship + –ment = shipment

Here, the suffix –*ment* begins with a consonant. Therefore, the final consonant is not doubled.

> benefit + –ed = benefited

Although this words ends in consonant + vowel + consonant, the accent is not on the last syllable.

> infer + –ence = inference

This words ends in consonant + vowel + consonant.

However, when the suffix is added, the accent is no longer on the first syllable.

Exercise 4-7

Add suffixes to each of the following words. When necessary, double the final consonant.

Example: refer + –ing   *referring*

1. fast + –est   _____

2. commit + –ment   _____

3. submit + –ed   _____

4. hot + –est   _____

5. regret + –able   _____

6. skip + –er   _____

7. fit + –ness   _____

8. occur + –ence   _____

9. weep + –ing   _____

10. fasten + –er   _____

Plurals

Changing singular words to plurals can be problematic. There are several guidelines used to make singular nouns plural. (For more about making nouns plural, see Lesson 1-1.) Here is a list of guidelines for making singular nouns plural.

▶ **For most words, simply add –s.**
   Examples:

   book / books   tree / trees

▶ **For words ending in s, ch, sh, x, or z, add –es.**
   Examples:

   bus / buses   church / churches
   box / boxes   buzz / buzzes

▶ **For words ending in o, add –es if the o is preceded by a consonant. Add –s if the o is preceded by a vowel.**
   Examples:

   potato / potatoes   hero / heroes
   rodeo / rodeos   zoo / zoos

   There are exceptions to this guideline. These words include:

   memo / memos   silo / silos

▶ **Words ending in f or fe. For some words ending in f or fe, change the f to v and add –s or –es.**
   Examples:

   calf / calves   self / selves
   life / lives   knife / knives

▶ **Words ending in y. For words ending in y, change the y to i and add –es if the y is preceded by a consonant.**
   Examples:

   theory / theories   berry / berries

Keep the *y* and add *–s* if the *y* is preceded by a **vowel** or if the noun is proper.

Examples:

> attorney / attorneys   Joey / Joeys

▶ **Irregular plurals.** Some words are irregular plurals. These words simply do not fit any guidelines. Some of these words follow.

Examples:

> alumnus/ alumni   man / men
> bacterium / bacteria   moose / moose
> child / children   mouse/ mice
> datum / data   tooth / teeth

▶ **Compound words.** For compound words that are written as one word, treat them as you would other nouns by making the last part of the noun plural.

Examples:

> briefcase / briefcases   mailbox / mailboxes

For compound nouns that are written as separate words or hyphenated, make the most important part of the noun plural.

Examples:

> bus stop / bus stops
> lieutenant governor / lieutenant governors
> leap year / leap years
> mother-in-law / mothers-in-law

Exercise 4-8

Make each of the following singular words plural.

Example: turkey   *turkeys*

1. self   _____   6. woman   _____

2. theory   _____   7. hoof   _____

3. flash   _____   8. brother-in-law _____

4. patio   _____   9. beach   _____

5. treaty   _____   10. fox   _____

Lesson 4-3: Vocabulary

Your English vocabulary consists of the words whose meanings you know and use, and those from which you can deduce meaning from context. This means that you have memorized the meaning for a body of words and that you can determine meaning for a larger group of words when they are used by someone else. Each word is comprised of sections, each with its own definition. This lesson deals with parts of words and their separate meanings, as well as their meanings when combined. It also highlights patterns that words take when prefixes and suffixes are added. Understanding the different sections of words and the patterns they follow allows you to constantly build your vocabulary.

Root Words

A word root is the main part of a word, but it is not a complete word in itself. A root is a word from which other words grow, usually through the addition of prefixes and suffixes. For instance, the Latin root *dict* is used for the words *predict, verdict, malediction, dictionary, dictate, dictum, diction,* and *indict*. English contains many Latin and Greek roots. Recognizing them will help to expand your vocabulary. The table on pages 141–142 contains some common root words, their meanings, and examples.

Exercise 4-9

Using the chart of roots on pages 141–142, try to determine the meaning for each of the following words.

Example: beneficial (bene = good) *something good*

1. jurist   _____

2. centenarian   _____

3. audiophile   _____

4. dermatologist   _____

5. scribe   _____

6. telecast   _____

7. terrace   _____

8. portfolio   _____

9. vacuous   _____

10. videophone   _____

Chart of Roots		
Root	**Meaning**	**Examples**
–am–	love	amiable, amity
–audi–	hear	audience, audio
–belli–	war	bellicose, belligerent
–bene–	good; well	benefactor, benevolent
–bio–	life	biography, biology
–brev–	short	brevity, abbreviation
–cap–	head	capitol, decapitate
–cent–	hundred	century, percent
–cog–	know	cognitive, recognize
–corp–	body	corporal, incorporate
–derm–	skin	dermatology, epidermis
–domin–	lord	dominate, dominion
–duc(t)–	lead; make	conduct, reproduce
–fac–, –fec–	do; make	factory, effect
–fin–	end	final, infinite
–fus–	pour	effusive, profuse
–gen–	race; birth	genealogy, genetics
–geo–	earth	geography, geophysics
–graph–	write	graphic, photography
–jac–, –jec–	throw	projection, reject
–junc–, –jug–	join	juncture, injunction
–jur–, –jus–	law	jurisdiction, justice
–juven–	young	juvenile, rejuvenate
–leg–	law	illegal, legislature
–log(o)–	word; thought	biology, logical

Chart of Roots

Root	Meaning	Examples
–loqu–	speak	circumlocution, loquacious
–luc–	light	lucid, translucent
–magn–	great	magnanimous, magnitude
–manu–	hand	manual, manufacture
–mit–, –mis–	to send	submit, transmission
–mor–	die	mortal, mortician
–nat–	born	prenatal, native
–path–	feel; suffer	pathetic, sympathy
–phil–	love	bibliophile, philosopher
–photo–	light	photography, telephoto
–port–	carry	portable, transport
–prim–	first	primal, primary
–psych–	soul	psychic, psychology
–scrib–, –script–	write	manuscript, transcribe
–sent–, –sens–	feel	sensation, resent
–sequ–	follow	consequence, sequel
–son–	sound	consonant, dissonance
–tele–	far away	telegraph, telepathy
–tend–	stretch	extend, tendency
–terr–	earth	terrain, territory
–tract–	draw; pull	contract, retract
–vac–	empty	evacuation, vacant
–verb–	word	proverb, verbose
–vid–, –vis–	see	video, visible
–vit–	life	revitalize, vitality

Prefixes

The word *prefix* explains its own significance. The prefix *pre–* means before. Prefixes are word elements attached to the beginnings of roots and base words to modify and expand their meanings. Recognizing prefixes can help to decipher and decode unfamiliar words. This tool will help build your working vocabulary. This is especially helpful because prefixes can make your writing more concise.

Examples

> Several groups <u>opposed to war</u> protested the invasion of Iraq. Other groups felt the troops received <u>a lack of support</u>.

These sentences can be written in a more concise manner.

> Several <u>antiwar</u> groups protested the invasion of Iraq. Other groups felt the troops were <u>unsupported</u>.

These subtle changes make the sentences clearer.

> Homes in coastal areas need appliances to <u>take the humidity out of</u> the air. Otherwise, the humidity is <u>impossible to tolerate</u>.

These sentences can also be clearer with the use of prefixes.

> Homes in coastal areas need appliances to <u>dehumidify</u> the air. Otherwise, the humidity is <u>intolerable</u>.

These sentences are more concise.

Prefixes can be grouped according to their meanings. There are six common groups of prefixes that are used. On the following pages, there are six tables of common prefixes for varying purposes. With each group, the spelling of the base word does not change. However, in some cases a hyphen is used between the prefix and the base. For example, a hyphen is always required after the prefix *ex–* when the base word is a proper noun or proper adjective. Consult a dictionary when you are unsure about whether or not to use a hyphen after a prefix.

Prefixes With Negative Meanings

Prefix	Meaning	Examples
a–, an–	without; not	atypical, anomalous
dis–	apart; away	disappear, dispatch
il–	not; without; lack of	illegal, illiterate
im–	not; without; lack of	immature, implacable
in–	not; without; lack of	incredible, indistinct
ir–	not; without; lack of	irrelevant, irrevocable
mal–	bad; wrong	malevolent, malfeasance
mis–	bad; wrong	misapply, miscarry
non–	not	nonconformist, nonsense
un–	not	unable, unfair

Exercise 4-10

For each of the following sentences, substitute one word for the under-lined phrase or clause. The one word should be a word from the phrase or clause combined with the prefix in parentheses.

Example:　Are some dogs <u>not capable</u> of being trained?
　　　　　　(in–)

　　　　　　Are some dogs *incapable* of being trained?

1. I felt <u>a lack of belief</u> as I watched the puppy run into the street.
   (dis–)

   _____

2. It appeared that the dog was <u>treated badly</u>.
   (mis–)

   _____

3. The thin puppy must have been <u>under nourished</u>.
   (mal–)

   _____

4. The dog's owner was <u>not courteous</u> to the crowd on the street.
   (dis–)

   _____

5. Could this person be <u>without morals</u>?
   (a–)

   _____

6. My anger was <u>beyond measure</u> as I approached him.
   (im–)

   _____

7. The conversation between us was <u>not productive</u>.
   (non–)

   _____

8. I was <u>not capable</u> of restraint as I spoke with the man.
   (in–)

   _____

9. The fact that he had papers for the dog was <u>not relevant</u> to me.
   (ir–)

   _____

10. Animal abuse in any form is <u>not legal</u>.
    (il–)

   _____

Prefixes That Reverse Actions

Prefix	Meaning	Examples
de–	to deprive of; to remove	depersonalize, deactivate
dis–	to take away; to remove	discredit, dislocate
un–	to deprive of	uncover, unravel

Exercise 4-11

For each of the following sentences, substitute one word for the underlined phrase or clause. The one word should be a word from the phrase or clause combined with the prefix in parentheses.

Example: Online purchasing can make shopping less personalized.
(de–)

Online purchasing can *depersonalize* shopping.

1. One scandal can remove the credibility of any politician.
(dis–)

_____

2. Harsh weather continues to remove people from farming communities.   (de–)

_____

3. The technician removed the cover from the computer.   (un–)

_____

4. Cable service to her area is no longer continued.   (dis–)

_____

5. Her gardener began to remove the load of gravel from his truck.
(un–)

_____

Prefixes That Show Time or Order

Prefix	Meaning	Examples
ante–	before	antebellum, antediluvian
ex–	previous; former	ex-President, ex-convict
neo–	new; recent	neoclassic, neophyte
post–	after	postwar, postscript
pre–	before	prewar, predetermine
re–	again; back	reschedule, review
syn–	at the same time	synonym, synchronize

Exercise 4-12

For each of the following sentences, substitute one word for the under-lined phrase or clause. The one word should be a word from the phrase or clause combined with the prefix in parentheses.

Example: Can you <u>determine</u> the number of guests <u>prior to arrival</u>? (pre–)

Can you *predetermine* the number of guests?

1. We will have to <u>schedule</u> your visit <u>for another time</u>. (re–)

2. The treatment <u>that took place following his diagnosis</u> was rigorous. (post–)

3. The <u>former President</u> spoke at the assembly. (ex–)

4. Scientist worked to establish <u>prior existence</u> of plant life in the region. (pre–)

5. The man, <u>previously a soldier</u>, tried to establish a new career. (ex–)

6. After the earthquake, the buildings were <u>constructed again</u> using steel.   (re–)

7. The coach's conversation <u>after the game</u> focused on maneuvering. (post–)

8. His <u>former wife</u> retained custody of the children. (ex–)

9. Some recipe ingredients are for sale <u>already mixed</u> in the package. (pre–)

_____

10. The government is <u>again exploring</u> the possibility of tax incentives. (re–)

_____

Prefixes That Show Location

Prefix	Meaning	Examples
aer–	air	aerodynamics, airplane
aster–, astro–	star	astrology, astronomy
circum–	around	circumvent, circumnavigate
inter–	between; among	interdisciplinary, intervene
intra–	within	intravenous, intracellular
mid–	in the middle of	midweek, midsection
sub–	under; beneath	subbasement, submarine
trans–	across; over	transport, transcontinental

Exercise 4-13

For each of the following sentences, substitute one word for the underlined phrase or clause. The one word should be a word from the phrase or clause combined with the prefix in parentheses.

Example: The meeting, <u>scheduled for the middle of the week</u>, was inconvenient. (mid–)

The *mid-week* meeting was inconvenient.

1. The explorer <u>navigated around</u> the globe. (circum–)

_____

2. The highway <u>that goes between the states</u> needed repair. (inter–)

_____

3. After he drank three beers, his intelligence was <u>below normal</u>.
    (sub–)

    _____

4. The employee's evaluation <u>during the middle of the year</u> showed
    improvement. (mid–)

    _____

5. Trips <u>across the continent</u> can be exciting.
    (trans–)

    _____

Prefixes That Show Number or Degree

Prefix	Meaning	Examples
bi–	two	bipolar, bilateral
hyper–	over; more than	hyperbole, hypertension
hypo–	under; less than	hypodermic, hypoglycemia
mega–	enlarge; large	megalomania, megaphone
micro–	small	microfilm, microscopic
milli–	thousand	milligram, millimeter
mono–	one; single	monotone, monosyllable
omni–	all	omniscient, omnipotent
out–	going beyond; more	outnumber, outscore
over–	excessive; too much	overanxious, overcrowded
semi–	half	semicolon, semifinal
sub–	lower than; less than	subhuman, subcommittee
super–	above; better than	superhuman, superimpose
tri–	three	triangle, trident
under–	insufficient; too little	underdeveloped, undersized
uni–	one	uniform, universal

Exercise 4-14

For each of the following sentences, substitute one word for the underlined phrase or clause. The one word should be a word from the phrase or clause combined with the prefix in parentheses.

Example: Conservationists love cars that are smaller than compact cars.   (sub–)

Conservationists love *subcompact* cars.

1. Bill is extremely sensitive about his thinning hair.   (hyper–)

   _____

2. Ellen estimated the number of ticket holders too high.
   (over–)

   _____

3. Advertising is present everywhere today, even in doctors' offices!
   (omni–)

   _____

4. The strange event seemed to be beyond natural occurrences.
   (super–)

   _____

5. There is one form of dress in the military.   (uni–)

   _____

6. Vanessa's favorite store has a sale twice a year.   (semi–)

   _____

7. The athletic contest consisting of three events was held in Miami.
   (tri–)

   _____

8. Brandon estimated the sales figures too low.   (under–)

   _____

9. The number of teachers was more than the number students at the
   game. (out–)

   _____

10. Words with one syllable are easy to pronounce.   (mono–)

   _____

Prefixes That Show Support or Opposition

Prefix	Meaning	Examples
anti–	against	antibody, antimatter
co–	together with; joint	co-author, cohesive
col–	with; together	collaborate, collate
com–	with; together	combine, combustion
con–	with; together	connection, conduct
cor–	with; together	correspond
contra–	against	contraband, contravene
counter–	return an action against	counterforce, counterproposal
pro–	before, forward	propel, project

Exercise 4-15

For each of the following sentences, substitute one word for the under-lined phrase or clause. The one word should be a word from the phrase or clause combined with the prefix in parentheses.

Example: Andrea and Charlene <u>were leaders</u> for the team <u>together</u>. (co–)

    <u>Andrea and Charlene were *co-leaders* for the team</u>.

1. Seditious people demonstrate behavior <u>that goes against the establishment</u>. (anti–)

  _____

2. <u>Evidence provided by the defense</u> disproved the prosecution's claim. (counter–)

  _____

3. <u>Laws to protect conservation</u> have been instituted by many states. (pro–)

  _____

4. The two professors <u>wrote a textbook together</u>. (co–)

  _____

5. The test results <u>went against</u> the doctor's initial diagnosis. (contra–)

___

Suffixes

Suffixes are attached to the ends of words and word roots to modify and extend meanings. In many cases, the part of speech is also altered when the suffix is added. In other words, by adding or changing a suffix, a noun can become an adjective, a verb can become a noun, an adjective can become an adverb, and so on.

Examples

She is a <u>real</u> person.

The word *real* in this sentence is an adjective. Notice how the part of speech changes by adding a suffix.

She is a <u>realist</u>.

With the addition of *–ist,* the adjective *real* becomes the noun *realist.*

In <u>reality</u>, she is compassionate.

With the addition of *–ity,* the adjective *real* becomes the noun.

She is a <u>really</u> compassionate person.

In this example, the suffix *–ly* changes *real* into the adverb *really.*

___

Using suffixes can increase your vocabulary by expanding words that you already know. Like prefixes, suffixes can also make your writing more concise. In the following examples, note how the sentences become clearer and more direct with the addition of suffixes.

Examples

<u>The fire that consumed the building turned the walls black. The people who occupied the building needed to find temporary housing.</u>

These sentences could be clearer with the use of suffixes.

<u>The consuming fire blackened the walls. The occupants needed to find temporary housing.</u>

By changing a few suffixes, these sentences are more concise.

___

Suffixes are grouped according to whether they derive nouns, adjectives, verbs, or adverbs. However, the main adverb-forming suffix is *–ly*. The suffix *–ly* can be added to many adjectives to form adverbs. The following pages contain tables that list common suffixes used to form nouns, adjectives, and verbs. Notice that a spelling change is sometimes required when a suffix is added to a base word. (For more about these spelling changes, review Lesson 4-2 on page 128.)

Suffixes That Form Nouns

Suffix	Meaning	Examples
–acy	state of or condition	democracy, intimacy
–age	result of action	marriage, drainage
–al	action	denial, rebuttal
–ance, –ence	state of or quality of	maintenance, preference
–ant, –ent	performer of action	occupant, superintendent
–ation	action; state; result	expectation, transformation
–dom	condition; domain	boredom, kingdom
–ee	receiver of action	employee, trainee
–eer	one involved in activity	auctioneer, mountaineer
–er, –or	performer of an action	competitor, investor
–ful	amount	cupful, mouthful
–hood	state of or condition of	childhood, widowhood
–ism	doctrine; system; belief	Buddhism, imperialism
–ist	one who does or follows	organist, physicist
–ity	quality; state; condition	absurdity, reality
–ment	state or condition	astonishment, government
–ness	quality or state of	cleanliness, deafness
–ship	position; quality; state	fellowship, leadership
–sion, –tion	state of being or action	digression, transition
–tude	quality or state	gratitude, multitude
–ure	act; means; result	exposure, pleasure
–y	quality; action; condition	jealousy, inquiry

Exercise 4-16

For each of the following sentences, substitute a noun for the underlined phrase or clause. The noun should be a word from the phrase or clause combined with the suffix in parentheses.

Example: All couples need <u>time to be private</u>.   (–acy)

All couples need *privacy*.

1. <u>The fact that he refused</u> help was admirable.   (–al)

_____

2. <u>A person who depends on others</u> may not succeed.   (–ent)

_____

3. He spoke with the <u>person being trained</u>.   (–ee)

_____

4. We needed <u>someone to read</u> manuscripts.   (–er)

_____

5. The <u>man who made it to the finals</u> dropped out of the competition. (–ist)

_____

6. <u>The idea over which they argued</u> was ridiculous.   (–ment)

_____

7. Molly was known throughout school <u>for being friendly</u>. (–ness)

_____

8. <u>The fact that they are friends</u> has affected both their lives. (–ship)

_____

9. The audience lost interest <u>when he digressed from the topic</u>. (–tion)

_____

10. Because <u>she was jealous</u>, Emily acted foolishly.   (–y)

_____

Suffixes That Form Adjectives

Suffix	Meaning	Examples
–able, –ible	capable of being	breakable, digestible
–al, –ial	characteristic of; pertaining	comical, denial
–ary	related to	planetary, elementary
–en	made of; like	golden, wooden
–esque	reminiscent of	picturesque, statuesque
–ful	full of; having quality of	colorful, hopeful
–ic	having nature of; pertaining	metallic, poetic
–ious, –ous	full of; characterized by	famous, nutritious
–ish	having the quality of	greenish, prudish
–ive	having the nature of	expressive, festive
–less	without; lacking	joyless, humorless
–like	similar to	childlike, doglike
–ly	like; characteristic of	friendly, heavenly
–some	like; tending to	loathsome, quarrelsome
–y	like; showing	dirty, healthy

Exercise 4-17

For each of the following sentences, substitute an adjective for the underlined phrase or clause. The adjective should be a word from the phrase or clause combined with the suffix in parentheses.

Example: The coupon to be redeemed was in the newspaper.   (–able)

The *redeemable* coupon was in the newspaper.

1. The expression on the baby's face was adorable.   (–ial)

_____

2. The diligent saleswoman gave me a lot of help.   (–ful)

_____

3. The recent archeology dig in Africa <u>had an impact on history</u>. (–ic)

_____

4. The hero, <u>filled with glory</u>, marched to victory.   (–ious)

_____

5. The gluttonous man at the buffet <u>seemed like a pig</u>.   (–ish)

_____

6. Eileen is <u>good at creating</u>.   (–ive)

_____

7. The movie seems <u>to have no end</u>.   (–less)

_____

8. My sister <u>acts like she is a friend</u> to everyone.   (–ly)

_____

9. The villain <u>who committed murder</u> was finally caught.   (–ous)

_____

10. The ice cream was <u>more like soup</u>.   (–y)

_____

Suffixes That Form Nouns and Adjectives

Suffix	Meaning	Examples
–an, –ian	belonging to; related to	American, republican
–ese	of a style or place	journalese, Viennese

Suffixes That Form Verbs

Suffix	Meaning	Examples
–ate	become; cause to become	activate, captivate
–en	become; cause to become	lengthen, quicken
–fy, –ify	cause to become	purify, terrify
–ize	become; cause to become	civilize, modernize

Exercise 4-18

For each of the following sentences, substitute a verb for the underlined phrase or clause. The verb should be a word from the phrase or clause combined with the suffix in parentheses.

Example: The school children watched the sugar-water become crystals. (–ize)
The school children watched the sugar-water *crystallize*.

1. The earthquake made the structure become weak.
   (–en)

_____

2. The scientist was able to change the gas into liquid.
   (–fy)

_____

3. Teams must work to unite their members.
   (–ify)

_____

4. The manager had to make sure the payments were regular.
   (–ate)

_____

5. We wanted to make the plans final.
   (–ize)

_____

Derivational Patterns

Certain types of words follow definite patterns in the suffixes they take. For example, just as *deceive* can become *deception* and *deceptive*, *receive* can become *reception* and *receptive*. These patterns allow writers to easily change the part of speech. In this case, the part of speech changes from verb to noun to adjective. Although a writer would not include several forms of the same word in one sentence, knowing different forms of each word can be a tremendous aid, especially at the revision stage. On the following pages there are tables for nine patterns of derivational suffixes. By learning these patterns you can expand your writing vocabulary because you can predict derived forms of words you already know.

Pattern I: –ment, –er

Verb	Noun	Noun
achieve	achievement	achiever
adjust	adjustment	adjuster
announce	announcement	announcer
appoint	appointment	appointer
encourage	encouragement	encourager
enforce	enforcement	enforcer
develop	development	developer
punish	punishment	punisher

Exercise 4-19

For each of the following sentences, insert the correct form of the word in parentheses into the space provided.

Example: An insurance company sends an *adjuster* to *adjust* a claim if it requires an *adjustment*. (adjust)

1. At the theater we heard the _____ give an _____ over the loudspeaker to _____ the end of intermission. (announce)

2. An worthwhile employer must also be an _____; he should use _____ to _____ his employees to succeed. (encourage)

3. The judge was known as an effectual _____; he would always _____ with the appropriate _____. (punish)

4. No matter what the goal, an _____ strives for _____ in order to _____ his or her objective. (achieve)

5. Law _____ personnel _____ the laws of the state, county, and nation. An _____ is an honorable profession. (enforce)

Pattern II: –ify, –ification, –ifier

Verb	Noun	Noun
amplify	amplification	amplifier
beautify	beautification	beautifier
clarify	clarification	clarifier
classify	classification	classifier
codify	codification	codifier
fortify	fortification	fortifier
justify	justification	justifier
modify	modification	modifier
nullify	nullification	nullifier
pacify	pacification	pacifier
simplify	simplification	simplifier

Exercise 4-20

For each of the following sentences, insert the correct form of the word in parentheses into the space provided.

Example: When the level of sound is too low, *amplification* is needed; use an *amplifier* to *amplify* the sound level. (amplify)

1. Vitamins and minerals contribute _____ to the body. They nourish and _____ with different _____(s). (fortify)

2. A _____ for the postal system will _____ different types of packages using _____. (classify)

3. To enhance outward appearance of a building, a _____ will _____ the outside of the structure. _____ improves the facades. (beautify)

4. Clear _____ is needed when traveling. Airport personnel will use an _____ to _____ travelers. (identify)

5. When a change or _____ is needed in your sentence, use a _____ to alter or _____ what you want to say. (modify)

Pattern III: –ize, –ization, –izer

Verb	Noun	Noun
authorize	authorization	authorizer
colonize	colonization	colonizer
modernize	modernization	modernizer
organize	organization	organizer
tranquilize	tranquilization	tranquilizer
vaporize	vaporization	vaporizer

Caution is necessary here. It has become trendy to add suffixes, in particular *–ize,* to words in order to sound scholarly or to make an allusion. (DNA selection can *Einstein-ize* the population.) This is erroneous. Be sure that your words correctly take the suffix or else you end up with gibberish.

Exercise 4-21

For each of the following sentences, insert the correct form of the word in parentheses into the space provided.

Example: *Authorization* is needed from an *authorizer* in order to *authorize* a change in service. (authorize)

1. When _____ began in this country, a typical _____ would _____ and develop a specific area. (colonize)

2. _____ of a location occurs when a _____ attempts to update and _____ a setting. (modernize)

3. The zookeeper will _____ an animal with a
   _____ if necessary. _____
   is a last resort. (tranquilize)

4. The teacher helped her students _____ their
   notebooks using _____. _____(s)
   are successful students. (organize)

5. _____ happens when solids turn to gas.
   To _____, use the _____
   in the laboratory. (vaporize)

Pattern IV: –ate, –ation, –ator

Verb	Noun	Noun
arbitrate	arbitration	arbitrator
calculate	calculation	calculator
cultivate	cultivation	cultivator
decorate	decoration	decorator
educate	education	educator
indicate	indication	indicator
legislate	legislation	legislator
navigate	navigation	navigator
violate	violation	violator

Both –er and –or have the same meaning: "one who does." The suffix –or is used to form a noun from verbs that end in *ate*.

Exercise 4-22

For each of the following sentences, insert the correct form of the word in parentheses into the space provided.

Example: *Arbitration* is used in legal cases where an *arbitrator* must *arbitrate* a decision. (arbitrate)

1. I used a _____ to _____ my
   mathematical _____ for my checkbook. (calculate)

2. _____ is a priority for most states. We must
    _____ students and train competent
    _____ (s). (educate)

3. The _____ light on the dashboard will
    _____ when a car needs oil. This
    _____ can save your transmission. (indicate)

4. To _____ a cake, a _____ will apply
    festive _____ (s) to the top and sides. (decorate)

5. The _____ must be trained in _____ in order
    to successfully _____ large bodies of water. (navigate)

Pattern V: –ation, –er

Verb	Noun	Noun
admire	admiration	admirer
explore	exploration	explorer
export	exportation	exporter
import	importation	importer
observe	observation	observer
preserve	preservation	preserver
reform	reformation	reformer
tempt	temptation	tempter
transform	transformation	transformer

Exercise 4-23

For each of the following sentences, insert the correct form of the word
in parentheses into the space provided.

Example: Lifeguards are trained to *preserve* lives; they use different
measures for *preservation*, including the life *preserver*.
(preserve)

1. I _____ someone with courage; my _____
    shows I am an _____ of strength. (admire)

2. The _____ of the New World came from the
   _____('s) need to _____ and
   discover new places. (explore)

3. A rug_____ deals with the _____
   and distribution of rugs; he or she must _____
   them from other countries. (import)

4. The director of the play made an astute _____. As
   an _____, her role is to _____
   the performers on stage. (observe)

5. The caterpillar is a _____. It undergoes a _____
   in order to _____ into a butterfly. (transform)

Pattern VI: –ion, –ive

Verb	Noun	Adjective
aggress	aggression	aggressive
connect	connection	connective
exhaust	exhaustion	exhaustive
express	expression	expressive
instruct	instruction	instructive
invent	invention	inventive
oppress	oppression	oppressive
prevent	prevention	preventive
restrict	restriction	restrictive

Exercise 4-24

For each of the following sentences, insert the correct form of the word
in parentheses into the space provided.

Example: An *aggressive* action by one party usually provokes
aggression from another party. (aggress)

1. A good cable _____ is important for computers.
   You must be sure to use sturdy _____ devices when
   you _____ your PC. (connect)

2. The _____ shopping excursion caused an _____ of finances as well. Be sure not to _____ all financial resources. (exhaust)

3. Debate fosters _____ speech. If careful _____ can influence an audience, be sure to _____ your ideas clearly. (express)

4. The _____ scientist created a marvelous _____. He was able to _____ an ice cream with no calories! Too bad it also had no flavor. (invent)

5. Fire _____ saves lives. It can _____ fires with _____ measures. (prevent)

This next table contains verbs that undergo almost the same kinds of changes as those in Pattern VI. However, in Pattern VII there is an additional spelling change when the derivational suffixes are added. Look for the changes in spelling when the word changes from verb to noun and verb to adjective.

Pattern VII: –ion, –ive

Verb	Noun	Adjective
adhere	adhesion	adhesive
compel	compulsion	compulsive
comprehend	comprehension	comprehensive
conclude	conclusion	conclusive
deceive	deception	deceptive
evade	evasion	evasive
explode	explosion	explosive
extend	extension	extensive
permit	permission	permissive
persuade	persuasion	persuasive
receive	reception	receptive
repel	repulsion	repulsive

Exercise 4-25

For each of the following sentences, insert the correct form of the word in parentheses into the space provided.

Example: I used _adhesive_ tape to wrap my holiday packages. The _adhesion_ was strong and the wrapping held tightly. (adhere)

1. My neighbor is a _____ cleaner. He has a _____ to clean every surface in his house. I wish I could _____ him to clean mine. (compel)

2. Reading _____ is concern in schools today. In order to determine what students _____, they must undertake _____ examinations. (comprehend)

3. The witches in *Macbeth* are _____. They use _____ to beguile and _____ the title character and his wife. (deceive)

4. _____ measures were used during the conflict. In order to _____ the overpowering enemy, military leaders planned an _____. (evade)

5. A grand _____ was planned to _____ the dignitaries from abroad. Both sides were _____ to the idea of the gala. (receive)

Pattern VIII: –ence, –ent

Verb	Noun	Adjective
depend	dependence	dependent
differ	difference	different
diverge	divergence	divergent
emerge	emergence	emergent
insist	insistence	insistent
persist	persistence	persistent
recur	recurrence	recurrent
reside	residence	resident
revere	reverence	reverent

Exercise 4-26

For each of the following sentences, insert the correct form of the word in parentheses into the space provided.

Example: _Persistence_ is frequently an admirable quality.
A _persistent_ person shows dedication to cause.
(persist)

1. Many people have _____
   dreams. The _____
   of certain images and patterns may prove that certain anxieties
   also _____.
   (recur)

2. The two friends _____ on
   many topics. They have _____
   styles of dress, but this _____
   has not cost them their friendship. (differ)

3. I watched the groundhog _____
   from his hole. His _____
   has become a tradition in weather forecasting. When the
   _____ animal saw
   his shadow, the crowd expected six more weeks of winter.
   (emerge)

4. The citizens of our town all _____
   our mayor. This _____
   woman has done a great deal for our community.
   _____ for her is widespread.
   (revere)

5. The two painters _____ in
   their new loft. Their _____
   has already been painted by Tammy, the _____
   artist. (reside)

In this next table, the derivation is a little different. Pattern IX shows how some nouns and adjectives are changed into other nouns and/or adjectives.

Pattern IX: –ist, –ism, –istic

Adjective or Noun	Noun	Adjective
fatal	fatalist, fatalism	fatalistic
future	futurist, futurism	futuristic
ideal	idealist, idealism	idealistic
legal	legalist, legalism	legalistic
material	materialist, materialism	materialistic
moral	moralist, moralism	moralistic
national	nationalist, nationalism	nationalistic
plural	pluralist, pluralism	pluralistic
rational	rationalist, rationalism	rationalistic
real	realist, realism	realistic
ritual	ritualist, ritualism	ritualistic
sensational	sensationalist, sensationalism	sensationalistic

Exercise 4-27

For each of the following sentences, insert the correct form of the word in parentheses into the space provided.

Example: *Idealism* is a theory posed by *idealist(s)* in order to make others believe in a Utopian, *idealistic* world. (ideal)

1. _____ people place _____, or the importance of _____ goods, above all else. (material)

2. The _____ nature of religion and its practicing _____(s) are intriguing. For most religions, _____ can be linked to previous millennia. (ritual)

3. In tabloid writing, the _____ will use
    _____ to sell papers. People are intrigued
    by _____ stories. (sensational)

4. The _____ atmosphere of the parade
    celebrated _____ and all for which our
    country stands. (national)

5. _____ is a personal level of belief. Do not
    preach; sometimes being _____ can make a
    person appear haughty. (moral)

Lesson 4-4: Diction

With the spoken word, diction is the manner in which you speak; it is
your enunciation. With the written word, diction represents words you
choose to express yourself; it means your writer's voice. The main focus
of diction with the written word is to choose words effectively based on
the writer's subject, audience, and purpose. What is appropriate for one
piece of writing might be totally inappropriate for another. Occupation,
social or ethnic group, region, and relationship can all have an impact on
the writer's diction. For example, the vocabulary you choose for an e-
mail to a friend is exceedingly different from the vocabulary you use for
a business letter. Do you use correct grammar and polysyllabic words in
your notes to friends? Would an associate or company with whom you do
business take you seriously if you wrote: "ur gr8 b/c ur funny - lol!"? This
section deals with the various forms of English that we use on an everyday basis.

Slang and Colloquial Language

Slang, or extremely informal language, is what you use with a small
group of people. Close friends and family use different terms that sometimes become obsolete quickly. Some slang expressions become com-
monplace and almost seem universal; they are so hackneyed that one
almost forgets that they are slang expressions. Some slang terms are other
words used in a different way. For instance, you can *finger* a suspect. The
words *cool, represent,* and *mellow* mean different things to different gen-
erations. Colloquial expressions, such as "he has *nerve*" and "we made a
killing with our investments" are more widely recognized. The differences
between slang and colloquial are who understands what you are saying, and
who these people are.

Using slang and colloquial language, write a paragraph describing your favorite activity. Be sure to include description and detail. Then, rewrite the paragraph using conventional English. Note the different effects that the language has on each paragraph.

Denotation and Connotation

Denotation is the general meaning of the word; basically, it is the definition. Connotation is the association that comes with the word. It can apply to mood and how the reader interprets what you are saying. For example, *average* and *mediocre* have similar denotations, but they have different connotations. *Average* represents the mean; it is normal. *Mediocre* is something that is not good enough. *Childish* and *childlike* both have the same denotation, someone like a child. The connotation for the word *childish* is negative. It implies that acting like a child is a bad thing. However, *childlike* has a positive connotation. It implies that the person is innocent and playful. These words are so similar, but they are inferred differently by the reader.

The writer must be careful. Some words change connotation in different circumstances. For instance, *old-fashioned* can be something charming and quaint, or antiquated and out-of-date. Connotation can also change with the audience. Certain groups of people may have different connotations based on their history. Connotations can also be personal. Each individual may have memories associated with words that affect their connotations. Although some connotation is out of the writer's control, he must be careful to explore connotation when selecting words and phrases.

Balancing General and Specific Diction

In some cases, general terms are the most appropriate. Other times, specific terms are needed. A writer must balance general diction with specific terminology in order to be effective. Consider the levels of specificity for the following examples.

General	Less General	Specific	More Specific
a car	a red car	a red Mustang	a 1965 Mustang convertible
a book	a textbook	a science textbook	an organic chemistry text
a house	a white house	a white colonial	the colonial on Main Street

When general descriptions are provided, the reader uses his imagination to fill in the blanks. When too much detail is given, the pace of the piece is slow. The writer must find a good balance where enough description is provided, but the main point does not get lost in all the detail. Notice the diversity is the following passages.

> "They prepared dinner and served it to their guests."

VS.

> "Ruby cut the heads off three chickens, for the yard was now so full of chicks they could hardly walk to the springhouse without stepping on one, and the population was such that they could anticipate a sufficiency of capons soon. They cut the chickens up and fried them, cooked pole beans, boiled potatoes and stewed squash. Ruby made a triple recipe of biscuits, and when supper was ready they called in the visitors and sat them at the dining-room table." Charles Frazier, *Cold Mountain*

The terseness of the first passage might be suitable for some purposes, but the imagery of the second passage affects the senses of the reader. You must determine the level that is suitable for each piece.

Exercise 4-29

Rewrite each of the following concise sentences to include more specific details.

Example: The book is on the desk.

The red antique, leather-bound book with gilded edges, once a treasured possession of my grandmother, lay open on the mahogany desk, its pages softly blowing and turning one by one as the gentle wind enters from the open window.

1. My car has a dent.

2. There is trash on the floor.

3. Sunday dinner was delicious.

4. The child was in the park.

5. At the store, I bought a toy.

Figurative Language

Some examples in the previous section contain figurative language, or figures of speech. Figurative language paints pictures in the minds of the reader. For instance, imagery, or figures of speech that affect the five senses, can be used to help describe an exact sound or a specific color. A house might be painted "the color of mud" or "cornflower blue." Her voice might be "as sweet as a nightingale," or it may sound "like a rooster with a nail puncturing its side." Some forms of figurative language include:

▶ **Similes:** These figures of speech compare two unlike things using *like* or *as*.

  Example:

> The child ran through the room like a freight train flying off its tracks.

▶ **Metaphor:** This type of figurative language compares two unlike things without using *like* or *as*.

  Example:

> Your heart is a stone.

▶ **Analogies:** These are used to compare similar features of two dissimilar things and are often extended to several sentences or paragraphs in order to incorporate details.

  Example:

> "Restaurants are to the nineties what theater was to the sixties." (from *When Harry Met Sally*)

▶ **Allusions:** Allusions are references to historical events, cultural events, works of art and literature, and people. They call upon a common body of knowledge to further describe something or someone. Remember, though, that an allusion is effective only when it is recognized by the audience.

  Example:

> The defensive end was the football team's *Achilles' heel*.

This allusion is a reference to the vulnerable spot.

When using figurative language, avoid two pitfalls. First, do not mix metaphors. A mixed metaphor is a comparison that is inconsistent. Instead of painting a clear image, it confuses the reader. Secondly, avoid clichés; trite expressions are no longer effective. Instead of saying "busy as a bee," try something unusual such as "busy as a postal worker during the catalogue season."

Exercise 4-30

For each of the following hackneyed expressions, create an original simile or metaphor.

Example: I'm so hungry I could eat a horse.
I'm hungry enough to eat day-old dog fur.

1. My love is like a rose.

_____

2. She's cute as a button.

_____

3. It is fresh as a newborn baby.

_____

4. It sparkles like a diamond.

_____

5. He is as happy as a kid in a candy store.

_____

Answers to Exercises

Exercise 4-1

1. (Their / There / <u>They're</u>) going to build (<u>their</u> / there / they're) new home over (their / <u>there</u> / they're) near the water.

2. Melissa likes (<u>to</u> / too) eat marshmallows (to / <u>too</u>).

3. The (begining / <u>beginning</u>) of this play is (definately / <u>definitely</u>) similar to the last play we saw.

4. The local (bussiness / <u>business</u>) (<u>received</u> / recieved) (<u>a lot</u> / alot) of coverage in the newspaper.

5. (Wheather / <u>Whether</u>) or not you (<u>believe</u> / beleive) her story, you must (<u>immediately</u> / immedietly) investigate the situation.

6. Some couples (devealop / <u>develop</u>) (seperate / <u>separate</u>) identities as they grow older.

7. The (<u>heroes</u> / heros) (acepted / <u>accepted</u>) (<u>their</u> / there / they're) award for "valor under (<u>truly</u> / truley) difficult circumstances."

8. She (<u>cannot</u> / canot) remove the (noticable / <u>noticeable</u>) stain from her carpet.

9. They (sucessfully / <u>successfully</u>) (<u>experienced</u> / expirienced) a peaceful holiday in a harmonious (enviroment / <u>environment</u>).

10. My (<u>professor</u> / proffesor) has an (arguement / <u>argument</u>) with a student (everyday / <u>every day</u>).

Exercise 4-2

1. The (personal / <u>personnel</u>) (hear / <u>here</u>) at this company are (scene / <u>seen</u>) as quite competent.

2. (Are / <u>Our</u>) (<u>principal</u> / principle) (through / <u>threw</u>) a holiday party for the faculty.

3. I (council / <u>counsel</u>) you to (<u>cite</u> / site) sources used on (<u>your</u> / you're) research paper.

4. In one (weak / <u>week</u>) we will (<u>buy</u> / by) (presence / <u>presents</u>) for the children.

5. The bus (fair / <u>fare</u>) went up for the (forth / <u>fourth</u>) time this year.

6. It is difficult to (<u>elicit</u> / illicit) responses from (board / <u>bored</u>) students.

7. Julia required (<u>plain</u> / plane) (stationary / <u>stationery</u>) on (<u>which</u> / witch) to write her letters.

8. We (<u>heard</u> / herd) the doctor (<u>compliment</u> / complement) the nurses' care of (patience / <u>patients</u>).

9. The (<u>eminent</u> / imminent) activist (<u>led</u> / lead) a march (threw / <u>through</u>) the streets.

10. We must (altar / <u>alter</u>) our (coarse / <u>course</u>) to get back on the (<u>right</u> / rite) track.

Exercise 4-3

1. sl *ei* gh
2. h *ei* ght
3. fr *ie* nd
4. ach *ie* ve
5. w *ei* rd
6. consc *ie* nce
7. for *ei* gn
8. p *ie* rce
9. br *ie* f
10. s *ei* ze

Exercise 4-4

1. *dis–*

accord	*disaccord*	honest	*dishonest*
believe	*disbelieve*	service	*disservice*
establish	*disestablish*	similar	*dissimilar*

2. *mal–*   adjusted   *maladjusted*   odorous   *malodorous*
        adroit   *maladroit*   practice   *malpractice*
        content   *malcontent*   treat   *maltreat*

3. *non–*   essential   *nonessential*   support   *nonsupport*
        fiction   *nonfiction*   union   *nonunion*
        stop   *nonstop*   violence   *nonviolence*

4. *pre–*   amble   *preamble*   determine   *predetermine*
        conceive   *preconceive*   dispose   *predispose*
        condition   *precondition*   eminent   *preeminent*

5. *trans–*   continental   *transcontinental*   fuse   *transfuse*
        figure   *transfigure*   plant   *transplant*
        form   *transform*   pose   *transpose*

Exercise 4-5

1. notice + –able   *noticeable*   6. gape + –ing   *gaping*
2. separate + –ness   *separateness*   7. shake + –en   *shaken*
3. implore + –ing   *imploring*   8. outrage + –ous   *outrageous*
4. acute + –ly   *acutely*   9. procure + –ment   *procurement*
5. bereave + –ment   *bereavement*   10. note + –ed   *noted*

Exercise 4-6

1. busy + –er   *busier*   6. happy + –ness   *happiness*
2. cry + –ing   *crying*   7. zany + –er   *zanier*
3. play + –ful   *playful*   8. defy + –ance   *defiance*
4. breezy + –ness   *breeziness*   9. duty + –ful   *dutiful*
5. boy + –ish   *boyish*   10. likely + –hood   *likelihood*

Exercise 4-7

1. fast + –est   *fastest*   6. skip + –er   *skipper*
2. commit + –ment   *commitment*   7. fit + –ness   *fitness*
3. submit + –ed   *submitted*   8. occur + –ence   *occurrence*
4. hot + –est   *hottest*   9. weep + –ing   *weeping*
5. regret + –able   *regrettable*   10. fasten + –er   *fastener*

Exercise 4-8

1. self — *selves*
2. theory — *theories*
3. flash — *flashes*
4. patio — *patios*
5. treaty — *treaties*
6. woman — *women*
7. hoof — *hooves*
8. brother-in-law — *brothers-in-law*
9. beach — *beaches*
10. fox — *foxes*

Exercise 4-9

1. jurist — (jur = law) *one who professes law*
2. centenarian — (cent = 100) *someone 100-years-old*
3. audiophile — (audio = hear) *one who loves to listen*
4. dermatologist — (derm = skin) *one who studies skin*
5. scribe — (scrib = write) *one who writes*
6. telecast — (tele = far) *sent far through television*
7. terrace — (terr = earth) *raised tract of ground*
8. portfolio — (port = carry) *flat case for carrying papers*
9. vacuous — (vac = empty) *unfilled*
10. videophone — (vid = see) *picture phone*

Exercise 4-10

1. I felt *disbelief* as I watched the puppy run into the street.
2. It appeared that the dog was *mistreated*.
3. The thin puppy must have been *malnourished*.
4. The dog's owner was *discourteous* to the crowd on the street.
5. Could this person be *amoral*?
6. My anger was *immeasurable* as I approached him.
7. The conversation between us was *nonproductive*.
8. I was *incapable* of restraint as I spoke with the man.
9. The fact that he had papers for the dog was *irrelevant* to me.
10. Animal abuse in any form is *illegal*.

Exercise 4-11

1. One scandal can *discredit* any politician.
2. Harsh weather continues to *depopulate* farming communities.
3. The technician *uncovered* the computer.

4. Cable service to her area is *discontinued*.

5. Her gardener began to *unload the* gravel from his truck.

Exercise 4-12

1. We will have to *reschedule* your visit.

2. The *post-diagnosis* treatment was rigorous.

3. The *ex-President* spoke at the assembly.

4. Scientist worked to establish *pre-existence*.

5. The *ex-soldier* tried to establish a new career.

6. After the earthquake, the buildings were *reconstructed* using steel.

7. The coach's *post-game* conversation focused on maneuvering.

8. His *ex-wife* retained custody of the children.

9. Some recipe ingredients are for sale *pre-mixed* in the package.

10. The government is *re-exploring* the possibility of tax incentives.

Exercise 4-13

1. The explorer *circumnavigated* the globe.

2. The *interstate* highway needed repair.

3. After he drank three beers, his intelligence was *subnormal*.

4. The employee's *midyear* evaluation showed improvement.

5. *Transcontinental* trips can be exciting.

Exercise 4-14

1. Bill is *hypersensitive* about his thinning hair.

2. Ellen *overestimated* the number of ticket holders.

3. Advertising is *omnipresent* today, even in doctors' offices!

4. The strange event seemed to be *supernatural*.

5. There is *uniform* dress in the military.

6. Vanessa's favorite store has a *semi-annual* sale.

7. The *triathlon* was held in Miami.

8. Brandon *underestimated* the sales figures.

9. The teachers *outnumbered* the students at the game.

10. *Monosyllabic* words are easy to pronounce.

Exercise 4-15

1. Seditious people demonstrate *anti-establishmentarian* behavior.

2. The defense's *counterevidence* disproved the prosecution's claim.

3. *Pro-conservation* laws have been instituted by many states.

4. The two professors *co-authored* a textbook.

5. The test results *contradicted* the doctor's initial diagnosis.

Exercise 4-16

1. *His refusal of* help was admirable.

2. *A dependent person* may not succeed.

3. He spoke with the *trainee*.

4. We needed *a manuscript reader*.

5. The *finalist* dropped out of the competition.

6. *Their argument* was ridiculous.

7. Molly's *friendliness* was known throughout school.

8. *Their friendship* has affected both their lives.

9. The audience lost interest *at his digression*.

10. Because *of jealousy*, Emily acted foolishly.

Exercise 4-17

1. *The baby's facial expression* was adorable.

2. The diligent saleswoman *was helpful*.

3. The recent archeology dig in Africa *was historic*.

4. The *glorious* hero marched to victory.

5. The gluttonous man at the buffet *was piggish*.

6. Eileen is *creative*.

7. The movie seems *endless*.

8. My sister *is friendly* to everyone.

9. The *murderous* villain was finally caught.

10. The ice cream was *soupy*.

Exercise 4-18

1. The earthquake made the structure *weaken*.

2. The scientist was able to *liquefy the gas*.

3. Teams must _unify_ their members.

4. The manager had to _regulate the payments_.

5. We wanted to _finalize the plans_.

Exercise 4-19

1. At the theater we heard the _announcer_ give an _announcement_ over the loudspeaker to _announce_ the end of intermission.

2. An worthwhile employer must also be an _encourager_; he should use _encouragement_ to _encourage_ his employees to succeed.

3. The judge was known as an effectual _punisher_; he would always _punish_ with the appropriate _punishment_.

4. No matter what the goal, an _achiever_ strives for _achievement_ in order to _achieve_ his or her objective.

5. Law _enforcement_ personnel _enforce_ the laws of the state, county, and nation. An _enforcer_ is an honorable profession.

Exercise 4-20

1. Vitamins and minerals contribute _fortification_ to the body. They nourish and _fortify_ with different _fortifier_(s).

2. A _classifier_ for the postal system will _classify_ different types of packages using _classification_.

3. To enhance outward appearance of a building, a _beautifier_ will _beautify_ the outside of the structure. _Beautification_ improves the facades.

4. Clear _identification_ is needed when traveling. Airport personnel will use an _identifier_ to _identify_ travelers.

5. When a change or _modification_ is needed in your sentence, use a _modifier_ to alter or _modify_ what you want to say.

Exercise 4-21

1. When _colonization_ began in this country, a typical _colonizer_ would _colonize_ and develop a specific area.

2. _Modernization_ of a location occurs when a _modernizer_ attempts to update and _modernize_ a setting.

3. The zookeeper will _tranquilize_ an animal with a _tranquilizer_ if necessary. _Tranquilization_ is a last resort.

4. The teacher helped her students _organize_ their notebooks using _organization_. _Organizer_(s) are successful students.

5. _Vaporization_ happens when solids turn to gas. To _vaporize_, use the _vaporizer_ in the laboratory.

Exercise 4-22

1. I used a *calculator* to *calculate* my mathematical *calculation* for my checkbook.

2. *Education* is a priority for most states. We must *educate* students and train competent *educator*(s).

3. The *indicator* light on the dashboard will *indicate* when a car needs oil. This *indication* can save your transmission.

4. To *decorate* a cake, a *decorator* will apply festive *decoration*(s) to the top and sides.

5. The *navigator* must be trained in *navigation* in order to successfully *navigate* large bodies of water.

Exercise 4-23

1. I *admire* someone with courage; my *admiration* shows I am an *admirer* of strength.

2. The *exploration* of the New World came from the *explorer*('s) need to *explore* and discover new places.

3. A rug *importer* deals with the *importation* and distribution of rugs; he or she must *import* them from other countries.

4. The director of the play made an astute *observation*. As an *observer*, her role is to *observe* the performers on stage.

5. The caterpillar is a *transformer*. It undergoes a *transformation* in order to *transform* into a butterfly.

Exercise 4-24

1. A good cable *connection* is important for computers. You must be sure to use sturdy *connective* devices when you *connect* your PC.

2. The *exhaustive* shopping excursion caused an *exhaustion* of finances as well. Be sure not to *exhaust* all financial resources.

3. Debate fosters *expressive* speech. If careful *expression* can influence an audience, be sure to *express* your ideas clearly.

4. The *inventive* scientist created a marvelous *invention*. He was able to *invent* an ice cream with no calories! Too bad it also had no flavor.

5. Fire *prevention* saves lives. It can *prevent* fires with *preventive* measures.

Exercise 4-25

1. My neighbor is a *compulsive* cleaner. He has a *compulsion* to clean every surface in his house. I wish I could *compel* him to clean mine.

2. Reading *comprehension* is concern in schools today. In order to determine what students *comprehend*, they must undertake *comprehensive* examinations.

3. The witches in *Macbeth* are *deceptive*. They use *deception* to beguile and *deceive* the title character and his wife.

4. *Evasive* measures were used during the conflict. In order to *evade* the overpowering enemy, military leaders planned an *evasion*.

5. A grand *reception* was planned to *receive* the dignitaries from abroad. Both sides were *receptive* to the idea of the gala.

Exercise 4-26

1. Many people have *recurrent* dreams. The *recurrence* of certain images and patterns may prove that certain anxieties also *recur*.

2. The two friends *differ* on many topics. They have *different* styles of dress, but this *difference* has not cost them their friendship.

3. I watched the groundhog *emerge* from his hole. His *emergence* has become a tradition in weather forecasting. When the *emergent* animal saw his shadow, the crowd expected six more weeks of winter.

4. The citizens of our town all *revere* our mayor. This *reverent* woman has done a great deal for our community. *Reverence* for her is widespread.

5. The two painters *reside* in their new loft. Their *residence* has already been painted by Tammy, the *resident* artist.

Exercise 4-27

1. *Materialistic* people place *materialism*, or the importance of *material* goods, above all else.

2. The *ritualistic* nature of religion and its practicing *ritualist*(s) are intriguing. For most religions, *ritualism* can be linked to previous millennia.

3. In tabloid writing, the *sensationalists* will use *sensation* to sell papers. People are intrigued by *sensational* stories.

4. The *nationalistic* atmosphere of the parade celebrated *nationalism* and all for which our country stands.

5. *Moralism* is a personal level of belief. Do not preach; sometimes being *moralistic* can make a person appear haughty.

Capitalization and Punctuation

Capitalization and punctuation are the mechanics of writing. They are not simply rules that we must memorize and follow; they are specific signals to the reader. These mechanics are used to determine meaning and to clarify intent. It is possible to change the connotation of a sentence by altering punctuation and/or capitalization. There is a popular story about punctuation. A college professor once wrote the following on the blackboard: "Woman without her man is nothing." He then gave directions to the students to use commas to punctuate the sentence. The result of the English class was that most females used two commas and most males used one comma. In other words, the females wrote: "Woman, without her, man is nothing." The males in the class wrote: "Woman without her man, is nothing." This story helps to show the importance of comma placement. Capitalization and other forms of punctuation are equally important. Capitalization can turn a common noun into a proper noun. This can be a clue to the reader whether he or she is reading about a specific person or something in general. A simple change in punctuation can change the entire meaning of the sentence. Subjects can be modified with a comma. The number of people or things can be changed with an apostrophe. Dialogue is attributed to certain people with the use of quotation marks. Each seemingly subtle change in the sentence amends the meaning. Therefore, we must adhere to the conventions so our intent is clear. This chapter highlights the different capitalization rules, the various punctuation marks, and the purposes and guidelines for these devices.

Lesson 5-1: Capitalization

Capitalization rules are not easy to follow. There are many words that can be capitalized or lowercase, depending on their meaning. For instance, earth is lowercase when it refers to soil, but it is frequently capitalized as the name of our planet. Father, mother, dad, and so on are common nouns; however, if they are specific people to whom you are referring or addressing, they become capitalized. Words such as *professor* or *dean* are common nouns, but in some instances they are capitalized. You must keep in mind if the noun signals a person or a position. The following sections cover some basic rules that will make capitalization clearer.

The First Word of a Sentence

The first word of every sentence is always capitalized. This rule never varies. Capitalizing the first word of each sentence signals the beginning of a new idea. This is always true in prose, but it is slightly different for poetry. Poets traditionally capitalize the first letter of each line, regardless of punctuation. This is because poetry focuses more on rhyme and meter, rather than typical conventions of capitalization and punctuation. By capitalizing the first word of each line, the poet can signal where a new line begins, rather than a new idea. For prose, regardless of the type of sentence, the first word is always capitalized.

Examples

The car is green.

The is capitalized as the first word in this declarative sentence.

Who cooked dinner tonight?

Even in an interrogative sentence, the first word is capitalized.

The Pronoun *I* and the Interjection *O*

The first-person singular pronoun *I* is always capitalized, regardless of where it appears in the sentence. A lowercase *i* would not be recognized as the first-person singular pronoun, I. It might be mistaken for a numeral. Also, the interjection *O* is also capitalized. *O* is mainly used in poetry and religious writing, usually before the name of the person or thing being addressed. The interjection *oh* is less formal and is therefore lowercase unless it is the first word in a sentence or in a line of poetry.

Examples

My brother and <u>I</u> drive red cars.

I is the first-person singular pronoun and is always capitalized, no matter where it appears in the sentence.

He asked if <u>I</u>'ve been well.

Even as part of the contraction for *I have*, the pronoun *I* must be capitalized.

Awake, <u>O</u> north-wind,
And come, thou wind of the South. (from Henry
Wadsworth Longfellow's "Christus: A Mystery")

The interjection *O* is capitalized wherever it appears in a line of poetry. *Awake* and *And* are both the first words in the line, and so they are also capitalized.

But it <u>o</u>'ertaketh him!

This line from the same poem has a lowercase *o*. This is not an interjection; it is a contraction of the word *overtaketh*.

<u>Oh</u> set me as a seal upon thine heart.

Oh is the first word of the line, and is therefore capitalized. It is only capitalized here because it is the first word of the line.

He bought her a present, and <u>oh</u>, what a gift it was!

Because it occurs in the middle of the line, there is no reason to capitalize *oh* in this sentence.

Exercise 5-1

Underline all of the letters that should be capitalized, including the first word of the sentence, the pronoun *I,* and the interjection *O.*

Example: <u>h</u>e asked me if <u>i</u> needed milk.

1. our physician is a compassionate person.

2. we met through a mutual friend.

3. she and i went to school together.

4. o say can you see?

5. his office is located next door.

6. where is the new student?

7. after dinner, i went out for ice cream.

8. she told me that i've never looked better.

9. before the movie, i need to call home.

10. will you dance with me?

Proper Nouns

A proper noun is the name of a particular person, place, or thing. Specific names are capitalized as proper nouns; if the noun is common, it is not capitalized.

Examples

Mr. Curran is having lunch at the Fernwood Diner.

Mr. Curran is the name of a specific person, and *Fernwood Diner* is the name of a particular thing. They are both proper nouns and are therefore capitalized. The common noun *lunch* is not capitalized. (For more about proper nouns, consult Lesson 1-1.)

Mary Kate and Anne live in Pennsylvania.

Mary Kate, Anne, and *Pennsylvania* are all proper nouns. Mary Kate and Anne are specific people, and Pennsylvania is a particular place. Therefore, they are all capitalized.

Proper Adjectives

Proper adjectives are adjectives formed from proper nouns. They are always capitalized. Proper adjectives include adjectives from names of people, specific places, ethnic groups, or political and religious terms.

Examples

My favorite genre of poetry is Victorian poetry.

Victorian is a proper adjective that comes from the name of a specific person, Queen Victoria; it must be capitalized.

Adele's delicious Sunday meals consist of various Italian dishes.

Italian is a proper adjective formed from the name of a specific place and must be capitalized. Notice that Adele and Sunday are capitalized, also. *Adele* is a proper noun, and *Sunday* is a date. (See Lesson 5-1.)

The <u>Congressional</u> hearings took place in a closed session.
Congressional is a proper adjective formed from a political term and must be capitalized.

Exercise 5-2

For each of the following sentences, underline all of the proper nouns and proper adjectives that should be capitalized.

Example: Mrs. <u>locasio</u> is studying <u>german</u> poetry.

1. I hope to travel to ireland next summer.

2. We met through andrew, a mutual friend.

3. Did you interview the republican candidate?

4. The puerto rican flag flies outside the embassy.

5. He hopes to purchase a persian carpet.

6. The building is made from imported grecian marble.

7. When I visit california, I will stop and see ms. murphy.

8. Her favorite meal is chinese food.

9. We like to walk to the bergmans' house.

10. We enjoy watching foreign films, including french movies.

Titles Before a Name and Abbreviated Titles

Titles used *before* a proper name are capitalized. Used alone or following a name, most titles are not capitalized. Consider whether the title is part of a name, and therefore a proper noun referring to a specific person, or if it is a common noun. Abbreviated titles, such as Mr., Ms., Jr., and Sr., and those indicating professions and academic degrees are always capitalized.

Examples

<u>Father</u> Anderson, our priest, led the mass on Sunday.
Father is a title and must be capitalized.

<u>Dr.</u> Emily Thompson led the surgical team.
Dr. is the abbreviation for doctor and is therefore capitalized. If the full term were used before the name (Doctor Emily Thompson), it would also be capitalized.

Emily Thompson, our <u>doctor</u>, led the surgical team.

In this case, *doctor* is not part of her name and remains lowercase.

<u>Rev</u>. Martin Luther King, <u>Jr</u>. stood for equality.

In this example, the abbreviations before and after the name are both capitalized.

The <u>President</u> held a press conference to explain the new tax bill.

President in this case refers to a specific person (the President of the United States). Whether referring to the position or the person, this is always capitalized. A position of this rank is not considered a common noun. The same is true for *king* and *queen* when they designate specific positions, such as Queen of England or King of Spain.

Exercise 5-3

Underline all of the letters that should be capitalized, including the names, titles, and abbreviations.

Example: We asked <u>mrs</u>. <u>e</u>dwards for a book recommendation.

1. Our physician, doctor bernstein, is a compassionate person.

2. We needed to speak to professor addabbo.

3. Our congresswoman is rep. schroeder.

4. The professor, ms. anderson, lives near dr. combs's office.

5. We must ask peter jr. for help in this matter.

6. The head of our school is dr. williams, e.d.

7. The judge for the district court is sam walters, j.d.

8. She consulted president cohen about the problem.

9. His father's name is edward simmons, sr.

10. The new parish priest is fr. bailey.

Days of the Week, Months of the Year, and Holidays

Dates are capitalized. This rule includes days of the week, months of the year, and specific holidays. Remember, though, that seasons are neither considered dates nor holidays, and so they remain lowercase.

Example

> Labor Day is the first Monday in September. It marks
> the unofficial end to summer.

Labor Day is a holiday. *Monday* is a day of the week. *September* is a month. These are all capitalized. Note that *summer* remains lowercase because seasons are not capitalized.

Historical Events, Eras, and Documents

Important dates, events, and elements of our history are capitalized. This includes names of events, such as major conflicts, and documents, such as treaties.

Examples

> Many poets wrote moving accounts about their
> turbulent experiences during World War I.

World War I is a historical event, and must be capitalized.

> The Renaissance brought about a new appreciation for
> many art forms.

Renaissance is an era.

> Our Constitution is amended as our society changes.

Constitution is a document and must be capitalized.

This rule can be problematic. We capitalize major events, but we also capitalize less significant events, such as the World Series or the Super Bowl. This is difficult because the writer must determine what is important. There are inconsistencies, but use your best judgment.

Major Words in the Titles of Books, Movies, Paintings, Musical Compositions, Magazines, and Articles

Titles of published items, such as music, pieces of writing, sculptures, and movies are capitalized. However, only the major words are capitalized; the rest are lowercase. Major words are usually words with more than two letters. This excludes articles, but includes pronouns and prepositions.

Examples

> *The Day of the Jackal,* the novel by Fredrick Forsyth, was
> made into a movie.

The is capitalized the first time because it is the first word in the title. It is lowercase the second time because it is **not** considered a major word.

> Vincent van Gogh's *Starry Night* was recently on display
> at the New National Gallery in Berlin.

Starry Night is capitalized as the title of a work of art. *New National Gallery* is the name of the museum and must be capitalized, as well as the other names in this sentence.

> Our local newspaper, *The New York Herald,* contains many
> interesting editorials. My favorite is "Why Talk is Cheap."

In this example, the major words in both the publication's title and the article's title are capitalized. (For more about the punctuation for these titles, see Lessons 5-8 and 5-11.)

Geographic Regions

The names of geographic regions, such as mountain ranges or sections of a country, are capitalized. However, directions are not capitalized. This means that north, east, south, and west are sometimes capitalized, depending on how the words are used.

Examples

> Billy traveled to the Catskill Mountains in New York for
> his hiking trip.

The *Catskill Mountains* designates a particular region in the state of New York.

> Photographers travel to the Himalayas to capture the
> panoramic images.

Himalayas is also a geographic region and must be capitalized.

> The Civil War pitted the North against the South. We
> traveled east to see some of the historic battlegrounds.

In this case, *North* and *South* are particular places, and are duly capitalized. *East* is simply a direction and remains lowercase.

Exercise 5-4

Underline all of the letters that should be capitalized in the following sentences, including dates, events, major words in titles, and geographic regions.

Example: I will visit the wyoming valley on easter sunday.

1. the fourth of july is a great time to travel.

2. people journey around the united states of america.

3. during the summer, the southwest becomes extremely warm.

4. places like texas are still popular, though.

5. travelers visit the alamo in san antonio.

6. sometimes we leave on a friday and return on a tuesday.

7. we enjoy researching the revolutionary war.

8. later, we go east to philadelphia.

9. there we can see the declaration of independence.

10. we read about possible destinations in *today's travel*, our travel guide.

Lesson 5-2: Periods

Periods are an important form of punctuation. They designate a full stop after words, phrases, and clauses. They can also signal that a word is abbreviated. Periods are also used with initials and as decimal points in writing numerals.

Periods at the End of Sentences

Periods are used at the end of declarative sentences and imperative sentences, including polite commands. They are also used for sentences containing an indirect question.

Examples

The dog is hungry.

This sentence is **declarative**; it states a fact. It ends in a period in order to designate a full stop or the end of that idea.

Give him some food.

This sentence is **imperative** because it gives a command. It also ends with a period. Even though the tone of a command is more intensive, both declarative and imperative sentences end with a period.

She asked them if the dog had been fed.

This declarative sentence contains an indirect question. Therefore, it ends in a period.

Periods After an Abbreviation or an Initial

Periods are always used after abbreviations in order to shorten the word. Periods are also necessary after initials that represent complete names.

Examples

Mr. D. Luhman traveled to the U.S.A. to study English.

Mr. is an abbreviation for Mister. *D.* is the initial for his first name. *U.S.A.* is the abbreviation for the United States of America.

He earned a B.A. in English Lit.

B.A. stands for Bachelor of Arts, a post-secondary degree. *Lit.* is the abbreviation for literature. It is capitalized here because it is the title of his major. In this example, *English* is a proper adjective, but it is also capitalized as a proper noun.

There are many common abbreviations we use. We capitalized them according to the same rules. If they are a title or a proper noun, they are capitalized. If they represent a common noun, they remain lowercase.

Some Frequently Used Abbreviations		
atty. = attorney	Dr. = Doctor	Mrs. = Mistress
ave. = avenue	doz. = dozen	no. = number
capt. = captain	memo = memorandum	pd. = paid
dept. = department	Mr. = Master	st. = street

Do not use periods with abbreviations of some businesses, organizations, and government agencies. Also, do not use periods with the two-letter abbreviations of states that are used with ZIP codes or with abbreviations of metric measurements. Do not use periods with acronyms, abbreviations that are pronounced as words.

Example

Mary is a member of <u>PETA</u>.

This acronym for *People for the Ethical Treatment of Animals* is pronounced as a word. Therefore, no periods are necessary.

Exercise 5-5

For each of the following sentences, place a period where required.

Example: Dr. Johnson has an M.D. from Yale.

1. He joined the U S Marines after graduation

2. William H Macy is an incredibly talented actor

3. To find the market, turn left on Main St at the first traffic light

4. Elliot called the complaint dept about the overage charges on his cell phone

5. Morgan earned a B A from Manhattan College

6. She studied French Lit for two years

7. Capt Thompson led the fighting in western U S territories

8. Natalia gave the school the phone no for emergencies

9. Mr and Mrs Anderson were married in May

10. L A County in C A is one of the wealthiest counties in the U S

Lesson 5-3: Exclamation Marks

Exclamation marks also designate the end of a sentence. Yet, they are reserved for the strongest examples of feeling, surprise, urgency, or emotion. They should be used sparingly. An exclamation mark is used after an **interjection** or an **exclamatory sentence** that expresses sudden emotion.

Example

Ouch! That hurts!

Ouch is an interjection. The sentence that follows is exclamatory. Each needs an exclamation mark.

Fire! Run!

Both of these exclamations express urgency. It is necessary to punctuate with exclamation marks.

Remember that is it usually better to use a period rather than an exclamation point in regular prose writing. The effectiveness of the exclamation depends on the frequency of its use.

Be sure not to overuse the exclamation mark.

Example:

Incorrect: Dakota Fanning made several movies before her eighth birthday!

Correct: Dakota Fanning made several movies before her eighth birthday.

Lesson 5-4: Question Marks

A question mark is also a full stop in punctuation. However, question marks have one specific function. A question mark is used after an **interrogative sentence.**

Examples

Where are you going? With whom will you go?

Both of these sentences are interrogative and require question marks.

There is one common error associated with the question mark, and that is where it is placed.

Always place the question mark at the end of the question.

Example:

Incorrect: How long ago? did you visit your sister.

Correct: How long ago did you visit your sister?

Exercise 5-6

Punctuate each of the following sentences with a period, an exclamation mark, or a question mark.

Example: How do you make potato pancakes?

1. I'll see you tomorrow

2. Hey Look out

3. Can you reach the telephone

4. Put the encyclopedia on the shelf

5. Whose books are these

6. Never forget your key

7. Where are your shoes

8. Call me when you get home

9. Run Get out of here

10. Did you understand that memo

Lesson 5-5: Commas

The comma has many different roles within the sentence. It can be used to separate words and phrases, or to clarify meaning within a sentence. Incorrect use of a comma can change the meaning of a sentence. When writing, it is important to place commas in the sentence correctly; do not place them where it sounds like you would pause during speech. When used in lieu of a semicolon or a period, you have a comma splice or a run on sentence. (For more about these errors, consult Lesson 2-5 on page 81 and Lesson 9-1 on page 307.) This section deals with the different places to use a comma.

Commas After Introductory Words, Expressions, Phrases, or Clauses

Commas are necessary after introductory elements, such as phrases and clauses. These introductory elements include nouns, adverbs, participles, infinitives, and various types of phrases. Commas are used to separate the **independent clause** from these introductory elements. (For more about adverbs, participles, and infinitives, review Chapter 1. For more about clauses and phrases, review Chapter 2.)

Examples

Slowly, the sun came out from behind the clouds.

Slowly is an **adverb** that is separated from the independent clause it modifies by a comma.

Therefore, it was possible to go swimming.

Therefore is a **conjunctive adverb** and must be followed by a comma.

Walking outside, the families noticed the heat from the sun.

Walking outside is a **participle phrase** that must be separated from the independent clause by a comma.

To swim, they needed bathing suits.

To swim is an **infinitive** and must be followed by a comma.

Because they were hot, the men immediately dove into the water.

Because they were hot is a **subordinate clause** and must be separated from the independent clause.

Use a comma to set off a single short introductory prepositional phrase only if the sentence would be misread without the comma.

Avoid overuse of commas with prepositional phrases.

Example:

Incorrect: In the pool, the swimmers splashed and swam.

Correct: In the pool the swimmers splashed and swam.

Correct: In the pool that holds many people, the swimmers splashed and swam.

Exercise 5-7

Insert a comma after the introductory words, expressions phrases, or clauses in each of the following sentences.

Example: Lately, I enjoy walking in the morning.

1. Needing decorations I looked to nature.

2. Cautiously I climbed the fence.

3. Looking around I saw violets.

4. Unfortunately there were no daisies.

5. However I did spy some clover.

6. Reaching into my bag I removed my scissors.

7. To make a bouquet I chose several varieties of flowers.

8. Carefully I avoided the sharp burrs and thorns.

9. Because they were wilting I put them in water.

10. Finally I have a beautiful table arrangement.

Commas Before Coordinating Conjunctions in a Compound Sentence

A comma is necessary before a coordinating conjunction in a compound sentence. It immediately follows the first complete clause and immediately precedes the coordinating conjunction.

Examples

The baby grew tired, <u>and</u> the mother put her to bed.
And is a coordinating conjunction; it must be preceded by a comma.

I wanted to leave, <u>but</u> I couldn't find my keys.
But is a coordinating conjunction and is preceded by a comma.

You may have tuna, <u>or</u> you may eat cheese.
Or is a coordinating conjunction, and it is preceded by a comma.

Remember that without the coordinating conjunction you simply have a comma splice, which you want to avoid. A comma splice is two independent clauses separated by a comma. You also have the option in these examples to omit the coordinating conjunction and replace the comma with a semicolon.

Example:

Incorrect: Dinner was finished, we went for a walk.

Correct:　Dinner was finished, *and so* we went for a walk.

Correct:　Dinner was finished; we went for a walk.

(For more about coordinating conjunctions, see Lesson 1-6. Learn more about semicolons in Lesson 5-6.)

Exercise 5-8

Place a comma in the appropriate places for coordinating conjunctions.
Example: It is difficult, but we must face the problem of hunger.

1. More food is produced today than ever before but only one third of the world is well fed.

2. Many people in the world are hungry and many children suffer from malnutrition.

3. Citizens are unaware of hunger in their own country for the hungry lack the means to publicize their condition.

4. The rich nations have overweight citizens and the poor nations have starving citizens.

5. Many people receive government assistance but they still do not have enough to eat.

6. Hunger is a monumental problem but it can be solved.

7. We need to develop more food sources and funds must be made available.

8. Money is not enough for research is also needed.

9. Health conditions must be studied and children must be protected.

10. Rich nations must do more to help the poor and poor nations must do more to help themselves.

Commas With Parenthetical Expressions

Use a comma to set off parenthetical expressions. Parenthetical expressions are unrelated words in the sentence that may interrupt the flow or thought of the sentence. In other words, a parenthetical expression is simply an extraneous expression. Beware of these expressions in formal writing. Usually the sentences should be revised for clarity.

Examples

Crime and Punishment, <u>we heard</u>, is Barbara's favorite novel.

In this sentence, *we heard* is a parenthetical expression that is separated from the rest of the sentence with commas.

She read it for the first time, <u>I believe</u>, in college.

In this example, *I believe* is a parenthetical expression.

There are two errors associated with the use of commas for parenthetical expressions.

> **When you use commas to set off an expression in the middle of a sentence, place a comma both *before* and *after* the expression.**

Example:

Incorrect: There is, however one other possibility.

Correct: There is, however, one other possibility.

Incorrect: During dance class, my favorite activity I heard beautiful music.

Correct: During dance class, my favorite activity, I heard beautiful music.

> **Do not place a comma before an indirect quotation or an indirect question.**

Example:

Incorrect: Nora said, that she needs a new guitar.

Correct: Nora said that she needs a new guitar.

Incorrect: Arial asked her brother, if he enjoyed playing baseball.

Correct: Arial asked her brother if he enjoyed playing baseball.

Commas With Words and Numbers in a Series

Use commas to separate nouns, verbs, adjectives, and adverbs in a series. This includes lists of numbers. Be sure to include the comma after the item that immediately precedes that final item in the list.

Examples

Red, white, and blue are the colors of our flag.

Red, white, and *blue* are nouns and must each be separated by a comma.

The young girls dance, act, and sing.

In this example, each verb is separated by a comma. If the second comma was omitted, one might assume that *dance* is independent from *act* and *sing*.

The winning lottery numbers are 7, 14, 23, and 32.

Each numeral is separated by a comma. The same would be true if the numbers were written out (seven, fourteen, and so on).

There are a few common errors with commas in lists.

> **In order to avoid confusion, always include last comma in a series.**

Be sure to include the comma after the item that immediately precedes that final item in the list. This rule is inconsistent; it varies according to the source. For instance, the *Chicago Manual of Style* considers the omission of the final comma in the series correct. You will also encounter newspapers and periodicals that omit the final comma. However, when writing for school, it is better to demonstrate knowledge of the traditional conventions. Also, whichever you choose, maintain consistency.

Example:

Incorrect: I like apples, oranges and bananas.

Correct: I like apples, oranges, and bananas.

Do not place an additional comma after the conjunction.

Example:

Incorrect: He bikes, runs, and, swims.

Correct: He bikes, runs, and swims.

Do not use commas between items in a series if they are joined by conjunctions.

Example:

Incorrect: The available sizes are seven, and nine, and eleven.

Correct: The available sizes are seven and nine and eleven.

Exercise 5-9

Place a comma in the appropriate spaces for parenthetical expressions and/or words and numbers in a series.

Example: I am the founder, owner, and president of a company.

1. This company sells shirts shorts pants and jackets.

2. We frequently buy two four or six cases of fabric at a time.

3. Orders can be shipped to Delaware New Jersey New York and Connecticut.

4. The shirts are available in sizes small medium large and extra large.

5. The colors I believe are limited.

6. Red blue and green are out of stock.

7. We also have yellow available I think in the warehouse.

8. Blue we were told is our most popular color.

9. The business I am sure is set for expansion.

10. We will hire new designers seamstresses managers and office personnel.

Commas With Appositives

An **appositive** is a word or group of words used to explain the noun or pronoun that it follows. In other words, it is an alternate way to refer to someone or something. Use a comma to set off an appositive unless it is essential to the meaning of the sentence.

Examples

Ms. Friedman, our teacher, is retiring next year.

Mrs. Friedman and *our teacher* are the same person. Therefore, it is necessary to set the **appositive** apart with commas. Notice how the meaning of the sentence is changed when one comma is removed.

Ms. Friedman, our teacher is retiring next year.

In this sentence, *Ms. Friedman* is being told that someone's teacher is retiring next year. *Ms. Friedman* and *our teacher* are two different people.

Do not use commas for an appositive that is essential to the meaning of the sentence. An appositive is considered essential if it gives necessary information about the noun or pronoun that it precedes or follows. In other words, if the meaning of the sentence changes by surrounding the appositive with commas, do not use them.

Examples

Louisa May Alcott's novel *Little Women* describes events from the author's own life.

The appositive in this case is not surrounded by commas because it would change the meaning of the sentence. Notice the difference with the commas.

Louisa May Alcott's novel, *Little Women,* describes events from the author's own life.

This sentence implies that *Little Women* is the author's only novel.

In *Little Women,* Jo mourns the loss of her sister Beth. Jo has more than one sister.

A comma after *sister* would change the meaning of the sentence.

In *Little Women,* Jo mourns the loss of her sister, Beth. In this example, it appears that Beth is Jo's only sister.

Exercise 5-10

For each of the following sentences, place a comma in the appropriate spaces for appositives. Do not use commas if the appositive is essential to the meaning of the sentence.

Example: The American writer Ernest Hemingway spent many years abroad. He lived in Paris with other expatriates, artists choosing to live abroad.

A comma is not needed for the first sentence, but it is required for the second sentence.

1. Ernest Hemingway was born on July 21, 1899, in Oak Park a suburb of Chicago Illinois.

2. His father Dr. Clarence Edmonds Hemingway was a fervent member of the First Congregational church.

3. His mother Grace Hall sang in the church choir.

4. The Red Cross a charitable foundation accepted Hemingway as an ambulance driver.

5. He boarded a ship the *Chicago* bound for Bordeaux, France.

6. From there he went to his final destination Italy.

7. He had his friend Theodore Brumback beside him.

8. He also met a new friend Howell Jenkins.

9. The trip from America to Italy was a long and tiring one.

10. On the morning of June 7, 1918, 18-year-old Hemingway stepped off a train at Garbaldi Station in Milan and assumed the duties of a Red Cross ambulance driver.

Commas With Nonrestrictive Elements

Nonrestrictive elements are clauses, phrases, and words that do not limit, or restrict, the meaning of the words they modify. These elements can be lifted from the sentence without changing the sentence's meaning. They may be participles, participial phrases, prepositional phrases, infinitive phrases, and so forth. Use commas to set off nonrestrictive elements.

Commas help to modify the meaning when the words cannot. Restrictive clauses do not need commas; their meaning is clear without punctuation.

Examples

> Susan, tired, went up to bed early.

The participle *tired* modifies but does not limit the meaning of Susan.

> The basket, in the back of the closet, was perfect to
> hold his magazines.

The prepositional phrase (*in the back of the closet*) modifies but does not limit the meaning of the basket.

> The military officers, demonstrating valor, earned
> recognition.

This is a *nonrestrictive* clause. In this case, *all* of the military officers represented have demonstrated valor and earned recognition. Notice how the meaning changes **without** the commas.

> The military officers demonstrating valor earned
> recognition.

This is a *restrictive clause*. We know from the sentence that not all military officers have demonstrated valor. However, recognition is *restricted* to those who have demonstrated valor. We do not need the commas here.

Exercise 5-11

Place a comma in the appropriate spaces for nonrestrictive words, phrases, and clauses. Some sentences do not require commas.

Example: Mary, who is one of my best friends, recently underwent a difficult period of time.

1. Our friend Mary a hard worker needs a new job.

2. Mary amazed learned her position was eliminated.

3. Her Chief Officer upset with the events released all of the executives.

4. All the executives because they needed employment searched online for jobs.

5. The online jobs available only to some required relocation.

6. Some executives after searching for months accepted lower-paying jobs.

7. All new store clerks who required training were sent to workshops.

8. The workshops especially those specializing in social skills were helpful.

9. Frank found one course "People to People" extremely helpful.

10. All new employment requiring adjustment can be stressful.

Commas With Quotations of Dialogue

Use a comma before or after a quotation of dialogue. In some cases, the comma is inside the quotation marks, and other times it is outside the quotation marks.

Examples

My teacher said, "Take your seat."
In this case the comma comes *before* the dialogue.

"No one may leave the room," commanded the teacher.
Here, notice the comma is *inside* the quotation marks.

"All I need," said the principal, "is to call your parents."
In this case, the quotation is separated. Notice the comma *inside* the first set of quotation marks and *before* the second set. Also, note that the period is *inside* the quotation marks. (For more about quotation marks, see Lesson 5-8.)

Commas With Addresses, Dates, and Numbers

Use a comma to separate information with addresses, dates, and numbers. The comma is used here to separate numbers and to clarify information. For dates, commas belong between the day of the week and the month, between the day of the month and the year, and between the year and the rest of the sentence. In addresses, a comma is used to separate each part of the address, except for the ZIP code. Commas are also used to separate numerals (every three digits, from right to left). This can be helpful to clearly see numbers larger than four digits. If the address or name of the place is in the middle of a sentence, place a comma after the last part to set it off from the rest of the sentence.

Examples

> Our child was born on December 21, 1982, in St. Louis, Missouri, after many months of waiting.

In this example, commas are used to separate the *day of the month* and the *year*, and the *year* from the rest of the sentence. Commas also separate the city from the state and the state from the rest of the sentence.

> My address is 4567 East Spring Street, Anytown, New York 20020.

Here, a comma is used to separate each part of the address except for the ZIP code. Notice how the street address, including the number and name of the street, is not separated by a comma.

> The home improvement store offers more that 35,000 varieties of paint.

In this sentence, the comma needed is to separate *more than three digits of numerals*.

Exercise 5-12

Place a comma in the appropriate places for dialogue, addresses, dates, and/or numbers.

Example: On Thursday, March 19th, Joanne turned 47 years old.

1. The first annual parade was held on May 28 1995 in Springville Missouri.

2. The bandleader cried "All fall in!"

3. "Harold lost his instrument" laughed Sally.

4. It looked like there were 10000 people in uniforms.

5. The firefighters met at Bob's house in Ellenville Missouri.

6. He lives at 23 Main Street Ellenville Missouri.

7. "Park around the corner" he cried "by the supermarket."

8. More than 60000 people were in attendance that day.

9. The press wrote "The parade was delightful."

10. "For fun, come to Springville Missouri" wrote the local paper.

2. Boiling vegetables removes some of the vitamins therefore, vegetables should be steamed.

3. Some foods are healthier raw eat several servings of raw vegetables per day.

4. Dairy products provide large amounts of calcium cheese and milk are especially good sources.

5. Beef is only about twenty-five percent protein you get more protein from soybeans, chicken, and turkey.

6. Turkey and chicken have less fat than beef moreover, they contain more protein.

7. Some foods are better in combination consequently, people should learn how to combine foods for the best health benefits.

8. Vitamin A is supplied by eggs and liver it can also be obtained from some fruits and vegetables.

9. Citrus fruits provide vitamin C oranges and grapefruits are particularly good sources.

10. Our bodies need protein and vitamins therefore, it is essential for us to know which foods provided them.

Lesson 5-7: Colons

A colon is used as an introduction to a list. It comes before things: an explanation, a series, or a quotation. A colon is also used as a separation. It can be used between numbers, or between letters, or between words in citations. A colon also follows a salutation in a formal letter. It can also be found when referring to sections of the Bible.

Examples

A traveler must carry the following items at all times: a passport, contact information, and local currency.

The colon is used here before a *series*.

Expectant mothers frequently ask themselves: "Am I ready for this?"

In this case, a colon is used before the *quotation*.

The Web address for the store's homepage is *http://fictitiousstore.address.no.*

We frequently use colons for Internet sites.

They wore the typical businessman's uniform: a charcoal suit, a white shirt, and a red tie.

In this case, the colon comes before the *explanation.*

Our train is scheduled to depart at 12:45 p.m.

In this example, the colon is used to separate the *numbers* related to tir

The teacher to student ratio at our school is 1:9.

In this case, the colon is used to separate numbers in order to demo strate ratio.

Exercise 5-14

In each of the following examples, insert a colon where appropriate.

Example: Camp teaches children many things: independence, athletic prowess, and social interaction.

1. Summer camps can be categorized by themes outdoor adventure, life skills, community service, or nature appreciation.

2. Some camps offer many activities swimming, archery, boating, and golf.

3. A good counselor-to-camper ratio is 1 12.

4. Many camps have "lights out" at 10 30 at night.

5. At sailing camp, there are different boats the sailboat, the sunfish, and the canoe.

6. Canoeing develops muscles the biceps, the triceps and the laterals.

7. I have many favorite activities fishing, swimming, canoeing, and rock climbing.

8. We always wake up at 7 15 in the morning.

9. My counselor calls her motto "Rise and shine."

10. When the summer is over, I come home to my family my mother, my father, my sister, and my dog.

Lesson 5-8: Quotation Marks

Quotation marks are used most frequently to indicate other people's words, but they are also used in citations. There are two types of quotation marks: double and single. Double quotation marks have several uses. They are used to signal specific quotations, show dialogue, and punctuate titles of smaller works, such as poems, articles, and short stories. Single quotation marks are used to enclose a quotation within a quotation. Remember that quotation marks are **not** used for paraphrasing someone else's words or for titles of major works such as novels, periodicals, or volumes of short stories or poetry.

Examples

John Keats once wrote: "Beauty is truth, truth beauty."

This quotation is from his poem "Ode on a Grecian Urn." In this example, the poem is quoted precisely, and therefore needs **quotation marks**. The title of the poem is in quotation marks because it is a smaller work, or part of a larger work. Notice the period belongs inside the quotation marks. Periods and commas always sit inside the quotation marks.

John Keats once wrote that beauty is the same as truth,
and truth the same as beauty.

In this case, the quote is *paraphrased*, and quotation marks are not required.

Eleanor says, "My favorite poem, 'I, Too,' was written
by Langston Hughes."

The single quotation marks are needed here to punctuate the poem's title within quotation marks.

"Make your beds up right," cried my mother.

In this example, the *dialogue* is indicated by quotation marks. Also, notice the comma inside the quotation marks.

The cab driver, to the rude couple, yelled, "Get out now!"

Notice the end punctuation is inside of the quotation marks in this example. That is because it is part of the quotation.

Where can I find Ralph Ellison's story, "Flying Home"?

In this case, the short story is in quotation marks, but the end punctuation, the question mark, is *outside* of the quotation marks. Question marks and exclamation marks belong *outside* of the quotation marks unless they are part of the quotation. If they are part of the quotation, they remain *inside* the quotation marks. As noted earlier, commas and periods always belong *inside* the quotation marks. Colons, semicolons, and footnote numbers always belong *outside* the quotation marks.

Exercise 5-15

Insert quotation marks where necessary into each of the sentences in this exercise.

Example: "Wrap the gift," she said, "before the party begins."

1. Time magazine had an article entitled Looking for Lois.

2. Unlock the front door, yelled my mother.

3. The Swede faintly smiled, wrote Stephen Crane in The Blue Hotel.

4. She asked me, Where are your shoes?

5. My dictionary defines loiter as to linger idly.

6. I can't believe he told me to mind my own business!

7. Do you know the story Rip Van Winkle?

8. David yelled, Get out!

9. Eddie said, The article, Name Brands for Nannies, is really interesting.

10. The movie review called his epic a mistake for the masses.

Lesson 5-9: Apostrophes

Apostrophes are used to designate a noun as possessive, which indicates ownership of something. They are also used to signal an omission, such as in a contraction, and to form the plural of letters, numbers, and signs used as words. There are various rules for using apostrophes.

Singular Possessive

In most cases, to show the possessive form of a singular noun, place an apostrophe after the last letter of the word and add *–s*.

Examples

The <u>plant's</u> roots were tangled in the diminutive pot.

Plant is a singular noun. Therefore, to show ownership of the pot by the *plant*, simply add an apostrophe followed by *s*. By moving the apostrophe, you move the meaning. If the sentence used *plants'* roots, you are writing about more than one plant.

The reception was held in the <u>school's</u> auditorium.

In this sentence, *school* is a singular noun. An apostrophe followed by *s* is required to show ownership.

I left my hat in <u>James's</u> car.

In this case, you also add an apostrophe followed by *s*. This rule is inconsistent, however. Some sources will tell you to only add an apostrophe if the singular noun ends in *s*. Other sources say to add an apostrophe followed by *s* if the noun is **one** syllable, and only the apostrophe if the noun is **more than one** syllable. Your goal here is to demonstrate that the noun is singular. To do this, you should always add apostrophe *s* to be sure that it is obvious when the noun is singular. Also, make sure you are always consistent within the document.

If two or more persons possess something jointly, use the possessive form of only the last nane mentioned. The names of businesses and organizations should also be treated this way.

Examples

I enjoyed playing with <u>Nora and Tony's</u> new puppy.

Although they are both people have ownership of the puppy, only the second noun is possessive because it is joint ownership.

Adam purchased <u>Wilson and Bell's</u> workout equipment.

In this example, the joint company produces the equipment. Therefore, only the second name is possessive.

If two or more persons or things each possess something individually, put each name in the possessive form.

Example

> I recently read <u>Hemingway's and Fitzgerald's</u> first novels.

This example is about two separate books by two separate authors, and so they are both possessive.

Plural Possessive

To show the possessive of a plural noun not ending in *s,* add the apostrophe followed by *s.* For a plural noun ending in *s,* simply add the apostrophe.

Examples

> The shoe store displayed only <u>men's</u> shoes in the window.

In this example, *men* is a plural noun that does not end in *s,* so an apostrophe followed by *s* is required.

> The <u>children's</u> shoes were in the back of the store.

In this sentence, *children* is a plural noun that does not end in *s,* so an apostrophe followed by *s* is required.

> The <u>girls'</u> shoes are available in many colors.

In this case, *girls* is a plural noun that ends in *s,* so only an apostrophe is required.

> We went to the <u>Sanseverinos'</u> house for Thanksgiving.

Here, *Sanseverinos* is a plural noun that ends in *s,* so only an apostrophe is required.

Keep in mind that your goal is your reader must be able to tell whether the possessive noun is *singular* or *plural.* Look at the difference between the following sentences.

> Check the <u>car's</u> brakes.

Here you have one car on which to check the breaks.

> Check the <u>cars'</u> brakes.

In this example, there are two or more cars that need their brakes checked. The change between sentences is slight; the apostrophe and the *s* are reversed. However, there is a difference in meaning between these sentences.

Exercise 5-16

For each of the following sentences, make the underlined noun possessive by either adding an apostrophe or an apostrophe followed by an *s*
and write the possessive form of the noun in the space provided.

Example: The children department carries many styles of sneakers.
children's

1. Susan friend, Mary, went away for the weekend. _____

2. Susan agreed to feed Mary cats. _____

3. She had to keep the cats bowls filled with food
   and water. _____

4. Mary also told her to check the bandage on the
   black cat leg. _____

5. It was necessary to seal the bandage seams. _____

6. Before leaving, Mary checked the doors locks. _____

7. The veterinarian office was closed, but Mary
   left a message. _____

8. Next, Mary left a message on her boss voicemail. _____

9. She also stopped by her neighbors house to
   leave a key. _____

10. They said they hoped their friend trip went well. _____

Contractions

Contractions use apostrophes to stand in place of missing letters.
When words are contracted together, some of the letters are lost and the
apostrophe marks where they were.

Examples

The hungry child couldn't wait to eat.

Couldn't stands for *could not* in this example. This contraction is obvious; some are more difficult.

My shoes won't stay tied.

In this sentence, *won't* replaces *will not.*

The following chart contains the most commonly used contractions.

Common Contractions		
can't = cannot	couldn't = could not	doesn't = does not
don't = do not	he'd = he would	he's = he has/is
I'd = I would	I'm = I am	I've = I have
it's = it is	let's = let us	o'clock = of the clock
there's = there is	they're = they are	wasn't = was not
we're = we are	weren't = were not	who's = who is/has
won't = will not	wouldn't = would not	you'll = you will

Using contractions signals an informal tone. (For more on tone, see Lesson 9-9 on page 329.) They are not appropriate in formal writing. They are suitable for letters, memos, and e-mails, but not for essays, reports, or other formal writing. Notice how the tone immediately changes in the next exercise.

Exercise 5-17

Rewrite each of the following sentences and change the underlined contraction to the full expressions.

Example: We'll be late unless you'll hurry and get ready.

We will be late unless you will hurry and get ready.

1.   I don't like pears, but the store didn't have any other fruit.

2.   Won't you wait for me?

3.   My father couldn't change the tire without the jack.

4.   Samantha wouldn't wait for her friend, or she'd be late for class.

5.   He's been so tired, lately.

6.   Perhaps he's coming down with a cold.

7.   It's always obvious when you're annoyed with me.

8.   I can't tell who's on the telephone.

9. I'm sure I'd rather be fishing right now.

10. Let's take your children to the beach.

Lesson 5-10: Parentheses

Parentheses are used to set off extra material. They can enclose words, phrases, or numbers that supplement, illustrate, or clarify material. They can act as an aside, where you have a chance to explain something either before or after the parentheses. They are also used in citations to help sort and separate information. Commas are also used to separate extra material. The difference with parentheses is the degree. Use parentheses for material that is not part of the main statement but is important enough to include.

Examples

We are all actors (although some of us have paying jobs).

The parentheses are used here to clarify a statement.

All current information is kept in the library's database. (Please note that all out of date material is kept on microfilm.)

In this example, the parentheses contain a complete sentence that gives additional, less important, material.

Roy, A. (1997). <u>The God of Small Things</u>. New York: Harper Collins.

This example shows the use of parentheses (as well as colon and underline) in an APA style citation.

As these examples show, a *period* can be placed **before** or **after** the closing parenthesis. If the entire sentence is contained within the parentheses, the period comes first. If the material inside the parenthesis is part of a larger sentence, the parenthesis comes first. A *comma*, however, is always placed outside a closing parenthesis. Also, you do not place a comma before the opening parenthesis.

In formal essay writing, avoid the use of parentheses when possible. For instances where clarity and precise writing is crucial, try to convey meaning in the main part of the sentence. Sometimes parentheses in formal writing seem like afterthoughts.

Exercise 5-18

Rewrite each of these sentences using parentheses where necessary.

Example: New parents frequently need help understanding their children's sleep needs (among other things).

1. On average, a young baby under six months of age needs around 17 hours of sleep per 24-hour period.

2. Newborns and young babies because of this need for sleep often become drowsy while they are feeding.

3. Older babies ages six months and older are less inclined to fall asleep while feeding.

4. They may also learn how to keep themselves awake, and parents in order to sleep themselves may have to devise new strategies to help their baby relax and go to sleep.

5. Toddlers need on average around 10 to 12 hours sleep per night and still need daytime naps.

6. A child's night-time sleeping routine if they sleep at all can be severely disrupted if he does not get enough sleep during the day, or if his afternoon nap is too close to bedtime.

7. Children of all ages and adults too need adequate sleep and rest.

8. Some babies those who have chronic sleep trouble may have trouble feeding properly or finishing their feeds.

9. Older babies and in many cases toddlers may be more difficult to handle, because tiredness often translates into crankiness and tears.

10. Even if your child sleeps well at night, he or she still needs a morning and or afternoon nap until at least around the age of two and a half to three years.

Lesson 5-11: Underline or Italics

Underline and italics are interchangeable as forms of punctuation. Nevertheless, italics and underline are both useful when typing, but underline is more useful when writing by hand. You may use either to punctuate the title of a larger work, such as a novel, collection of short stories, a movie, or a volume of poetry. Underline has been used traditionally, but with the widespread use of computers, italics are becoming more popular.

Examples

My favorite novel is <u>The God of Small Things</u> by Arundhati Roy.

Here, underline is used to designate the novel as a major work of literature.

My favorite novel is *The God of Small Things* by Arundhati Roy.

In this sentence, italics punctuate the novel.

Both of the examples are correct. Remember that quotation marks would not be correct for this example.

In addition, you may also use italics for special emphasis of words, phrases, and numbers. Foreign words are frequently in italics, and Latin words are always in italics.

Examples

An unusual species of orchid is the *Coeloglossum virdie* because it can withstand arctic temperatures.

Coeloglossum virdie is the Latin name and is therefore italicized.

Elliot's employer *claims* to be independently wealthy.

There is extra emphasis on the word *claims* in this sentence. Using italics changes the tone of the word, implying disbelief.

Additionally, italics are used for words, numbers, signs, and letters used to represent themselves.

Examples

Be careful not to mix up the words *elicit* and *illicit*.

Elicit and *illicit* are italicized because they represent themselves.

The *1* and the *4* on my phone are completely worn off.

These numbers are italicized because they represent themselves.

As you can see, there are few rules regarding underline and italics. You must use italics to specify Latin words, and you must signal a major work with underline or italics. Other than these cases, you may use these devices to accent words, phrases, or numbers. As with any other situation involving choices, implement a variety of techniques and punctuation to keep your writing interesting.

Exercise 5-19

For each of the following sentences, underline the word or words that should be italicized.

Example: The French expression <u>joi de vivre</u> describes my mood today.

1. She crossed all her t's and dotted all her i's.

2. Why do some people think the number 7 is lucky and 13 is unlucky?

3. Americans use the $ sign to express amounts of money.

4. I legally changed my name from Patricia to Tricia.

5. The sempervirens in my garden are evergreens.

6. The chrysantha contorta are twisted, yellow flowers.

7. Her license plate has three 8's and two Y's.

8. The English word odyssey comes from Odysseus, the title character in The Odyssey.

9. The postal worker delivered the package tout de suite.

10. The banker wrote denied on the applicant's loan papers.

Lesson 5-12: Hyphens

Hyphens have several specific purposes. They are used to divide words at the end of the line for spacing, they are used with compound words, they are used for clarity, and they are with certain prefixes and suffixes.

Examples

Frank bought a gift for his <u>two-year-old</u> daughter.

Two-year-old is a **compound word,** so it takes a hyphen. Compound numbers between twenty-one and ninety-nine and fractions also take a hyphen.

Rita and Andrew have been married for thirty-seven years.

Thirty-seven is a **compound number** and takes a hyphen.

Comments made during the election were considered by some to be un-American.

In this sentence, *un-American* is hyphenated because the word taking the prefix is capitalized. In most cases, there is no hyphen after prefixes or before suffixes.

Anti-inflation measures were a hot issue with the politicians.

Anti-inflation is hyphenated for clarity.

The pitcher on the all-state baseball team injured his left shoulder.

All-state is hyphenated because adding the prefix gives the word a specific meaning. However, most words with prefixes do not require a hyphen.

Hyphens are also used to divide words the end of a line. Computers are eliminating this need when the words are typed, but there is still sometimes a need to divide a word at the end of a line. Remember that words separated at the end of a line with a hyphen *must* be divided between syllables.

Example

The pitcher cannot complete the season, because his rota-tor cuff needs surgery.

Rotator has a hyphen between the second and third syllable for spacing purposes.

There are several rules to keep in mind when dividing words at the end of a line.

Do not divide one-syllable words or a single syllable within a word.

Example:

Incorrect:	ask-ed	Incorrect:	gasoli-ne
Correct:	asked	Correct:	gas-o-line

In general, divide multi-syllable words that have double consonants between the double consonants.

Example:

Incorrect:	puzz-led	Incorrect:	poss-es
Correct:	puz-zled	Correct:	pos-ses

If a suffix such as *–ing* or *–est* has been added to a word that ends in two consonants, divide the word after the two consonants.

Examples:

Incorrect:	pres-sing	Incorrect:	tal-lest
Correct:	press-ing	Correct:	tall-est

If a word contains two consonants standing between two vowels, divide it between the consonants.

Examples:

Incorrect:	princ-ess	Incorrect:	powd-er
Correct:	prin-cess	Correct:	pow-der

Divide a word with a prefix or a suffix after the prefix or before the suffix.

Examples:

Incorrect:	unt-ie	Incorrect:	squea-mish
Correct:	un-tie	Correct:	squeam-ish

To divide a compound noun or compound adjective that is generally written as one word, place the hyphen between the two base words.

Examples:

Incorrect:	ho-memade	Incorrect:	keeps-ake
Correct:	home-made	Correct:	keep-sake

Do not divide proper nouns, proper adjectives, or abbreviations.

Example:

Incorrect:	Washing-ton	Incorrect:	Swed-ish	Incorrect:	PE-TA
Correct:	Washington	Correct:	Swedish	Correct:	PETA

Exercise 5-20

Decide whether or not each of the following words could be divided if it occurred at the end of a line. In the space provided, rewrite the word that can be divided, adding hyphens at the point or points of division.

Example: storyteller   *story-teller*

1. greatest   _____

2. complaining _____

3. walked   _____

4. Columbian   _____

5. pothole   _____

6. abbrev.   _____

7. feasible   _____

8. UNICEF   _____

9. eat   _____

10. regenerate   _____

11. Bradbury   _____

12. trapping   _____

13. Kennedy   _____

14. repeat   _____

15. lumber   _____

16. returnable   _____

17. food   _____

18. wriggled   _____

19. beaten   _____

20. slipper   _____

Answers to Exercises

Exercise 5-1

1. our physician is a compassionate person.

2. we met through a mutual friend.

3. she and i went to school together.

4. o say can you see?

5. his office is located next door.

6. where is the new student?

7. after dinner, i went out for ice cream.

8. she told me that i've never looked better.

9. before the movie, i need to call home.

10. will you dance with me?

Exercise 5-2

1. I hope to travel to <u>ireland</u> next summer.
2. We met through <u>andrew</u>, a mutual friend.
3. Did you interview the <u>republican</u> candidate?
4. The <u>puerto rican</u> flag flies outside the embassy.
5. He hopes to purchase a <u>persian</u> carpet.
6. The building is made from imported <u>grecian</u> marble.
7. When I visit <u>california</u>, I will stop and see <u>ms</u>. <u>murphy</u>.
8. Her favorite meal is <u>chinese</u> food.
9. We like to walk to the <u>bergmans</u>' house.
10. We enjoy watching foreign films, including <u>french</u> movies.

Exercise 5-3

1. Our physician, <u>d</u>octor <u>b</u>ernstein, is a compassionate person.
2. We needed to speak to <u>p</u>rofessor <u>a</u>ddabbo.
3. Our congresswoman is <u>r</u>ep. <u>s</u>chroeder.
4. The professor, <u>m</u>s. <u>a</u>nderson, lives near <u>d</u>r. <u>c</u>ombs's office.
5. We must ask peter jr. for help in this matter.
6. The head of our school is <u>d</u>r. <u>w</u>illiams, <u>e.d.</u>
7. The judge for the district court is <u>s</u>am <u>w</u>alters, <u>j.d.</u>
8. She consulted <u>p</u>resident <u>c</u>ohen about the problem.
9. His father's name is <u>e</u>dward <u>s</u>immons, <u>s</u>r.
10. The new parish priest is <u>f</u>r. <u>b</u>ailey.

Exercise 5-4

1. <u>t</u>he <u>f</u>ourth of july is a great time to travel.
2. <u>p</u>eople journey around the <u>u</u>nited <u>s</u>tates of <u>a</u>merica.
3. <u>d</u>uring the summer, the <u>s</u>outhwest becomes extremely warm.
4. <u>p</u>laces like <u>t</u>exas are still popular, though.
5. <u>t</u>ravelers visit the <u>a</u>lamo in <u>s</u>an <u>a</u>ntonio.
6. <u>s</u>ometimes we leave on a <u>f</u>riday and return on a <u>t</u>uesday.
7. <u>w</u>e enjoy researching the <u>r</u>evolutionary <u>w</u>ar.
8. <u>l</u>ater, we go east to <u>p</u>hiladelphia.
9. <u>t</u>here we can see the <u>d</u>eclaration of <u>i</u>ndependence.
10. <u>w</u>e read about possible destinations in *today's travel*, our travel guide.

Exercise 5-5

1. He joined the U.S. Marines after graduation.

2. William H. Macy is an incredibly talented actor.

3. To find the market, turn left on Main St. at the first traffic light.

4. Elliot called the complaint dept. about the overage charges on his cell phone.

5. Morgan earned a B.A. from Manhattan College.

6. She studied French Lit. for two years.

7. Capt. Thompson led the fighting in western U.S. regions.

8. Natalia gave the school the phone no. for emergencies.

9. Mr. and Mrs. Anderson were married in May.

10. L. A. County in C.A. is one of the wealthiest counties in the U.S.

Exercise 5-6

1. I'll see you tomorrow.

2. Hey! Look out!

3. Can you reach the telephone?

4. Put the encyclopedia on the shelf.

5. Whose books are these?

6. Never forget your key.

7. Where are your shoes?

8. Call me when you get home.

9. Run! Get out of here!

10. Did you understand that memo?

Exercise 5-7

1. Needing decorations, I looked to nature.

2. Cautiously, I climbed the fence.

3. Looking around, I saw violets.

4. Unfortunately, there were no daisies.

5. However, I did spy some clover.

6. Reaching into my bag, I removed my scissors.

7. To make a bouquet, I chose several varieties of flowers.

8. Carefully, I avoided the sharp burrs and thorns.

9. Because they were wilting, I put them in water.

10. Finally, I have a beautiful table arrangement.

Exercise 5-8

1. More food is produced today than ever before, but only one third of the world is well fed.

2. Many people in the world are hungry, and many children suffer from malnutrition.

3. Citizens are unaware of hunger in their own country, for the hungry lack the means to publicize their condition.

4. The rich nations have overweight citizens, and the poor nations have starving citizens.

5. Many people receive government assistance, but they still do not have enough to eat.

6. Hunger is a monumental problem, but it can be solved.

7. We need to develop more food sources, and funds must be made available.

8. Money is not enough, for research is also needed.

9. Health conditions must be studied, and children must be protected.

10. Rich nations must do more to help the poor, and poor nations must do more to help themselves.

Exercise 5-9

1. This company sells shirts, shorts, pants, and jackets.

2. We frequently buy two, four, or six cases of fabric at a time.

3. Orders can be shipped to Delaware, New Jersey, New York, and Connecticut.

4. The shirts are available in sizes small, medium, large, and extra large.

5. The colors, I believe, are limited.

6. Red, blue, and green are out of stock.

7. We also have yellow available, I think, in the warehouse.

8. Blue, we were told, is our most popular color.

9. The business, I am sure, is set for expansion.

10. We will hire new designers, seamstresses, managers, and office personnel.

Exercise 5-10

1. Ernest Hemingway was born on July 21, 1899, in Oak Park, a suburb of Chicago, Illinois.

2. His father, Dr. Clarence Edmonds Hemingway, was a fervent member of the First Congregational church.

3. His mother, Grace Hall, sang in the church choir.

4. The Red Cross, a charitable foundation, accepted Hemingway as an ambulance driver.

5. He boarded a ship, the *Chicago*, bound for Bordeaux, France.

6. From there he went to his final destination, Italy.

7. He had his friend Theodore Brumback beside him. *- no commas are necessary*

8. He also met a new friend, Howell Jenkins.

9. The trip from America to Italy was a long and tiring one. *- no commas are necessary*

10. On the morning of June 7, 1918, 18-year-old Hemingway stepped off a train at Garbaldi Station in Milan and assumed the duties of a Red Cross ambulance driver. *- no commas are necessary*

Exercise 5-11

1. Our friend Mary, a hard worker, needs a new job.

2. Mary, amazed, learned her position was eliminated.

3. Her Chief Officer, upset with the events, released all of the executives.

4. All the executives, because they needed employment, searched online for jobs.

5. The online jobs, available only to some, required relocation.

6. Some executives, after searching for months, accepted lower-paying jobs.

7. All new store clerks who required training were sent to workshops. *- no commas are necessary*

8. The workshops, especially those specializing in social skills, were helpful.

9. Frank found one course, "People to People," extremely helpful.

10. All new employment requiring adjustment can be stressful. *- no commas are necessary*

Exercise 5-12

1. The first annual parade was held on May 28, 1995, in Springville, Missouri.

2. The bandleader cried, "All fall in!"

3. "Harold lost his instrument," laughed Sally.

4. It looked like there were 10,000 people in uniforms.

5. The firefighters met at Bob's house in Ellenville, Missouri.

6. He lives at 23 Main Street, Ellenville, Missouri.

7. "Park around the corner," he cried, "by the supermarket."

8. More than 60,000 people were in attendance that day.

9. The press wrote, "The parade was delightful."

10. "For fun, come to Springville, Missouri," wrote the local paper.

Exercise 5-13

1. Food should be fresh; in fact, it should be organic when possible.

2. Boiling vegetables removes some of the vitamins; therefore, vegetables should be steamed.

3. Some foods are healthier raw; eat several servings of raw vegetables per day.

4. Dairy products provide large amounts of calcium; cheese and milk are especially good sources.

5. Beef is only about twenty-five percent protein; you get more protein from soybeans, chicken, and turkey.

6. Turkey and chicken have less fat than beef; moreover, they contain more protein.

7. Some foods are better in combination; consequently, people should learn how to combine foods for the best health benefits.

8. Vitamin A is supplied by eggs and liver; it can also be obtained from some fruits and vegetables.

9. Citrus fruits provide vitamin C; oranges and grapefruits are particularly good sources.

10. Our bodies need protein and vitamins; therefore, it is essential for us to know which foods provided them.

Exercise 5-14

1. Summer camps can be categorized by themes: outdoor adventure, life skills, community service, or nature appreciation.

2. Some camps offer many activities: swimming, archery, boating, and golf.

3. A good counselor-to-camper ratio is 1:12.

4. Many camps have "lights out" at 10:30 at night.

5. At sailing camp, there are different boats: the sailboat, the sunfish, and the canoe.

6. Canoeing develops muscles: the biceps, the triceps and the laterals.

7. I have many favorite activities: fishing, swimming, canoeing, and rock climbing.

8. We always wake up at 7:15 in the morning.

9. My counselor calls her motto: "Rise and shine."

10. When the summer is over, I come home to my family: my mother, my father, my sister, and my dog.

Exercise 5-15

1. *Time* magazine had an article entitled "Looking for Lois."
2. "Unlock the front door," yelled my mother.
3. "The Swede faintly smiled," wrote Stephen Crane in "The Blue Hotel."
4. She asked me, "Where are your shoes?"
5. My dictionary defines loiter as "to linger idly."
6. I can't believe he told me to "mind my own business"!
7. Do you know the story "Rip Van Winkle"?
8. David yelled, "Get out!"
9. Eddie said, "The article, 'Name Brands for Nannies,' is really interesting."
10. The movie review called his epic "a mistake for the masses."

Exercise 5-16

1. <u>Susan</u> friend, Mary, went away for the weekend.   *Susan's*
2. Susan agreed to feed <u>Mary</u> cats.   *Mary's*
3. She had to keep the <u>cats</u> bowls filled with food and water.   *cats'*
4. Mary also told her to check the bandage on the black <u>cat</u> leg.   *cat's*
5. It was necessary to seal the <u>bandage</u> seams.   *bandage's*
6. Before leaving, Mary checked the <u>doors</u> locks.   *doors'*
7. The <u>veterinarian</u> office was closed, but Mary left a message.   *veterinarian's*
8. Next, Mary left a message on her <u>boss</u> voicemail.   *boss's*
9. She also stopped by her <u>neighbors</u> house to leave a key.   *neighbors'*
10. They said they hoped their <u>friend</u> trip went well.   *friend's*

Exercise 5-17

1. I <u>don't</u> like pears, but the store <u>didn't</u> have any other fruit.
   I do not like pears, but the store did not have any other fruit.
2. <u>Won't</u> you wait for me?
   Will you not wait for me?
3. My father <u>couldn't</u> change the tire without the jack.
   My father could not change the tire without the jack.
4. Samantha <u>wouldn't</u> wait for her friend, or <u>she'd</u> be late for class.
   Samantha would not wait for her friend, or she would be late for class.
5. <u>He's</u> been so tired, lately.
   He has been so tired, lately.

6. Perhaps <u>he's</u> coming down with a cold.
    Perhaps he is coming down with a cold.

7. <u>It's</u> always obvious when <u>you're</u> annoyed with me.
    It is always obvious when you are annoyed with me.

8. I <u>can't</u> tell <u>who's</u> on the telephone.
    I cannot tell who is on the telephone.

9. <u>I'm</u> sure <u>I'd</u> rather be fishing right now.
    I am sure I would rather be fishing right now.

10. <u>Let's</u> take your children to the beach.
    Let us take your children to the beach.

Exercise 5-18

1. On average, a young baby (under six months of age) needs around 17 hours of sleep per 24-hour period.

2. Newborns and young babies (because of this need for sleep) often become drowsy while they are feeding.

3. Older babies (ages six months and older) are less inclined to fall asleep while feeding.

4. They may also learn how to keep themselves awake, and parents (in order to sleep themselves) may have to devise new strategies to help their baby relax and go to sleep.

5. Toddlers need (on average) around 10 to 12 hours sleep per night and still need daytime naps.

6. A child's night-time sleeping routine (if they sleep at all) can be severely disrupted if he does not get enough sleep during the day, or if his afternoon nap is too close to bedtime.

7. Children of all ages (and adults too) need adequate sleep and rest.

8. Some babies (those who have chronic sleep trouble) may have trouble feeding properly or finishing their feeds.

9. Older babies (and in many cases toddlers) may be more difficult to handle, because tiredness often translates into crankiness and tears.

10. Even if your child sleeps well at night, he or she still needs a morning and or afternoon nap (until at least around the age of two and a half to three years).

Exercise 5-19

1. She crossed all her <u>t's</u> and dotted all her <u>i's</u>.

2. Why do some people think the number <u>7</u> is lucky and <u>13</u> is unlucky?

3. Americans use the $ sign to express amounts of money.

4. I legally changed my name from Patricia to Tricia.

5. The sempervirens in my garden are evergreens.

6. The chrysantha contorta are twisted, yellow flowers.

7. Her license plate has three 8's and two Y's.

8. The English word odyssey comes from Odysseus, the title character in The Odyssey.

9. The postal worker delivered the package tout de suite.

10. The banker wrote denied on the applicant's loan papers.

Exercise 5-20

1. greatest	*great-est*	11. Bradbury	no division
2. complaining	*complain-ing*	12. trapping	*trapp-ing*
3. walked	*walk-ed*	13. Kennedy	no division
4. Columbian	no division	14. repeat	*re-peat*
5. pothole	*pot-hole*	15. lumber	*lum-ber*
6. abbrev.	no division	16. returnable	*return-able*
7. feasible	*feas-ible*	17. food	no division
8. UNICEF	no division	18. wriggled	wrig-gled
9. eat	*no division*	19. beaten	*beat-en*
10. regenerate	*re-generate*	20. slipper	*slip-per*

The Writing Process

All effective writing is well planned. A writer must determine what he wants to say and how he wants to say it. The writer has a responsibility to convey ideas in the clearest way possible. Writing is a process with steps that must be followed. These steps include determining the topic, planning, drafting, editing, revising, and proofreading. Without this process, valuable information could be lost to the reader. This chapter addresses the different stages of the writing process and follows the progression from beginning to end.

Lesson 6-1: Subject, Audience, and Purpose

A writer must ask himself three questions:

▷   *What is my subject?*
▷   *Who is my audience?*
▷   *What is my purpose?*

The answers to these three questions will determine his product. Each variable plays a role in determining the final product.

The Subject

This is the topic of the written work. There are an infinite number of subjects about which to write. Once the subject is determined, it should be honed and made specific. The subject should be as narrow as possible for each given assignment; clear writing is concise. Broad topics leave room for extraneous information. As a rule, the more specific the topic is, the more precise the article or essay.

Examples

Boats

This is an expansive subject. Volumes of work could be written on this topic. Even if the planned piece is prodigious, this topic is too general.

Sailboats on the Atlantic Ocean

This subject is much more limited than *boats*. At first glance, it appears to be a sound subject. However, what is the planned length of the piece of writing? Is it possible to fit everything about sailboats on the Atlantic Ocean into one essay? What about one book?

The safety of sailboats under twenty feet in length on the Atlantic Ocean

This topic is specific enough to cover in one article or essay. The topic is concise, and it allows the writer to address pertinent information.

Exercise 6-1

For each of the general topics listed, create a specific subject for an article or essay.

Example: Scary movies
The impact of violence in scary movies for teens.

1. The beach _____

2. Automobiles of the 1920s _____

3. Children's clothing_____

4. School safety _____

5. Literature of today _____

6. Skateboarding _____

7. Different forms of art _____

8. Birds of the Northeast_____

9. Medieval homes _____

10. Candles _____

The Audience

This is the person or people who will read the piece. Considering the audience will help determine content, language, and tone. Some audiences require more background information about the topic than others. Some audiences understand content-specific vocabulary. The level of vocabulary and tone can be different with varied groups of individuals. For example, does a teenager speak to her friends the same way she speaks to her teacher or employer? Are the topics of conversation the same? Is the language the same? When speaking, we modify topics and language according to whom we are addressing. The same is done for writing. Consider three different audiences for an article on music.

Examples

A music article published in *Teen People* magazine

The audience in this case is teenagers. The subject of this article must be music geared toward teenagers. The vocabulary must be accessible to teenagers; the language would be level appropriate for adolescents, and it could possibly include vernacular.

A music article published in *Time* magazine

The audience is different here; the readers of this article would be older. The music itself would differ for this group of audience. The vocabulary would be more varied, and the language would be more formal.

A music article published in a music magazine

This article has a specific audience of music listeners. This audience shares a common body of knowledge that allows for tacit omission of detail. Genre-specific vocabulary could be used. A reader of *Teen People* or *Time* magazines may not fully understand the content or vocabulary in this article.

The Purpose

This is the goal of the written word. There are many different purposes for writing. Perhaps the article or essay denounces someone or something. The purpose may be to persuade others to the author's way of thinking. The article might simply tell a good story for the purpose of entertaining the reader. The article might highlight an injustice and therefore be a call to action for the audience. The purpose for writing must be clear from the start. Let's look at some purposes with the previous example of the music article published in *Teen People* magazine.

Examples

A review of a new song release

The purpose of this article is to review a song. The reviewer could either praise the music or criticize it, and therefore persuade the reader to the writer's way of thinking. It would be filled with either positive or negative adjectives that describe the music.

An article highlighting a band's recent tour

This article's purpose is to regale the reader with interesting stories about a group of musicians. This article should therefore be entertaining. It should contain language that evokes emotions in the reader.

An exposition of racist lyrics in a song

The purpose of this piece is to draw attention to the band's malevolent message. It should not only denounce the band and its lyricist, it must urge the reader to take action against the band. This article should contain persuasive language that incites the reader.

Think of each component: subject, audience, and purpose as variable. Changing any one of these components changes the entire article or essay. The writer must be clear about each of these components before beginning the writing process.

Exercise 6-2

Generate ideas to include in each of the following assignments. Notice how the details differ depending on audience and purpose.

1. You have been asked to write a description of your local library for middle school and high school students. Your purpose is to encourage more teenagers to use the library. What information do you include? What details of the library do you highlight for teenagers?

2. You have been asked to write a description of your local library for local businesses. Your goal is to generate rent for the use of meeting rooms. What information do you include? What details of the library do you highlight for businesses?

3. You have been asked to write a description of your local library for the government. Your purpose is to apply for available library grants to purchase new books. What information do you include? What details of the library do you highlight for the government?

Lesson 6-2: Exploring a Topic

It is necessary to explore a topic before writing. A writer must assess what is known and what needs to be discovered. Ideas must be generated before writing. There are several common techniques used to accomplish this. Some of these techniques include brainstorming, freewriting, and clustering.

Brainstorming

This technique is used to generate ideas about a given topic. This strategy involves tossing out ideas as they occur. Two or more people can combine to generate ideas. This allows for others to hear, react, and build upon ideas. This can be done through discussion or correspondence. It can happen all at once, or over a period of time. If no one else is available, it is possible to brainstorm alone. Follow these simple steps:

▷ Set a time limit of five to 10 minutes to write down in list form every word or phrase that comes to mind about the topic. Use key words or phrases, not complete sentences. Much of what is on the list will not be used, but that does not matter. It is important to write everything down now and dismiss certain ideas later.

▷ Writer's block sometimes occurs even at the brainstorming stage. One solution is to focus on the opposite side of the argument or topic. Then, use the list to start building in the right direction.

▷ When the time is up, review the list. Look for clusters, patterns, or groups of ideas that can be used in your article.

Exercise 6-3

Choose one of the following topics to brainstorm. Write the topic at the top of your paper, set a time limit of five to 10 minutes, and write down everything that comes into your head.

1. The worst vacation ever

2. A famous athlete

3. The most memorable President

4. My best/worst job

5. How to deal with rude people

Freewriting

This method uses a stream-of-consciousness technique to explore possible topics. It is helpful when you are unable to come up with an idea for an article or essay. For a limited period of time, write down everything known about a general subject without thinking. Here are the steps:

> ▷ Set a time limit of no more than 10 minutes. Think about the subject, and let your mind wander as you write down *everything* that comes to mind. Write in complete sentences when possible, but do not worry about grammar at this point. Do not stop until the time is up. If you become blocked, continue writing about how you are blocked until something about the topic occurs to you.

> ▷ When the time is up, review what you have written. Eliminate all irrelevant information, and assess what remains. Determine possible topics, and transfer all pertinent statements to a new page.

Exercise 6-4

Choose one of these words to create a topic through freewriting. Set a time limit of no more than 10 minutes, and write everything that comes to mind about one word. When your time limit ends, underline all ideas generated about that one word. Choose one that seems interesting.

1. animals

2. automobiles

3. homes

4. children

5. science

Clustering

This technique uses a visual scheme to generate and organize ideas. Also called *webbing*, this strategy is useful for understanding the relationships among a broad topic, allowing for division into subtopics. This is a built in aid to writing about precise topics. The procedure is:

▷ Write down your topic in the middle of a blank piece of paper and circle it.

▷ In a ring around the topic circle, write down the main aspects of the topic. Circle each aspect and draw a line to connect it to the topic circle.

▷ As you generate ideas, examples, or facts about each part of the main topic, write them down in a ring around each aspect of the main topic. Circle the details and draw a line to connect it to the relevant circle. Your paper should begin to resemble a web of lines and circles.

▷ Repeat this process until you are no longer able to generate ideas about the main topic, aspects of the main topic, or ideas, examples, or facts about each aspect.

Exercise 6-5

Choose one of the following words to create a topic through clustering. Write the word in the center of your page and circle it. Keep writing down associations and clustering until you have filled the page.

1. technology

2. history

3. heroes

4. exercise

5. movies

After this process of exploring a topic is complete, the writer is able to measure what is known, and what, if anything needs to be determined. This will guide the research process. (For more about research, see Chapter 8.)

Once a topic is chosen and is made as specific as possible, and once information has been gathered through exploration or research, the main idea of the paper or article must be determined. The main idea is called the thesis statement.

Lesson 6-3: Creating a Thesis Statement

The thesis statement is one complete sentence that states the main idea of the piece of writing. It focuses the subject because it clearly states the writer's central point. A thesis statement may change as writing progresses, but a working thesis should be created early on. It occurs early on in the essay; it acts as a reference to the reader about what he or she will encounter. The thesis must be general enough to include all of the relevant information, but as the subject is, it must be as specific as possible. By writing a specific thesis statement, you focus on your subject and give your reader a clear idea of what will follow in the essay.

Examples

The company's president is a bad employer.

This thesis is too vague. Notice the general word *bad*. Where is the area of focus? This thesis needs to be revised.

The company's president ignores the needs of his employees.

This thesis is better. The topic is limited to needs of the employees. The main idea is more specific, and the reader will have a better idea about the content and structure of the article.

The company's president must modify the employee health care options.

This thesis is the best choice of the three examples. The topic is not all of the employees' needs; it is limited to the healthcare options.

In order to create a specific thesis, focus on description and direction. First, give focus to the paper by avoiding general topics. Choose a specific area to develop in your writing. Second, avoid vague terms and use precise description. Do not use words such as *bad* or *good*; use concise terms. Also, sharpen the thesis to give it direction. Make the area to cover as narrow as possible. Let's try revising some thesis statements.

Exercise 6-6

Revise each of the following thesis statements, making them more specific.

1. Our local library needs improvement.

2. Marriage is a good idea.

3. Healthy cooking is important.

4. Baseball is a fun sport.

5. I like my job.

6. You can learn a lot by watching children.

7. Summer is my favorite season.

8. Drag racing is a bad idea.

9. Recycling is important.

10. Students should always complete their homework.

Lesson 6-4: Organization

Once you have gathered the necessary information for you paper, you must be sure to organize it so it is presented in a way that makes sense to your reader. Information must be separated into groups, and each group must have its own paragraph or section of the essay. Information should be ordered in a way that makes sense for your topic. Different methods of organization include chronological, spatial, order of importance, and logical.

Chronological Organization

If the information you are presenting takes place over a period of time or involves a process that includes steps, the best order in which to present it is chronologically. In other words, help your reader understand what happened by telling the story from beginning to end. The sequence should begin with the initial event, and it should continue in order of events until the conclusion. This allows the reader to easily follow the progression of the article. Sometimes however, it can also be effective to present the events in reverse sequence. This may be helpful to explain why things occurred. Also, this can have a dramatic effect on the writing. With either method, sequencing from beginning to end, or from end to beginning, chronological organization is useful.

Careful use of time helps to prevent confusing sentences such as this: Before that happened, he also did something else. Transitional words and phrases such as *first, then, after that, soon, following, next, moments later, before, during,* and *finally* add clarity to chronological organization.

Examples

Before painting, clear the area of unnecessary items. Next, tape around windows and molding. After that, you are ready to begin.

This example gives a series of directions, but you can use time to tell a story sequentially.

The painter entered the house. Soon he began to work. First, he set up his supplies. He mixed paints while his assistant cleared the area. Next, he applied his first coat. After that, he painted the trim. Finally, the work was done.

Exercise 6-7

Arrange the following details according to chronological order.

_____ 1. Next, he became a commissioned lieutenant colonel, where he fought the first skirmishes of what grew into the French and Indian War.

_____ 2. Born in 1732 into a Virginia planter family, George Washington learned the morals, manners, and body of knowledge requisite for an 18th-century Virginia gentleman.

_____ 3. George Washington finally took office on April 30, 1789, while standing on the balcony of Federal Hall on Wall Street in New York.

_____ 4. The following year, as an aide to Gen. Edward Braddock, he escaped injury although four bullets ripped his coat and two horses were shot out from under him.

_____ 5. At 16, he helped survey Shenandoah lands for Thomas, Lord Fairfax.

Spatial Organization

If the information you have gathered is descriptive, it makes sense to organize the details using space. You should describe a person, a thing, or a place by following a direction, such as top to bottom, left to right, or background to foreground. In other words, if you were describing a room, it would be confusing to the reader to begin the description with the left wall, then jump to the floor, and then move to the table. You should guide your reader through the room by following a certain direction. This direction can differ according to need or focus, but it must make sense. Perhaps you want to describe an item on a table. You might begin with the overall placement of the table within the room, then move in towards the table, and finally describe the item. It would not make sense to describe the room, then the item, and finally the table's placement within the room.

Careful use of space helps the reader picture the setting. Transitional words and phrases such as *on the left, on the right, beyond, next to, above, below,* and *beside* aid clarity to spatial organization.

Example

The town's largest park was recently converted into a playground for children of all ages. Recreational equipment now covers the field. Near the entrance, swings are set at various heights. A large, brightly colored carousel sits in the center of the park. To the right of the carousel is a set of wooden monkey bars. At the far end, a sandbox shaped like a turtle provides enjoyment for the toddlers. For a day of fun, bring the family to the new playground.

Exercise 6-8

For each of the following examples, arrange the details according to space order.

_____ 1. The beige, red, and gold carpet beneath the furniture is a reproduction of an early-19th-century French Savonnerie carpet.

_____ 2. All the fabrics now in the Red Room were woven in the United States from French Empire designs.

_____ 3. Above it all sits the 13-light French Empire chandelier, fashioned from carved and gilded wood in 1805.

_____ 4. The Red Room of the White House was furnished between the years 1810 and 1830.

_____ 5. Behind the furniture hang 19th-century-inspired draperies made of gold satin with red silk valances and handmade gold and red fringe.

_____ 6. The walls are covered with a red twill satin fabric that has a gold scroll design in the border.

_____ 7. The furniture, like the American Empire sofa, is upholstered in a silk of the same shade of red.

Order-of-Importance Organization

If the information you are presenting will be used to persuade your reader with a series of examples, it is sometimes necessary to classify data into order of importance. It can be effective to begin with the most significant idea or event and continue to the least significant, therefore putting your strongest evidence first. You could also reverse the order and start with the least significant event to build to a climax. Either way, the order of importance must be determined. This can change according to the focus of your essay. For instance, you may determine one event more significant than another because of the idea you are attempting to prove.

Carefully using order of importance helps guide the reader and give coherence to the paragraph. Transitional words and phrases such as *first, next, another, even more, last,* and *least of all* allow for organization through order of importance.

Example

Thomas Jefferson achieved many goals throughout his lifetime. He wrote the Statute of Virginia for Religious Freedom. <u>Another</u> accomplishment was he founded the University of Virginia. However, he was known for <u>even greater</u> endeavors. For instance, Jefferson was the third president of the United States. <u>Even more importantly</u>, he was the author of the Declaration of Independence.

Exercise 6-9

For each of the following examples, arrange the details in order of importance from least to most significant.

1. _____ Children should not be exposed to inebriated adults.

2. _____ Games would be more pleasant without the rowdiness brought about by the consumption of alcohol.

3. _____ Possibility for violence and even death increases when alcohol is at hand.

4. _____ Littering increases when alcohol is available.

5. _____ Alcohol should not be sold at sporting events.

6. _____ More injuries occur at sporting events where alcohol is present.

Logical Organization

Some writing requires establishing logical relationships in your information. These relationships can be based on similarities, differences, or causes and effects. Some of the patterns used in logical organization include classification, comparing and contrasting, and cause-effect analysis.

▶ **Classification** means grouping separate items of information about a topic together. When you are faced with details that are diverse but must be presented in the same piece of writing, classification can help. Find characteristics about your information to establish groups, then simply classify, or group, similar items together within each paragraph. Use topic sentences to clue the reader in on each separate classification per paragraph.

▶ **Comparing and contrasting** is a technique that focuses on both similarities and differences between subjects. Comparison highlights similarities, wheras contrast illustrates differences. Used together, you can organize information on topics. Organization for comparing and contrasting include first presenting the similarities and then the differences between your subjects, or alternating between the two subjects.

▶ **Cause-effect analysis** either examines why something happens or happened by looking at its causes, or looks at a set of conditions and explains what results will occur. In other words, it analyzes what causes something or what effects are expected. This technique can be used for expository writing, technical writing, or persuasive writing.

Lesson 6-5: The Paragraph

A paragraph is a group of sentences that expounds one main idea. Usually five to 12 sentences in length, a paragraph occurs mostly with other paragraphs in a longer piece of writing, such as an essay, an article, or a letter. The paragraph is an important component in writing. Each paragraph or unit of the essay must be concise; only information that belongs should be included. It must be structured in a way that makes sense to the reader. Also, it must serve a purpose within the larger piece of writing. This lesson deals with ways to write clear, concise paragraphs.

The Topic Sentence

Each paragraph contains one main idea. This idea is generally expressed in the **topic sentence**. The body of the paragraph develops the topic sentence with details and examples. Here is an example of a typical paragraph. Note that the first line of the paragraph is indented five spaces. This is a rule of layout. With most writing, each new paragraph is denoted by an indentation of five spaces, or one *Tab* on the keyboard. Paragraphs should not be separated by additional space; do not leave a line between paragraphs when you indent.

Example

The night of the gala was spectacular. The cool, dry air, the essence of freshness, possessed a subtle fragrance of honeysuckle. The sky was a blanket of splintered mirrors.

In the background, clinking glasses and undistinguishable murmurs were heard. Figures moved about like gliding shapes of color. Music was drifting out from somewhere near the patio. The dance floor at the end of the dock slowly filled with dancers. The party tapered off into a dream.

The first sentence of this paragraph is the **topic sentence**; it states the main idea of the paragraph. The topic sentence tells us that *the night of the gala was spectacular*. The rest of the paragraph, the **body**, develops the idea set forth in the topic sentence. The body shows us details of how the night was spectacular.

The topic sentence is always more general than the body sentences. It must be specific to the idea but general enough to fit all of the sentences under it. There is a helpful method to visualize the topic sentence and the body sentences. Place the topic sentence next to each sentence in the paragraph. Do the two sentences make sense side by side? If not, consider whether the topic sentence is too narrow or whether the body sentence should be eliminated.

Examples

The night of the gala was spectacular. The sky was a blanket of splintered mirrors.

These two sentences make sense next to each other.

The night of the gala was spectacular. Music was drifting out from somewhere near the patio.

These sentences also make sense side by side.

The topic sentence sets the concept for the entire paragraph. Therefore, it should come first in the paragraph. This is helpful to the reader. He can understand the idea early on in the paragraph, and the idea builds as he reads along. In most cases, the topic sentence appears first. Occasionally, the topic sentence is the *second* sentence; there is a brief setup before the topic sentence. Rarely, you will find the topic sentence at the end of the paragraph. Some sophisticated writers choose to place the topic sentence as the last sentence for effect. These cases are infrequent. When writing, the proper place is the most obvious location for the reader, the beginning of the paragraph.

Exercise 6-10

From the following sentences, choose the topic sentence and write the corresponding letter in the space provided.

_____ 1. a. Cell phones and pagers can cause distractions in class.

b. Arriving promptly to class aids the teachers' attendance procedure.

c. Following school policies keeps our environment operating smoothly.

d. With headphones off, students are better able to concentrate.

e. When food remains in the cafeteria, the hallways remain clean.

_____ 2. a. He barks whenever he smells coffee.

b. Buddy incessantly chews his water dish.

c. In the evening, he runs laps around the yard.

d. Our puppy, Buddy, has developed some strange habits.

e. After eating breakfast, the puppy falls fast asleep.

_____ 3. a. Children look for their socks.

b. Parents look for their keys.

c. As the alarm resounds, the chaos begins.

d. Lunches are packed in a blitz of motion as the family prepares to leave.

e. Mornings are hectic at our house.

_____ 4. a. In 1788, the state of Maryland ceded the land to Congress.

b. The United States Capitol has an interesting history.

c. Before 1791, the federal government had no permanent site.

d. The Capitol has been built, burned, rebuilt, extended, and restored.

e. Commissioners accepted the design of Dr. William Thornton on April 5, 1793.

_____ 5. a. It is thought a Chinese cook accidentally mixed common kitchen ingredients.

b. The discovery of fireworks, or the formulation of gunpowder, is believed to have occurred by chance some 2000 years ago.

c. When the powder was ignited, a large bang was heard.

d. This crude, early mixture has come to be known as gunpowder.

e. These were heated over a fire, and dried to become a black, flaky powder.

_____ 6. a. Rock climbing in New Zealand stems from mountaineering.

b. In preparation for the next peak, mountaineers would climb shorter but more extreme peaks.

c. This drove climbers to develop better safety equipment and new rock climbing techniques.

d. Climbers tried progressively more extreme peaks.

e. Initially, this activity was considered training, but it evolved into a sport in its own right.

_____ 7. a. Frequently, many uncommon ingredients are combined.

b. Agreeable results depend not just on ingredients, but steps.

c. Following the process precisely is sometimes imperative.

d. Cooking is complex.

e. Procedure can make the difference between unpalatable and scrumptious.

_____ 8. a. On the fifth floor, the sculptures are exquisite.

b. Many genres of painting are represented downstairs.

c. This museum contains many fine pieces.

d. The entire left wing is devoted to Egyptian art.

e. My favorites are the Impressionists.

_____ 9. a. There is little strain on the ankles and shins.

b. Cardiovascular exercise helps maintain a healthy heart.

c. Heart rate and pulse can be adjusted through routes and resistance.

d. Bicycling works the leg muscles, and it is aerobic.

e. Bicycling boasts many health benefits.

_____ 10. a. Our neighbor, Sheila, is a strange woman.

b. Strange sounds emanate from her apartment at night.

c. Her favorite food is olive-loaf.

d. She never leaves her trash in the community trash bin.

e. Her cat looks like it has gone through a blender.

Generating Ideas for the Body

Once the topic sentence is selected and refined, ideas must be generated for each paragraph. One method used to generate body sentences is brainstorming. Take your topic sentence and jot down ideas relating to the topic sentence. Later, you can choose from these ideas. Let's look at a sample topic sentence.

Example

Smoking is a filthy habit.

With this topic sentence, it is easy to generate ideas for body sentences.

1. It causes cancer.

2. Smoking stains teeth.

3. It gives you bad breath.

4. Cigarettes are expensive.

5. Your hair smells.

6. Smoking banned from many public places.

7. Smoking causes clothing to smell.

8. It yellows the fingers.

9. Ashes create mess.

10. Cigarette butts litter the ground.

11. Smoking is illegal for those under age of twenty-one.

12. The house and car smell like smoke.

Not all of these ideas fit the topic sentence: Smoking is a filthy habit. Therefore, we must select and drop ideas according to how they fit into our paragraph.

Selecting and Dropping Ideas

After generating ideas for a paragraph, they must be assessed for relevance. As suggested earlier, one technique is to place each sentence next to the topic sentence and ask the question, "Do they work together?" Look at the sentences in the previous example regarding smoking. Which ones would you eliminate?

Sentences 4, 6, and 11 pertain to smoking, but they do not match the topic sentence. Therefore, the paragraph would make more sense if they were eliminated.

Exercise 6-11

In the space provided, place an **X** next to the sentences that match the topic sentence about automobile safety.

Topic sentence: *Automotive safety measures have improved over the past decade.*

_____ 1. Automatic brake systems allow for less skidding.

_____ 2. Seats are now more comfortable.

_____ 3. Air bags cushion passengers upon impact.

_____ 4. The cost for a new automobile has risen fifteen percent.

_____ 5. Tire tread patterns allow for better control and endurance.

_____ 6. Digital speedometers give drivers more accurate readings.

_____ 7. Windshields have changed in shape and form.

_____ 8. Children should always sit in the back seat.

_____ 9. Additional lights allow for better visibility during inclement weather.

_____10. Many styles of hubcaps are now available.

_____11. Automobile frames can sustain minor crashes to protect occupants.

_____12. Many vehicles offer built in child-safety seats.

_____13. Suspension systems make potholes and other obstacles less hazardous.

_____14. Power steering enables drivers to make difficult turns.

_____15. Innovative strides have been made in the development of safety glass.

Lesson 6-6: The Outline

Every piece of writing needs a plan, and the outline is the plan. The outline is crucial to any piece of writing. It designates the structure of the piece. It must be done for every article or essay, whether long or short. For shorter pieces, some writers keep an outline in their heads, but this is not suggested. The outline can be revised as you work, but it helps you keep focus while you write. The outline consists of three major parts: the introduction, the body, and the conclusion.

The Introduction

The introduction establishes the main idea of the piece. It is used to give background information on the subject, to present and overview of the topic, and to state the main idea of the writing. It should guide the reader into the piece by providing necessary knowledge to familiarize him with the topic. The introduction must also contain a clear thesis statement that conveys the main idea.

There is no one best method for organizing an introduction; however, you should never begin with explanations such as "This essay is going to be about" or "I will be discussing." Do not tell the reader what you will be writing; just write. Here are six different ways to organize the introduction effectively.

1. Begin with a single-sentence thesis statement.

This can be effective because it quickly sets the tone and states the main idea of the piece. The rest of the introduction will contain supporting evidence for the thesis.

Example:

Children in America need more supervision.

This simple thesis clearly states the main idea of the piece. It would be followed by general information about children in America. The body would contain supporting evidence about the topic.

2. Begin with a general idea and gradually narrow your topic toward the main idea.

Sometimes called the funnel method, this technique starts with a wide scope and then draws the reader towards the thesis.

Example:

More parents work today than ever before. With the ever-rising cost of living and the growing number of single-parent households, the stay-at-home parent is a thing of the past. After-school programs can be expensive or overcrowded. Children of working parents are left to care for themselves an average of six hours a week. Researchers, policy-makers, and child advocates say that unsupervised time increases the risk of injury, crime, drug use, or falling behind in studies. <u>Children in America need more supervision.</u>

This technique allows for a wide range of interested readers. The broad topic at the beginning of the introduction then gradually narrows.

3. Begin with an illustration.

By setting the tone with a narration, the introduction is accessible.

Example:

Imagine a 10-year-old child alone at home. Mom is on her way home from work. The helpful child begins her routine of preparing a snack to eat while doing her homework. The child's favorite treat is apple slices with peanut butter. Mom forgot to slice the apples this morning. No problem, thinks the child. She reaches for the large knife that Mommy always uses... <u>Children in America need more supervision.</u>

This technique allows the reader to visualize an image before encountering the thesis.

4. Begin with a surprising fact or idea.

This will help to immediately catch the reader's attention.

Example:

According to a report released by the U.S. Census bureau, 2.4 million children under the age of 12 are home alone before or after school. Seven million 5- to 14-year-olds of working parents are left to care for themselves for an average of six hours a week. Thirteen percent of these children are home alone for 10 hours a week, according to the report. <u>Children in America need more supervision.</u>

These facts convey a sense of urgency to the reader. Faced with these facts the reader can agree with the thesis before even moving on to the body of the written piece.

5. Begin with a contradiction.

This method can pique the reader's interest and then sway him to another way of thinking.

Example:

> Growing children do not need to be supervised. Adult guidance can hinder freedom; it can limit choices. With constant adult presence, children lose the ability to discover new things. They do not have the opportunity to consume alcohol and drugs, commit crimes, or accidentally injure themselves. Adult guidance and intervention can prevent all of these things. <u>Children in America need more supervision.</u>

This example begins with a contradiction of what the writer and many others actually believe. This technique immediately grabs the attention of the reader with an opposing opinion.

6. Begin with a direct quotation.

The quotation can be familiar or simply dramatic. It will catch the reader's attention immediately.

Example:

> "Protecting one's own children is a biological imperative – it is how our species sustains itself. When an animal fails to protect its babies, they do not survive." —Andrew Vachss. Without protection, children cannot survive. If we plan on continuing as a race, we must care for our young. Why then are so many children left home alone? <u>Children in America need more supervision.</u>

This example begins with someone else's idea. It is an effective technique because it shows the reader that you have researched what other people feel about your topic.

The Body

The body is the main part of the written piece. Organization of the body will vary depending on the type of written work. It varies in length but usually consists of several paragraphs. Each should include a different supporting point. Regardless of the type of work, paragraphs are used to separate information. Each paragraph must contain only one idea, and it must begin with a topic sentence.

The Conclusion

The conclusion signals the end of the essay and leaves the reader with a final thought. Think of the conclusion as the final taste left in the reader's mouth. If it is effective, the reader will walk away with the essence of the written work. There are many ways to write a convincing conclusion, but avoid the obvious. Never begin the conclusion with "As stated earlier" or "In conclusion." Here are three methods to powerfully organize the conclusion.

1. End with a call to action.

The call to action should persuade the reader to make a change or act to improve the situation.

Example:

Someone must look out for the children of our nation. We must work together to preserve the future. It takes a village to raise a child; if each community takes responsibility for its own, perhaps we can make a difference. Individuals must be willing to help in any way possible. Employers must make concessions for the single parent. Neighbors must maintain communication. Schools must provide safe havens. We all must contribute to the future.

This example ends on a positive note because it provides a solution, as well as imbuing a sense of community. The reader should not only recognize the problem and agree with the thesis statement, he should experience a desire to help solve the problem.

2. End with a final point.

The final point can tie up all of the other ideas in the essay or article. It shows the reader that the entire work has been leading up to this conclusion.

Example:

Without question, children who are supervised will thrive. With an adult around, the child will have appropriate guidance. Not only will major catastrophes such as crime or injury be avoided, the child will have the opportunity to safely develop and experiment. The benefits of supervision for children are obvious and without doubt necessary for our country's survival.

This example sums up the intent of the piece. The final flavor left with the reader is one of understanding and agreement.

3. End with a rhetorical question.

A question leaves the reader with something to think about. It gives meaning to the piece of writing.

Example:

Millions of children in this country are not receiving proper supervision. This has left a vast number of children in dangerous situations. They face crime, neglect, and injury on a daily basis. When and how will this problem be resolved? At what point do we say, "Enough"?

This example leaves the reader with a question to mull over. With this technique, the reader holds onto the written work while pondering the author's question.

Lesson 6-7: Editing and Revising

After the work is complete, it must be edited to improve clarity or errors. It must be looked at with a fresh eye. Sometimes, this can be achieved by having someone else read and edit the piece. However, this is not always possible or practical. Before editing your own work, you must take time to gain objectivity. The amount of necessary time will vary for each person, but everyone must take the chance to clear his mind and get some distance. When it is time again to approach your work, do your best to maintain your objectivity. Also, do not simply reread the work; you must focus on different things.

When re-reading your work, concentrate on meaning and clarity. Question whether points are clearly made to the reader. Also, keep in mind the subject, audience, and purpose. Just as you did when you initially wrote the piece, you must edit with these variables in mind. Do you maintain the appropriate tone throughout the piece?

When all of this is complete, conduct a final proofread for surface errors. These errors include spelling, grammatical, punctuation, and typing errors.

Answers to Exercises

Exercise 6-1

Possible answers

1.	The beach	*Health benefits of time spent at the beach*
2.	Automobiles of the 1920s	*Hazardous road conditions for these autos*
3.	Children's clothing	*The current quality of children's clothing*
4.	School safety	*The difference in safety from the 1940s*
5.	Literature of today	*Bestsellers in the mystery genre this year*
6.	Skateboarding	*Skateboarding as an indoor sport*
7.	Different forms of art	*The use of multiple mediums in New York City*
8.	Birds of the Northeast	*The migrating habits during the winter months*
9.	Medieval homes	*The connections between shelter and disease*
10.	Candles	*Techniques for creating molded candles*

Exercise 6-2

Possible answers

1. *computers, quiet space to study, books, videos, desks – a fun, popular place*

2. *spacious rooms, technology, availability, cost, privacy, furnishings – a businesslike environment*

3. *lack of books, use by patrons, need for funds – a deprived atmosphere*

Answers to Exercise 6-3 through Exercise 6-5 will differ.

Exercise 6-6

1. Our local library needs improvement.

   (**possible thesis**) *The technology of our local library is outdated and no longer meets the needs of our community.*

2. Marriage is a good idea.

   (**possible thesis**) *Married couples are entitled to more financial benefits than non-married couples.*

3. Healthy cooking is important.

   (**possible thesis**) *There are many health reasons to choose broiling over frying.*

4. Baseball is a fun sport.

   (**possible thesis**) *Baseball is a sport that allows for camaraderie as well as competition.*

5. I like my job.

   (possible thesis) *My job is satisfying because I continually learn while helping others.*

6. You can learn a lot by watching children.

   (possible thesis) *Analyzing childhood patterns provides valuable information about adult social behavior patterns.*

7. Summer is my favorite season.

   (possible thesis) *The summer climate provides the best environment for many outdoor sports.*

8. Drag racing is a bad idea.

   (possible thesis) *Illegal racing of automobiles creates unnecessary danger for both participants and spectators.*

9. Recycling is important.

   (possible thesis) *Recycling programs provide long-term financial benefits for our community.*

10. Students should always complete their homework.

    (possible thesis) *Homework provides educational advantages to all students.*

Exercise 6-7

   3   1. Next, he became a commissioned lieutenant colonel, where he fought the first skirmishes of what grew into the French and Indian War.

   1   2. Born in 1732 into a Virginia planter family, George Washington learned the morals, manners, and body of knowledge requisite for an 18th-century Virginia gentleman.

   5   3. George Washington finally took office on April 30, 1789, while standing on the balcony of Federal Hall on Wall Street in New York.

   4   4. The following year, as an aide to Gen. Edward Braddock, he escaped injury although four bullets ripped his coat and two horses were shot from under him.

   2   5. At 16 he helped survey Shenandoah lands for Thomas, Lord Fairfax.

Exercise 6-8

   6   1. The beige, red, and gold carpet beneath the furniture is a reproduction of an early-19th-century French Savonnerie carpet.

   2   2. All the fabrics now in the Red Room were woven in the United States from French Empire designs.

   7   3. Above it all sits the 13-light French Empire chandelier, fashioned from carved and gilded wood in 1805.

___1___   4. The Red Room of the White House was furnished between the years 1810 and 1830.

___5___   5. Behind the furniture hang 19th-century-inspired draperies made of gold satin with red silk valances and handmade gold and red fringe.

___3___   6. The walls are covered with a red twill satin fabric that has a gold scroll design in the border.

___4___   7. The furniture, like the American Empire sofa, is upholstered in a silk of the same shade of red.

Exercise 6-9

___4___   1. Children should not be exposed to inebriated adults.

___2___   2. Games would be more pleasant without the rowdiness brought about by the consumption of alcohol.

___6___   3. Possibility for violence and even death increases when alcohol is at hand.

___3___   4. Littering increases when alcohol is available.

___1___   5. Alcohol should not be sold at sporting events.

___5___   6. More injuries occur at sporting events where alcohol is present.

Exercise 6-10

1.	c	6.	a
2.	d	7.	d
3.	e	8.	c
4.	b	9.	e
5.	b	10.	a

Exercise 6-11

Topic sentence: **Automotive safety measures have improved over the past decade.**

___X___   1. Automatic brake systems allow for less skidding.

_____   2. Seats are now more comfortable.

___X___   3. Air bags cushion passengers upon impact.

_____   4. The cost for a new automobile has risen fifteen percent.

___X___   5. Tire tread patterns allow for better control and endurance.

___X___   6. Digital speedometers give drivers more accurate readings.

_____   7. Windshields have changed in shape and form.

_____   8. Children should always sit in the back seat.

   X   9. Additional lights allow for better visibility during inclement weather.

        10. Many styles of hubcaps are now available.

   X   11. Automobile frames can sustain minor crashes to protect occupants.

   X   12. Many vehicles offer built in child-safety seats.

   X   13. Suspension systems make potholes and other obstacles less hazardous.

   X   14. Power steering enables drivers to make difficult turns.

   X   15. Innovative strides have been made in the development of safety glass.

Types of Essays

For most students, the standard form of writing is the essay. However, each essay serves a different purpose. They vary in purpose, length, content, and tone. Over the course of an educational career, students are expected to understand the different forms of essays and choose the appropriate form for different assignments. This chapter explains the differences between the types of essays and highlights the best essay form for different assignments.

Lesson 7-1: The Expository Essay

The expository essay is used to explain, illustrate, or teach information about a topic. This type of essay, also called the illustration essay, is one of the most frequently used in both the educational field and in business. It develops a main point or idea using information and examples. Its main idea could be related to an aspect of business or a subject in school. This form of writing is used for everything from job applications to psychology and health publications.

Here are some guidelines to consider when writing an expository essay:

▷ Make sure your thesis can be developed with examples.

▷ Devote one paragraph to one topic.

▷ Include all necessary details.

▷ As with several other types of essays, always use simple present tense.

Here is an example of an expository essay:

"Flooding Precautions"

Flooding is a hazard that is generally the result of excessive precipitation. There are two main categories of floods: flash floods, which are the product of heavy localized precipitation in a short time period over a given location; and general floods, caused by precipitation over a longer time period and over a given river basin. Flash floods occur within a few minutes or hours of heavy amounts of rainfall, from a dam or levee failure, or from a sudden release of water held by an ice jam. These dangerous deluges can destroy buildings and bridges, and uproot trees. Heavy rains that produce flash floods can also trigger mudslides. Most flash flooding is caused by slow-moving thunderstorms, repeated thunderstorms in a local area, or by heavy rains from hurricanes and tropical storms. Although flash flooding occurs often along mountain streams, it is also common in urban areas where much of the ground is covered by impervious surfaces. Roads and buildings generate greater amounts of runoff than typical forested land. Fixed drainage channels in urban areas may be unable to contain the runoff that is generated by relatively small, but intense, rainfall events. Therefore, residents of urban and suburban areas must take proper precautions for their safety.

In areas prone to flooding, residents should be aware of proper procedures recommended by the local utility companies. During and following flooding, these companies should be contacted for information and advice on precautions and safety measures to be taken. Electrical cords or appliances that are connected should not be touched if the current is still on. If electricity is connected to an appliance that has had the motor controls submerged, a qualified service company representative should examine the appliance before it is turned on. Open flames should not be present in an enclosed area where gas fired or oil fired appliances are located before they are back in service.

Cleaning up after a flood requires extra care. During the cleanup of basements or other enclosed areas, as much ventilation as possible must be provided. Windows and doors should be opened to allow moist air to flow out. Anything that has been in contact with floodwaters should be considered contaminated and must be cleaned and disinfected. All surfaces that can be washed and disinfected may be salvaged by thoroughly washing in soap and warm water, followed by disinfecting with a chlorine solution. Chlorine bleach is an effective disinfectant, but it should never be mixed with ammonia since this combination produces poisonous gas. Surfaces that cannot be thoroughly washed and disinfected should either be discarded, or a professional cleaning and salvaging firm must be consulted.

Following a flood, all water and food must be evaluated for safety before consumption. Water from wells located in flooded areas may be unsafe for drinking; it must be boiled for at least ten minutes or treated by chlorine. To treat water with chlorine, add one teaspoon of liquid laundry bleach to five gallons of water, mix well, and let stand for thirty minutes before drinking. All food items that were in direct contact with floodwaters must be discarded. Jars, bottles, and similar containers with lids or covers must be thrown away; they cannot be relied on to prevent contamination.

Personal hygiene is also important after a flood. The bacteria associated with flooding can be deadly. The spread of these bacteria can be prevented by frequently washing hands in warm water and in chlorinated water, particularly before eating. Sewage-contaminated floodwaters must not be tracked into areas that are clean. All clothing should be washed at the end of the day and a hot shower taken.

Flooding is the most common environmental hazard, due to the widespread geographical distribution of river valleys and coastal areas, and the popularity of the regions. Usually, presidential declarations of major disasters are associated with flash and general floods. In order to survive these dangerous natural conditions, certain precautions must be taken during and after flooding. With these safety measures, many lives can be saved.

Exercise 7-1

Answer the following questions about the preceding expository essay.

1. The thesis statement of an expository essay states the writer's central idea for the essay. This idea is developed through examples. Which sentence in the introductory paragraph is the thesis statement?

2. How many examples support the central idea? What are they?

3. What are the topic sentences for each supporting paragraph?

Exercise 7-2

Choose a topic from the following list and write an expository essay.

1. Interesting ways in which people choose their jobs or professions
2. Television programs that portray teenagers (or another group) in a negative or positive light
3. Ways in which people dress to attract attention
4. People who have overcome educational, professional, emotional, or physical obstacles
5. The evolution of a policy at your school

Lesson 7-2: The Narrative Essay

The narrative essay relates a story or tells about an event. It is frequently used for English and history compositions. It can also be used for the college essay. This type of essay retells a meaningful event, either historical or personal. It must contain relevant details and be well organized in a chronological manner.

Guidelines to consider when writing a narrative essay include:

▷ Organize all the incidents and details in chronological order.

▷ Begin with the earliest event in the sequence.

▷ Supply any necessary background information.

▷ Use transitional expressions that indicate time order.

Example

Here is an example of a narrative essay:

"The Life of Harriet Tubman"

Harriet Ross was born into slavery in 1819 or 1820, in Dorchester County, Maryland. Given the names of her two parents, both held in slavery, she was of purely African ancestry. She was raised under harsh conditions and subjected to whippings even as a small child. At the age of twelve she was seriously injured by a blow to the head, inflicted by a white overseer for refusing to assist in tying up a man who had attempted escape. At the age of twenty-five, Harriet married John

Tubman, a free African American. Five years later, fearing she would be sold to the South, she made her escape. This escape became the major turning point in her life.

Mrs. Tubman was given a piece of paper by a white neighbor with two names and told how to find the first house on her path to freedom. At the first house she was put into a wagon, covered with a sack, and driven to her next destination. Following the route to Pennsylvania, she initially settled in Philadelphia, where she met William Still, the Philadelphia stationmaster on the Underground Railroad. With the assistance of Still and other members of the Philadelphia Anti-Slavery Society, she learned about the workings of the Underground Railroad.

After freeing herself from slavery, Harriet Tubman returned to Maryland to rescue other members of her family. In all she is believed to have conducted approximately 300 people to freedom in the North. The tales of her exploits reveal her highly spiritual nature, as well as a grim determination to protect her charges and those who aided them. She always expressed confidence that God would aid her efforts and threatened to shoot any of her charges who thought to turn back.

Her success was wonderful. Time and again she made triumphant visits to Maryland on the Underground Railroad. She would be absent for weeks at a time, running daily risks while making preparations for herself and her passengers. Great fears were entertained for her safety, but she seemed truly devoid of personal fear. The idea of being captured by slave-hunters or slaveholders never seemed to enter her mind. While she maintained utter personal indifference, she was much more watchful with regard to those she was piloting. She would not suffer one of her party to whimper once, about "giving out and going back," however wearied they might be by the hard travel day and night. She had a very short and pointed rule or law of her own, which implied death to any who talked of giving out and going back. Thus, in an emergency she would give all to understand that "times were very critical and therefore no foolishness would be indulged in on the road."

Closely associated with Abolitionist John Brown, Harriet Tubman was also well acquainted with the other Upstate abolitionists, including Frederick Douglass, Jermain Loguen, and Gerrit Smith. She worked closely with Brown and reportedly missed the raid on Harper's Ferry only because of illness.

Following the outbreak of the Civil War, Tubman served as a soldier, spy, and a nurse, for a time serving at Fortress Monroe, where Jefferson Davis would later be imprisoned. While guiding a group of black soldiers in South Carolina, she met Nelson Davis, who was 10 years her junior. When the war ended, Harriet Tubman returned to Auburn, New York. Denied payment for her wartime service, she was forced, after a bruising fight, to ride in a baggage car. In Auburn she married Nelson Davis; they lived in a home they built on South Street. This house still stands on the property and serves as a home for the resident manager of the Harriet Tubman Home.

After her death, Harriet Tubman was buried in Fort Hill Cemetery in Auburn with military honors. She has since received many honors, including the naming of the Liberty Ship Harriet Tubman, christened in 1944 by Eleanor Roosevelt. On June 14, 1914, a large bronze plaque was placed at the Cayuga County Courthouse, and a civic holiday was declared in her honor. Freedom Park, a tribute to the memory of Harriet Tubman, opened in the summer of 1994 at 17 North Street in Auburn. In 1995, Harriet Tubman was honored by the federal government with a commemorative postage stamp bearing her name and likeness.

Exercise 7-3

Answer the following questions about the preceding narrative essay.

1. What introductory information is given in the first paragraph?

2. The thesis statement of a narrative essay states the writer's central idea for the essay. Which sentence in the introductory paragraph is the thesis statement?

3. The topic sentences in the third, sixth, and seventh paragraphs demonstrate chronological order for this essay. What are these topic sentences?

Exercise 7-4

Choose a topic from the following list and write a narrative essay.

1. A family event that changed your view of yourself
2. An incident where you or someone you know acted with courage or cowardice

3. A successful struggle to achieve by someone you admire
4. An amazing real-life incident you witnessed
5. The turning point in your life

Lesson 7-3: The Descriptive Essay

The descriptive essay is used in both school and business to portray something. It can be used to depict a person, a setting, an experience, an event, or even a science experiment. Writers use descriptive essays to garner the imagination of the reader. Descriptive writing portrays people, places, things, moments, and theories with enough vivid detail to help the reader create a mental picture of what is being written.

Here are some guidelines to consider when writing a descriptive essay:

▷ Think of an instance that you want to describe. Why is this particular instance important?

▷ Focus on the other things happening around you. Does anything specific stand out in your mind?

▷ Determine the location of objects in relation to where you were.

▷ Build on prior knowledge. How did the surroundings remind you of other places you have been? Can you think of another situation that was similar to the one you are writing about? How can it help explain what you are writing about?

▷ Recall the sights, smells, sounds, and tastes in the air.

▷ Analyze your feelings at that time.

▷ Consider if you have felt this way before.

▷ Determine your objectives for the reader of this paper.

▷ Establish what types of words and images can convey this feeling.

▷ Be certain there is enough detail in your essay to create a mental image for the reader.

▷ Use simple present tense consistently.

Example

Here is an example of a descriptive essay:

"Wintertime at the Bronx Zoo"

Listen closely. A whistle is blowing; a steam engine is chugging along. Off in the distance there's a bell softly ringing. The crisp autumn air chills our noses as we enter the gates of New York's famous Bronx Zoo. Seas of color spill down the walkway towards the exhibits as adults and children, bundled in coats, hats, and scarves of every hue search out their favorite animals. Aromas of coffee, hot cocoa, and funnel cakes from The Dancing Crane Cafe mix together and tempt us with their promise of warmth. In addition to the usual pleasures of this welcoming venue, hundreds of thousands of lights sparkle as they cover over one hundred and forty animal, dinosaur, and holiday sculptures as the Bronx Zoo's Holiday Lights opens.

In a fairytale setting of meandering lighted pathways, reindeer and camels welcome Bronx Zoo guests. New for this year is a special treat—dinosaurs in lights! Meet the Bronx Zoo's own brontosaurus, stegosaurus, and an animated dimetrodon. Although a bustling metropolis is just yards away, there is an illusion of a fairyland in this wonderful setting. An entire evening of pleasure can be derived from wandering down seemingly endless paths of lights and shapes. However, there are many other magnificent things to see.

The animals at the zoo are always a must-see. A special sea lion feeding each evening at 7 p.m. is fun for visitors of all ages. The slipper fish are tossed as the gleeful, hungry sea lions display their unusual personalities. The dark entrance to the World of Reptiles contrasts the twinkle of the holiday lights. Crossing through the blackened threshold, your auditory sense is suddenly heightened. The sounds of nighttime can be scary for some, but the beautiful colors of the snakes and reptiles are dazzling. At the Monkey House, feeding time is messy. Hear the screeching of the animals while they swing and hang to entertain their audience.

In addition to the lights, animals, and tempting zoo cuisine, there is also a theater at the Bronx Zoo. "The Polar Express Experience" is a performance that should not be missed. Zoo-goers can enjoy a magical evening complete with an opportunity to watch as the Wildlife Theater Players perform their own whimsical version of award-winning children's author Chris Van Allsburg's *The Polar Express.* LuAnn

Adams engages little ones with stories and songs about wildlife and winter, while local choral groups perform a blend of seasonal favorites from around the world.

Several other attractions can be enjoyed as visitors amble around the zoo. Visitors can watch as a master ice carver composes extraordinary creations from huge blocks of ice. The enchanting Alice Farley Dance Company stilt-walkers are sure to delight visitors as they welcome guests nightly. Costumed characters including Tommy Turtle and Tasha the Tiger greet guests each evening, posing for photos in this dazzling setting.

Wintertime at the Bronx Zoo has something for everyone. It is a magical place that satiates the senses with music, food, lights, and laughter. The imagination grows in this special pocket of magic in the midst of an urban environment. The Bronx Zoo in winter contains the best of many worlds, yet it is like no other place in the world.

Exercise 7-5

Answer the following questions about the preceding descriptive essay.

1. The thesis statement of a descriptive essay explains what will be described and sometimes gives an overall impression of it. Which sentence in the introductory paragraph is the thesis statement?

2. Each paragraph in the body of this essay describes one scene or aspect of the topic. How many scenes or aspects are described and what are they?

3. What are some transitional phrases in this essay that help to link these aspects together?

Exercise 7-6

Choose a topic from the following list and write a descriptive essay.
1. Life in the 21st or any other century
2. Your favorite place in your hometown or neighborhood
3. A person or animal you have closely observed
4. Your first memory
5. What the concept of home is to you

Lesson 7-4: The Compare or Contrast Essay

The compare or contrast essay is used to highlight similarities or differences between two or more people or things. It is used frequently in English class to compare or contrast literary features. For example, two settings, symbols, or characters from one or more works of literature can be contrasted. This type of essay is common to other subjects as well. In psychology, theories or treatments can be compared. In history class, great leaders and their actions can be contrasted.

Guidelines to consider when writing a compare or contrast essay include:

▷ Consider that the most interesting essays usually compare two things that are different or contrast two things that are similar.

▷ Avoid the obvious.

▷ Do not state that the two people or things are the same or different. Use your thesis to form the comparison or contrast.

▷ Keep ideas separate as you prepare your outline.

▷ Stay in present tense throughout the essay.

Example

Here is an example of a compare or contrast essay:

"Athena and Artemis – Two Daughters of Zeus"

Zeus is not known for his restraint. As the ruler of the universe, he took whatever he desired. What he most wanted was female companionship. As a result, Zeus fathered many children with many different mothers. Two of his most famous daughters are Athena and Artemis. The stories of their births are as different as the goddesses themselves. Although both are strong females, these two sisters have little else in common.

Athena, Zeus's favorite daughter, is often described as the gray-eyed goddess. Daughter of the Titaness Metis, she is said to have sprang fully grown and in full armor from her father's head. Always depicted with her unmistakable helmet and the ever-present spear, Athena is perhaps the most recognizable of the gods. Because she was Zeus's favorite she was allowed to use his weapons and armor, including the awful aegis, his buckler, and even his thunderbolt. Athena is the embodiment of wisdom, purity, and reason, as well as the patron of the handicrafts, sciences, and agriculture. She is credited with teaching mathematics to man. She created many farm implements as well as the trumpet, the flute, the pot, the ship, and the chariot. Of the three virgin goddesses, a title Athena shared with Artemis and Hestia, she is chief and called the Maiden.

Artemis, Athena's virgin goddess sister, was born to Leto, another Titaness. Although hunted by Hera, Zeus's wife, Leto proudly bore Zeus twins: Artemis and Apollo. Known as a fierce hunter as well as protector, Artemis is one of the major Greek goddesses. When she was born, she asked Zeus for many names so that she would never become bored. That is why Artemis is known as the goddess of the night, the huntress, the maiden of the silver bow, the goddess of childbirth, Lady of the Beasts, the woodland goddess, the bull goddess, the personification of the moon, and the eternal virgin. While Athena is known for wisdom, Artemis is known to be more punitive in her encounters with humans. These personality traits are depicted in two different bathing stories.

While out walking one day, a young boy, Teiresais, encountered a bathing Athena. The boy knew he had no right to look upon the naked goddess, but entranced by her beauty, Teiresais was unable to look away. The goddess Athena caught him spying on her and immediately punished Teiresais by blinding him. When Athena realized the severity of the reprisal, she bestowed on Teiresais the gift of prophecy. Artemis was not as gracious when she found herself in a similar situation. A hunter, Actaeon, was hunting with his dogs in the mountains when he came across the goddess, bathing naked in a stream. Artemis was infuriated with the man, who, like Teiresais, was unable to divert his eyes from the beautiful figure in front of him. Artemis immediately turned Actaeon into a stag. His dogs, no longer recognizing him, tore him to pieces.

Both Athena and Artemis share a father, but they share few other traits. They are both virgin goddesses and protectors, but their temperaments separate them. Perhaps Zeus's favoritism for Athena allowed her a sense of maturity. Possibly the greatest attribute that divides them is intelligence. With Athena's wisdom, she stands out as a compassionate benefactress to man.

Exercise 7-7

Answer the following questions about the preceding compare and contrast essay.

1. The thesis statement of a comparison or contrast essay explains what two persons or things will be compared or contrasted. Which sentence in the introductory paragraph is the thesis statement?

2. Will this essay highlight similarities or differences? What words give evidence of this?

3. What is the outline for this essay? Are the ideas mingled or separated?

Exercise 7-8

Choose a topic from the following list and write a compare or contrast essay.

1. Two interesting people that you know or who are famous
2. Two of your favorite places to go
3. Someone else's background or history and your own
4. Two classes you have taken
5. Two cars, games, computers, and so on.

Lesson 7-5: The Persuasive Essay

The persuasive essay is one of the most commonly used in college or business. Frequently in school, business, or life in general, we are asked to take a stand on issues. In persuasive or argumentative writing, we try to convince others to agree with our facts, share our values, accept our argument and conclusions, and adopt our way of thinking.

Here are some guidelines to consider when writing a persuasive essay:

▹ Establish facts to support an argument.

▹ Clarify relevant values for your audience.

▹ Prioritize, edit, and/or sequence the facts and values in importance to build the argument.

▹ Form and state conclusions.

▹ Convince your audience that your conclusions are based upon the agreed-upon facts and shared values.

Example

Here is an example of a persuasive essay:

"The Homework Debate"

The homework debate, the argument about whether homework should be assigned, has been going on since the concept of education was founded. More than one hundred years ago, Edward Bok, the editor of *Ladies' Home Journal*, launched a campaign against homework. He argued that it was detrimental to students' physical, mental, and emotional health. The U.S. Commissioner of Education agreed, telling Congress that homework was "a prolific source of abuse." A year later, dozens of local school districts across the United States banned homework for any public school child younger than 15. Today, concern about homework is again in the forefront. This argument over homework is a familiar part of the nation's ongoing debate over education. Like everything else in our society, trends come and go. One generation of educators worries that students are not getting enough homework, and the next generation worries that children are overworked and overscheduled and that their social development is being ignored. The current perception is that children have too much homework. However, homework is a useful tool that must remain part of the educational program.

The average child today spends less than one hour a day on homework, and this is not unique to our times. It is nostalgic fantasy to think that there was a time when most American kids, willingly or unwillingly, did lots of homework. Since World War II, the proportion of high school students spending a substantial amount of time studying has generally varied from 7 percent to 13 percent. Homework amounts peaked briefly during the 1970s, but even then, the number of high school students who studied for more than two hours a night was less than 25 percent. There was never a time where children came home and dutifully studied for hours on end.

Second, it's not true that most parents object to homework. Today, as in the past, most parents strongly support it. A Public Agenda poll in 2000 found that only 10 percent of parents thought their children had too much homework, whereas 25 percent thought they had too little and 64 percent thought the amount was about right. The media can make it seem that parents are against homework. News reports can dramatize a few irate parents who feel their children are overwhelmed, but this does not mean that most parents feel this way.

Third, and most important, the homework debate focuses on how much and not what is assigned. Rather than worry about quantity, parents and educators alike should focus on quality. Why is the work assigned? How is it relevant to the curriculum? What are the benefits? Homework must be beneficial to the student's progress in school. If the homework is of sound quality, perhaps the amount of time it takes to complete is in itself an assessment of the student's progress.

Homework is a useful tool for students, parents, and teachers. For the student, it reinforces the work covered in class. For the parent, it provides a window into the classroom and the school-life of the child. For teachers, homework is a valuable assessment tool. In addition to promoting academic achievement, homework can inculcate habits of self-discipline and independent study. Homework must continue to be assigned and supported in schools.

Exercise 7-9

Answer the following questions about the preceding persuasive essay.

1. The thesis statement in a persuasive essay clearly states the issue to be discussed and the writer's position on it. Which sentence is the thesis statement?

2. This introduction includes facts, such as quotations, or data. What facts are included here?

3. How many details does this writer use to support his argument? What are they?

Exercise 7-10

Choose a topic from the following list and write a persuasive essay.
1. Illegal immigrants to this country should (or should not) be provided basic healthcare
2. Same-sex couples should (or should not) be allowed to adopt children
3. A college education is (or is not) worth the time and money
4. Teenage suicides should (or should not) be reported in the media
5. Social promotion in schools is (or is not) beneficial for the students

Lesson 7-6: The Process Essay

The process essay explains the steps involved in doing something. It is used to explain an action or a job and describes in detail the full process of completing the action. The details must be vivid and the organization must be clear in order for someone who has never done this process before to clearly follow the steps to completion.

Guidelines to consider when writing a process essay include:

 ▷ Find a specific and interesting topic.

 ▷ Use vivid details about the elements involved in the process.

 ▷ Avoid the verb to be; use specific action words.

 ▷ Organize the steps clearly.

Example

Here is an example of a process essay:

"How to Change Your Own Engine Oil "

Besides the regular check-ups that you should be doing every week or month on your car, there are a few items that come up several times a year. One of these routine maintenance procedures is an engine oil change. This is something that people do every 3,000 miles or so. With the right equipment and a little common sense, changing oil in an automobile can be a relatively easy job.

Before beginning, make sure the engine oil is warm enough so that it will drain out easily, but not too hot or you'll burn your skin or create a dangerous situation. Oil can become extremely hot inside your car engine, so this is an important step to take. Let the car run for a few minutes before the oil change. If you've driven your car already, let it cool off for a few hours before you start.

First, raise the front of your car so you can access under the hood, where most cars have oil filters and oil drain plugs. This can be done with car ramps or jacks. Remember to do it on a level surface, preferably on concrete. As a safety measure, remember to put your car in park and engage the parking brake. Also, put something wedge-shaped behind each of the rear wheels to prevent the car from sliding back.

Second, drain the old oil. You'll need to locate the oil pan and the drain plug that is attached to this pan. This varies from car to car.

Place the oil drain pan underneath the drain plug, but about five inches forward of center. This is because the oil will not pour out straight down, but outwards. Use a wrench to loosen the plug and use your fingers to take it completely off. Try to hold on to the plug; otherwise, it will drop into the pan. Allow all the oil to drain. After all the oil has been drained, screw the plug back in with a wrench. Screw the plug in tightly, but make sure you will be able to unscrew it the next time.

Third, you must remove the oil filter. Usually it is attached to the engine itself. Sometimes the filter is hidden behind wires and tubes, and other times it is halfway up the engine and difficult to see. Sometimes the filter is accessible from the top, with your hood open. Put the oil drain pan right underneath the filter before removing it. Try to unscrew it with your hands first. If that does not work, then use the oil filter wrench or socket wrench. When it is loose, carefully take the filter out with the open side on top, like a glass of water. Be careful because the filter contains oil. Pour the oil out into the pan. If any oil dripped during this process, wipe down the engine parts and wires. Before putting in the new filter, take a drop of new engine oil and, with your finger, coat the rubber seal on the filter. Screw the filter back in with your hands. Tighten the filter to a point where it is barely in there, and then turn it an additional quarter-turn. You should be able to unscrew it with your hands next time. Next, take a paper towel or rag and wipe down the underside of the car so it is free of engine oil.

Fourth, funnel the used oil into plastic milk bottles until you are ready to take them to a recycling center. Never throw these into a public flood drain, your toilet, or your sink. You must always recycle engine oil. Most auto parts stores will take the oil free of charge, and your local recycling center will take them as well.

Finally, check underneath the car to make sure there is no oil dripping. Take your car off the ramps or jacks and drive the car for about for about five minutes. Park it and put a clean cardboard underneath the engine. After thirty minutes, check for drips or leaks.

This process should take about forty minutes to complete. Like any other process, the more times you complete it, the easier it will be. Continue to change your engine oil every three thousand miles, or every three months, whichever comes first. If you follow these simple steps, you will be changing oil like a professional.

Exercise 7-11

Answer the following questions about the preceding process essay.

1. The thesis statement in a process essay tells the reader what process will be described. What is the thesis statement of this essay?

2. What is the outline for this essay?

3. How many steps are outlined in this process? What are they?

Exercise 7-12

Choose a topic from the following list and write a process essay.
   1. How someone became a success
   2. How to plan a theme party
   3. How to prepare for a vacation or trip
   4. How to train a pet
   5. How to prepare for college

Lesson 7-7: The Thematic Essay

The thematic essay is used frequently in English and social studies classes. It is also used for essay examinations, by the school, by the state, or by college entrance examiners. This type of essay is used for analysis of literature, current events, historical events, and their impact on society. When analyzing, a thesis or main idea must be formed. Just as with other types of essays, the goal here is to illustrate your point of view and conclusions.

In English class or for an examination for English, you are sometimes given a theme from which to create your thesis. For instance, you may be given the topic of *good versus evil*. You may be asked to relate this topic to a work you have read, or you may be instructed to relate this topic to a specific work, such as William Shakespeare's *Macbeth*. From there, you would create a thesis statement based on this topic. Your thesis may be general, such as: *Macduff, the archetype of good, conquers Macbeth, the epitome of evil, because in literature, virtue must prevail*. It might also be more specific, such as: *In Shakespeare's Christian society, Macbeth is an unredeemable character because he loses his faith in God*. Remember: The more specific the thesis, the better the essay. The outline for this essay would include the introduction including title, author, and thesis statement, three body paragraphs that include evidence from the text that supports your thesis, and the conclusion.

An additional challenge with writing about literature is **tense**. A work of literature can be opened at any time to any page; therefore, it remains in the **present tense**. This rule is true for all parts of the work. For instance, Act I is not in the past simply because you have already read it. This technique is really a habit you must develop; it becomes second nature once you grasp it. The same rule applies to the author. Although Shakespeare met his demise almost four centuries ago, we refer to his work as a writer in the present. For example: *Shakespeare uses his society's Christian faith to reinforce Macbeth's lack of redemption.*

For history or global studies, the concept is similar. You may be given a topic, such as: *Geographical features can have a positive or negative impact on the development of a nation or region.* You may also be provided with a specific task, such as: *Select one geographic feature from your studies and explain this feature's positive or negative effect on the development of two nations or regions.* The outline for this essay would include the introduction containing the thesis statement, two to four body paragraphs with evidence supporting your thesis, and the conclusion.

Here are some guidelines to consider when writing a thematic essay:

▷ Create a specific thesis relevant to the theme.

▷ Make observations about the topic using facts, reasoning, and argument.

▷ Keep ideas separate as you prepare your outline.

▷ Use transitions to guide your reader.

▷ Include all necessary and relevant details.

Example

Here is an example of a thematic essay based on the global studies outline:

"The Impact of Geographical Features on Great Britain and Japan"

Two of the most powerful nations in the world are Great Britain and Japan. As islands, both of these nations' historical developments were influenced by the unique attributes of this geographic feature.

For example, both nations were isolated or protected for a time because they are surrounded by water, and both eventually practiced imperialism around the world due to their natural harbors. Although located in different areas of the world, the geographical features of both Great Britain and Japan have brought about similar historical events.

As an island nation, the sea has provided Great Britain with a natural barrier that protected it from invasion. In the late 16th century, King Phillip II of Spain launched the famed Spanish Armada with orders to invade England. In the battle that ensued, the Spanish were defeated and England was not invaded. The sea presented too great an obstacle for most armies. This condition lasted for several centuries. Until the relatively recent advancements in aeronautic technology, any nation wishing to take over England would need to attack by sea.

Ports and harbors are abundant in the British Isles. This allowed the natural development of a powerful navy and shipping industry. This is but one of the factors that led to the start of the Industrial Revolution in Great Britain. Britain's success with industrialization became a driving force for the nation; this eventually led to the practice of imperialism. In order to obtain cheap natural resources, Britain overpowered other nations. Britain emerged as a world super-power with its empire stretching across the globe in areas such as India, Africa, and China.

Japan was one area that did not face imperialism by Great Britain. Because of its island status, Japan followed a policy of isolationism for more than 200 years. This policy was easily enforced due to the vast seas surrounding the island nation. The Japanese felt secure in their isolation until the arrival of Commodore Matthew Perry in the 1850s.

Representing the United States, Perry demanded that Japan open itself to trade, and soon other European nations followed suit. Fearing the imperial conquest that had happened to the neighboring Chinese, the Japanese began a massive policy of industrialization called the Meiji Restoration. They soon realized that they lacked abundant natural resources necessary to sustain industrialization. Therefore, they decided to take advantage of their position in the sea to build a modern navy. This allowed them to utilize Korea, China, and eventually most of the Pacific Rim for their needs.

As islands, both Great Britain and Japan have been protected from outside forces. The oceans provided a natural barrier that allowed each culture to fully develop. Despite differences in how industrialization occurred, both island nations found that their location and natural ports allowed the development of naval power. This eventually led both to practice imperialism to sustain industrialization. Despite being thousands of miles apart, it is interesting to note the similarities in the development of these two vastly different cultures.

Exercise 7-13

Answer the following questions about the preceding thematic essay.

1. The thesis statement in a thematic essay outlines what will be covered in the essay. What is the thesis statement of this thematic essay?

2. What is the outline for this essay?

3. What are some of the facts that support the thesis?

Exercise 7-14

Choose a topic from the following list and write a thematic essay.

1. The portrayal of characters in a specific setting
2. Economic effects on different nations
3. The impacts of the author's life on literature
4. The author's use of symbolism
5. The impact of technology on society

Lesson 7-8: The Definition Essay

The definition essay can be used for a variety of reasons. Sometimes it is used in courses to define terminology. For instance, you may be asked to define a psychological term or condition such as the Oedipal complex. It can also be used as an assessment for understanding. For instance, a teacher might assign a definition essay on a topic like segregation. Other times this type of essay is used to provide personal insight on topics such as life and love.

Guidelines to consider when writing a definition essay include:

▷ Choose a generic topic rather than a specific topic.

▷ Divide the subject into parts and define each part separately.

▷ Consider the physical characteristics, traditional thoughts, and other distinguishing attributes.

▷ Narrate illustrations that can clarify a group, theory, or object.

▷ Evaluate and include origins and causes of the topic.

▷ Discuss the consequences and uses of the subject.

Example

"Winning"

The dictionary defines winning as "achieving victory over others in a competition, receiving a prize or reward for achievement." However, some of the most meaningful wins of my life were not victories over others, nor were there prizes involved. Winning does not have to be about being the best or getting the biggest reward. To me, winning means overcoming personal, professional, and educational obstacles.

My first experience of winning occurred in elementary school. Physical education class was usually a challenge for me. Nearly every day, after the warm up of push-ups and squat thrusts, we were forced to run relays. Although I suffered from asthma as a child, my team won many of the races. My chest would burn terribly for several minutes following these races, but it was worth it. I felt proud, not because I had beaten others, but because I had overcome a handicap. I managed to be a part of a team, to participate with everyone else successfully, even though I had a chronic condition that affected my breathing.

In high school, I had another experience of winning. Although I loved reading about biology, I could not bring myself to dissect a frog in lab. I hated the smell of anything dead. To be faced with it and breathe in the odor would be bad enough; the idea of actually cutting open a frog repulsed me. Every time I tried to take the scalpel to the frog, my hands would shake and my stomach would turn. Worst of all, my biology teacher reacted to my futile attempts with contempt. After an upsetting couple of weeks, I decided to take control. I realized that I was overreacting. With determination, I walked into lab, went straight to the table, and with one swift stroke, slit open the frog. After that incident, I excelled in biology. I had conquered a fear of the unknown and discovered something new about myself. I had won again.

Today, I am experiencing a different type of winning. I am a college student. In order to get here I had to overcome many obstacles, both internal and external. I had to overcome my anxiety about leaving family and friends behind. I had to choose a school that had the curriculum I wanted. I had to meet the entrance requirements for this school. I had to find a way to finance my education. All of these barriers were difficult to overcome, but I succeeded. Once again, I am a winner.

These examples show what winning is to me. I know I will always have goals, and with these goals may come obstacles, but I am not afraid. In fact, I now know that I appreciate life more if I have to sacrifice to overcome these impediments. This knowledge is the spirit of winning.

Exercise 7-15

Answer the following questions about the preceding definition essay.

1. The thesis statement in a definition essay tells the reader what term will be defined and usually defines it as well. What is the thesis statement of this thematic essay?

2. What are the topic sentences for the body paragraphs?

3. What type of order does the writer use for the body paragraphs?

Exercise 7-16

Choose a topic from the following list and write a descriptive essay.
   1. A true friend
   2. A good teacher
   3. A healthy lifestyle
   4. A positive role model
   5. Courage

Answers to Exercises
Exercise 7-1
1. Thesis statement:

    Therefore, residents of urban and suburban areas must take proper precautions for their safety.

2. Four examples that support the central idea:
   1. *Appliances could become possible hazards. Utility companies' procedures should be followed.*
   2. *Flooding can leave deadly bacteria. All surfaces must be cleaned.*
   3. *Food and water that have been exposed to flood waters should be thrown away.*
   4. *Deadly bacteria may also be on the body. Personal hygiene is crucial.*

3. Topic sentences:
   1. *In areas prone to flooding, residents should be aware of proper procedures recommended by the local utility companies.*
   2. *Cleaning up after a flood requires extra care.*
   3. *Following a flood, all water and food must be evaluated for safety before consumption.*
   4. *Personal hygiene is also important after a flood.*

Exercise 7-3

1. Introductory information:

   This paragraph provides details about place and approximate date of birth. It gives details about her parents and the conditions she faced as a child. This paragraph also states when Harriet Tubman married, and when and why she made her escape.

2. Thesis statement:

   This escape became the turning point in her life.

3. Topic sentences of paragraphs containing chronological detail:

   Paragraph 3. *After freeing herself from slavery, Harriet Tubman returned to Maryland to rescue other members of her family.*

   Paragraph 6. *Following the outbreak of the Civil War, Tubman served as a soldier, spy, and a nurse, for a time serving at Fortress Monroe, where Jefferson Davis would later be imprisoned.*

   Paragraph 8. *After her death, Harriet Tubman was buried in Fort Hill Cemetery in Auburn with military honors.*

Exercise 7-5

1. Thesis statement:

   In addition to the usual pleasures of this welcoming venue, hundreds of thousands of lights sparkle as they cover over one hundred and forty animal, dinosaur, and holiday sculptures as the Bronx Zoo's Holiday Lights opens.

2. Scenes or aspects of the topic:

   There are four different scenes in the body of this essay. They are the lights in shapes of animals and dinosaurs, the animals, the theater, and various attractions that are located throughout the zoo.

3. Transitional phrases include:

   However, there are many other magnificent things to see.

   In addition to the lights, animals, and tempting zoo cuisine, there is also a theater at the Bronx Zoo.

   Several other attractions can be enjoyed as visitors amble around the zoo.

Exercise 7-7

1. Thesis statement:

   Although both are strong females, these two sisters have little else in common.

2. This essay highlights differences between the goddesses. Words that give evidence:

   The stories of their births are as different as the goddesses themselves...these two sisters have little else in common...two different bathing stories...they share few other traits.

3. Outline: (Notice each goddess is separated. Do not go back and forth between ideas.)

   Paragraph 1. *Introduction and thesis contrasting Athena and Artemis*

   Paragraph 2. *Background on Athena*

   Paragraph 3. *Background on Artemis*

   Paragraph 4. *Stories with strong contrast about each goddess*

   Paragraph 5. *Conclusion*

Exercise 7-9

1. Thesis statement:

   Homework is a useful tool that must remain part of the educational program.

2. Facts:

   There is mention of specific people, Edward Bok, and the U.S. Commissioner of Education with a quotation. There is reference to an action against homework at the turn of the 20th century.

3. Supporting details:

   The first detail is that children do not spend great amounts of time on homework. The second detail is that parents do not argue with the need for homework. The third detail is that it is not quantity, but quality of homework that is important.

Exercise 7-11

1. The thesis statement:

   With the right equipment and a little common sense, changing oil in an automobile can be a relatively easy job.

2. The process described:

   How to change your oil

3. The steps are outlined in this process:

   There are five steps outlined in this process essay.

   1. Raise the front end of the car.

   2. Drain the old oil.

   3. Remove, drain, and replace the oil filter.

   4. Funnel old oil into jugs and bring to a recycling center.

   5. Check for drips and leaks.

Exercise 7-13

1. The thesis statement:

   Although located in different areas of the world, the geographical features of both Great Britain and Japan have brought about similar historical events.

2. The outline: (Notice that each nation is separated. Do not go back and forth between ideas.)

   Paragraph 1. *Introduction and thesis about geographical features of both Great Britain and Japan*

   Paragraph 2. *Great Britain's protection by being an island nation*

   Paragraph 3. *Ports and harbors aided Britain's industry*

   Paragraph 4. *Japan's isolation as island nation*

   Paragraph 5. *Trade industry in Japan*

   Paragraph 6. *Conclusion*

3. Supporting facts:

   King Phillip II launched the Spanish Armada. Without new technology, any nation wishing to take over England would need to attack by sea. Ports and harbors are abundant in the British Isles. Japan followed a policy of isolationism for more than 200 years. Commodore Matthew Perry arrived in the 1850s. Representing the United States, Perry demanded that Japan open itself to trade. Japan began a massive policy of industrialization called the Meiji Restoration. They built a modern navy.

Exercise 7-15

1. Thesis statement:

   To me, winning means overcoming personal, professional, and educational obstacles.

2. Topic sentences:

   1. My first experience of winning occurred in elementary school.

   2. In high school, I had another experience of winning.

   3. Today, I am experiencing a different type of winning.

3. The type of order is used for the body:

   The writer uses chronological order for the body paragraphs. The first body paragraph deals with elementary school, the second deals with high school, and the third deals with college.

Research and Citation

Research is basic exploring and learning. We spend our lives searching for answers to questions. Research is the method that we use. Methods of research vary depending on what we want to know, what we already know, and why we want to know. Research is how we find our answers. Techniques for research today are easier than ever. All it takes is a search engine to answer most questions. What a responsible researcher will do, however, is consider the source or sources of the information. This chapter explores the many ways to conduct research, methods for organizing and presenting data, how to evaluate different sources, how to gather relevant data, and how to cite sources effectively.

Lesson 8-1: Planning Your Research
Choosing a Subject

Many high school and college courses require a research component. You may be asked to collect data, compile your information, and present it in the form of a research paper. This could consist of an author research paper for English class, a statistical paper for a math course, an historical research paper for a history course, or a scientific research paper for a subject in that field. Regardless of the course, some teachers assign topics, and others allow students the opportunity to explore their interests. If your assignment does not specify a topic, you can best begin with what interests you. With the amount of time you will be spending on this project, think about a subject on which you would like to become knowledgeable. After considering a general field, think about the specifications about purpose, audience, scope, length, and deadline. All of these factors should play a role in your decision.

The parameters of the project will influence your decision because they determine why you write the paper, who will be reading the paper, the scope of the research, the length of the paper, and how much time you really have to research and write it. Bear in mind how much time you actually have to work on this assignment. How many hours will you spend researching and writing outside of class? When is your deadline? One way to help manage your time is to keep the topic as limited as possible.

Narrowing a Topic

Any topic you choose to research must be manageable. Not only must you complete it in the time allowed, you must also be able to write an in-depth paper in a limited amount of words or pages. Accomplishing this feat requires narrowing the topic. As you reduce your subject towards a narrower topic, consider a governing question that will guide your research. What are you looking to discover? The governing question is what you want to know. One method for finding a governing question is to brainstorm a series of questions about your subject. From this list, you can choose an interesting question that can be answered by a hypothesis, a statement of what you anticipate your research will show.

An example of a broad subject is *education*. This subject can be narrowed through questions such as: What is wrong with today's schools? How are schools funded? Does this funding work? What aspect of education can be improved with more money? Now imagine the final question is your governing question. Can you create a statement that tentatively answers the question? A sample hypothesis might be: *The mismanagement of school funding has lead to the problems in education today.* As you gather information and begin reading sources, your hypothesis will become more refined. Only after you have explored it through close reading and writing, your hypothesis will become a working thesis. Your sample hypothesis may evolve into a thesis such as: *Budget cuts, which led to the dismantling of both athletic and art programs, have had a larger negative impact on females than on males.*

Scheduling

One of the most important elements for a successful research project involves time management. Some data can only be collected periodically, some research requires hours of wading through sources, some research requires interviews or observations that must be planned in advance, and some projects require a large amount of reading in preparation for writing. Plan to devote enough time to the project so that you do not cut corners in your research. Also, you must allow enough time for outlining, drafting, editing, revising, and proofreading your paper. The best method for this is to devise a schedule. The following chart shows a typical schedule for a research project. Try to use a checklist such as this one to plan your project in advance. The best way to do this is consider the final due date and work backwards.

Assignment title: _____

Step:	Complete by:
Analyze the assignment; select and limit subject.	_____
Arrange library and Internet time; decide on methods of research.	_____
Complete general online searches; do background reading.	_____
Narrow topic if necessary; determine research question.	_____
Start bibliography; find library and online sources.	_____
Develop a working thesis and rough outline.	_____
Read and evaluate sources; take notes.	_____
Create explicit thesis and outline.	_____
Prepare first draft of paper.	_____
Obtain and evaluate critical responses.	_____
Find more sources, if necessary.	_____
Revise draft; prepare list of works cited.	_____
Edit revised draft.	_____
Prepare final draft; proofread.	_____
Submit completed project.	_____

Lesson 8-2: The Research Paper

The purpose of research is to discover the facts about a subject. The research paper is the organized presentation of these facts. A research paper is an extensive, formal composition using information taken from a number of sources.

Although many research papers are purely informational, there is usually an attempt to draw a conclusion based on the information gathered. In other words, instead of simply presenting findings, many teachers expect students to analyze the results and make decisions based on the evidence. For example, a research paper on the discovery and condition of stone circles in Ireland could be purely informational. However, to speculate on the construction, purpose, and people who created and used these stone circles would require drawing conclusions. Some research topics a student might encounter and analyze might be the effectiveness of the death penalty on the crime rate, conditions and solutions for the world's hunger problems, or the social ramifications of recent legal actions. These, as can many topics, can be researched, but they also require speculation on the part of the writer to tie the evidence to the result.

The Steps in Writing a Research Paper

The steps to be followed for writing a research paper are similar for those used in other forms of writing. (For more about these steps, see Chapter 6.) The main difference is that when writing a research paper, you must find different sources, extract information from these sources, and give credit to the authors of these sources. Here is a list of steps for writing a research paper. Look over these steps before beginning the process.

The 7 Steps in Writing a Research Paper

1. Prepare a governing question, form a hypothesis, and narrow the topic.

2. Prepare a working bibliography (a list of sources).

3. Create a working thesis and a rough outline.

4. Read research material and take notes.

5. Organize information and write thesis and final outline.

6. Write the first draft and the Works Cited or References page.

7. Write and proofread the final draft.

Conducting Research

Once your topic has been chosen, you should immediately get started on your research. The library is the best place for this stage of the writing process. There are a great many print materials available: books, journals and periodicals, reference materials. In addition, the library has many electronic catalogues and databases. Through computer terminals, you can gain access to medical libraries, newspaper search engines, and college databases. Another added benefit of the library is that libraries are connected via the Internet, and they share materials with other branches in the system. That means you can access information from many libraries simply by visiting your own library.

There are so many types of reference materials available at the library. The most commonly used include encyclopedias, biographical dictionaries, summaries of current events, and book indexes. These are used to find the latest research and publications. These materials are obtainable either online or on CD-ROM; your librarian can help you gain access to them.

Before diving into research, develop a strategy. You must consider how many and what type of sources you need. You must also consider the most current resources, as well as the most specific. Ask yourself the following questions:

▶ **Will I need primary sources, secondary sources, or both?**

Primary sources are firsthand accounts. They are the most reliable sources. Primary sources include historical documents, literary works, diaries, letters, raw data from experiments, and eyewitness accounts of events. Secondary sources are secondhand accounts. These include accounts by other investigators, lab reports from other researchers, biographies, or reviews.

▶ **What kinds of sources does the assignment require?**

If you must use primary or non-print resources, find out where they are and when they are available. Some reference materials are only for use in the library building; you may not check them out. Therefore, it is crucial that you set enough time to explore these sources. If you need Internet sources, make sure you have access to a computer with Internet services. Due to the wide range of what is available online, some schools limit Internet use through software. Make sure you have the access that you need. If you need secondary resources, such as your own fieldwork, surveys, or observations, be sure to incorporate time for these projects into your plan.

▶ **How current do my sources need to be?**

If you are researching a contemporary topic, you should use the most up-to-date data. This means that periodicals, such as medical and technical journals, might be the best material for you. Also, there are usually recent postings on the Web, but you must evaluate the source. If your topic is less progressive, you can use books. This data changes at a much slower rate.

▶ **Do I need to consult sources contemporary with an event or a person's life?**

If your research about a topic also includes the effects of a time period, you may need time-specific materials. This information can be found in magazines, newspapers, and books from the time period. They can be found at the library; they are stored using different methods. There are periodical catalogues available for these materials, but sometimes they are difficult to locate. If necessary, ask the librarian for assistance.

▶ **Are my sources reliable?**

In this age of the Internet, it is more important than ever to question your sources. Almost anyone can publish almost anything online, but this also pertains hard copy publications as well. You must develop a critical attitude toward your sources, especially when you are writing about controversial subjects. Ask yourself these questions:

⬦ What do I know about the author?

⬦ Whom does this person represent?

⬦ To what organization does he or she belong?

⬦ When was this published?

As a researcher, you must be aware of the motivation behind the source.

▶ **How many sources should I consult?**

You should expect to look at many more resources than you will end up using. As your thesis develops, you may need to find more relevant sources. Keep a working bibliography during this stage. Also, check to see whether your assignment requires a minimum number of sources.

Conducting Field Research

For many research projects you will need to collect field data. The "field" could be many things, depending on the project. You might be expected to take a survey in one of your classes, you might have to conduct an experiment in a laboratory, or you might simply make observations of groups of people. As a field researcher, you will need to discover where you can find relevant information, how to gather it, and who might be the best sources for this information.

Observation

The first type of field research is observation. This sounds easier than it is. First, the observer should not directly or indirectly influence the behavior of those he or she observes. If the subject of the observation is nervous or is aware of the observer, he or she might change normal behavior patterns. Second, remember that the observation is never neutral. The observer is watching the situation with preconceived ideas, and that might influence either what he sees or how he perceives it. Before you conduct any observation, decide exactly what you want to discover and anticipate what you are likely to see. After that, be as objective as possible. Here is a list of suggestions for conducting observations:

▷ Determine the purpose of the observation, and be sure it relates to your research question and hypothesis.

▷ Make plans as far in advance as possible. Consider what you want to see and when the best time is to observe, and leave ample time to accomplish the observation. Remember that so many variables are out of your control (weather, travel, and so on).

▷ If necessary, make appointments and gain permission to observe. With any observations involving children, speak with the parents beforehand. It is also considered professional to plan in advance and to ask permission from any subject. Of course, if you are attempting to observe conditions unobtrusively but in the open, permission is not necessary.

▷ Develop a suitable system for recording data. When conducting field research, it can be difficult to write down a good deal of notes. Figure out a system that works for you. Sometimes a worksheet or pre-planned check list can help.

▷ Collect and record data using as many methods as possible. You could use a tape recorder, a video camera, or notes depending on the situation.

▷ After taking notes, go back and question your observations, remaining open to interpretations. Sometimes you see things differently the first time around.

Interviewing

Some information is best collected through the interview. This can be done in person, on the phone, or even through e-mail. Your research might require a sampling of people to be interviewed, or you might have to interview experts about your research question and hypothesis. When looking for people to interview, see if your research has generated any names or positions of people to interview. If not, you can interview those in similar positions or those affected by your hypothesis. Be sure to compose questions in advance. These questions should be factual questions. In other words, they should be based on fact, rather than opinion. Also, the questions should be answered with facts, not opinions. Factual questions elicit specific answers; they are not open-ended and subject to multiple direction and opinion.

Here is a list of suggestions for interviews:

▷ Determine your exact purpose for the interview; be sure it relates to your research question and hypothesis.

▷ Set up the interview in advance. Remember that people's schedules are subject to change; leave time to reschedule if necessary. Also, ask permission in advance if you plan to record the session.

▷ Prepare a written list of questions in advance. This will save time and keep you on track during the interview.

▷ Be prepared, be prompt, and be professional. Remember that other people's time is precious too. Have your questions and materials ready, be there on time, and appear dressed in a manner appropriate to the interview. Also, feel free to show your appreciation with a thank-you note or e-mail. Let the person you interview know that you appreciate his or her time.

Survey

The survey, or questionnaire, is another common way to gather data. This is an efficient method for collecting information from multiple sources. The key to a successful survey is to pose the right questions to the right people. The questions should be clear and easy to understand. They should be designed for easy answer and no interpretation. For example, a simple yes or no question works well, or a range question. Also, be sure to gather information from relevant sources; do not give surveys to people who are unaffected by the issue. Here is a list of suggestions for interviews:

▷ Consider your purpose and review your research question and hypothesis before writing the survey questions.

▷ Determine the audience for your questionnaire, and determine how you will reach your potential respondents. Who should fill out the survey? Will it be completed via the telephone, e-mail or regular mail, or in person? Will you distribute questionnaires to your audience and ask them to return them, or will you collect them immediately?

▷ Draft your questions and check to see that each question calls for a short, specific answer.

▷ If the questionnaire is to be distributed by mail, write a brief cover letter. If it is to be sent electronically, write a short e-mail explaining your survey. Make sure the directions, including the deadline and the method for return, are clear.

▷ Proofread everything before sending it out.

The Preliminary Outline

Before going any further in the writing process, take the time to organize your notes and develop a preliminary outline. A preliminary outline is not an outline of your paper; it is a guide for your reading and note-taking. It represents the topics you will most likely cover in your paper. As your reading leads to new topics, you can insert them in the outline. As you find that some topics are no longer relevant, remove them from the preliminary outline.

At this point you have gathered many sources of information. You probably have dozens of photocopies of pages from reference books as well as printouts from the computer. What you need here is organization.

One of the most helpful tools during this process is the note card. Using an index card for each source aids in the organization; this can also serve as your working bibliography. On one side of the card, write the general topic and cite the source. On the other side of the card, take notes in your own words. When you begin looking for information, you can simply look through your stack of cards.

It is important to keep notes on the backs of these cards, and the best way to do this is to write down the information in your own words. A research paper is not a list of quotations from sources; it must contain your ideas and your words. This means you must analyze the information that you gather. If you do not take the time to process the information as you collect it, there will be more work for you later. Processing also allows you to filter extraneous information. The writing process will be much faster if you are not burdened with sifting through the data at that time. Quote verbatim only when the words of the source are extremely important.

Regardless of whether you quote or paraphrase, remember to acknowledge your sources. Quotations and citations are an easy cure for avoiding plagiarism, but what about when you paraphrase? If you incorporate notes directly from a source, even if you attempt to paraphrase, you still run the danger of using someone else's words or style. The best way to avoid the appearance of plagiarism is to take notes in your own words. The use of note cards can help. If you start by taking notes in your own words, you will develop your own style that will be consistent throughout the paper.

The Final Outline

When you are satisfied that you have enough sources, arrange your notes into the order in which you will use them. Review your hypothesis. Can you shape it into a more specific thesis statement? Organize all of your sources in a manner that makes sense. You can accomplish this by sifting through your note cards. This simple task will aid you in the organization of your paper. As you prepare this outline, some of your topics may be discarded. Remember: Effective writing means only including relevant information.

The 1st Draft

The first draft of your paper is the compilation of your research. This is where you assemble and connect all of your information. Do not write it as if it is the final paper; this is simply a part of the process. As you piece together the information from your sources, your thesis may still become more specific. Do not worry about writing an introduction first; focus on the body and see where your data takes you.

The Body

As you incorporate ideas from your notes, make certain that you indicate the source in your paper. Whether you paraphrase or use quotations, you must list the source in the body. Do not wait until the paper is complete; you will save a great deal of time if you do it now. Also, you do not want to run the risk of omitting a source. To avoid plagiarizing, document any source material with a citation within your text and an entry in your list of sources.

Transitions are also important when piecing together your ideas and your research. Quotations need to be smoothly and clearly linked to the surrounding sentences in your essay. One way to accomplish this is with signal verbs. These verbs can characterize the author or researcher's viewpoint while allowing you to incorporate quotations and to connect ideas.

Examples

In *The Stranger*, the heat affects Mersault. "The sun was shining almost directly overhead onto the sand, and the glare on the water was unbearable." (Camus 52).

This example would be more effective with the transition of a signal verb.

In *The Stranger*, Camus emphasizes the power of the heat on Mersault. "The sun was shining almost directly overhead onto the sand, and the glare on the water was unbearable." (52).

The second example clearly shows that the quotation came from Camus. It is not always necessary to mention the source within the text, but in this case it achieves another goal; it also accomplishes a point of view that is not present in the first example. The signal verb also aids in the transition. By stating that Camus *emphasizes* the power, there is a preconceived idea while reading the quotation. Also note that the citation is different in the two examples. (For more about citations, see Lesson 8-3 on page 295.)

Signal Verbs

acknowledges	concludes	disputes	opposes
advises	concurs	emphasizes	remarks
agrees	confirms	expresses	replies
allows	criticizes	interprets	reports
answers	declares	lists	responds
asserts	describes	objects	reveals
believes	disagrees	observes	suggests
claims	discusses	offers	thinks

When your body is roughly put together with your research and examples incorporated, it is time to focus on the introduction and the conclusion.

The Introduction

The introduction should draw the reader into the essay and provide background needed to understand the topic before reading the paper. There are several effective methods for writing an introduction. One method is to open with a question, perhaps the research question that initially led you to your hypothesis. Another technique is to include highlights of what the reader will encounter in the paper. Some writers include personal experience that establishes credibility. The reader might be interested in what makes the writer an expert on the topic.

The Conclusion

The conclusion also serves an important role in the research paper. It shows the reader what he or she has learned. It does not persuade the reader to agree with your findings; the body should have done that. The conclusion has an impact because it leaves the reader with final thoughts. There are a few specific strategies when writing a conclusion for a research paper. First, you can begin your conclusion by restating your thesis and then expand to a more general conclusion about the topic. Another method is to remind readers of your main points in your conclusion. This will leave them with a strong impression of the evidence. Some writers conclude with a rhetorical question, a call to action, or a hypothetical condition that leaves a lasting impression on the reader. (For more ideas about introductions and conclusions, see Lesson 6-6 on page 247.)

The Final Draft

Because a research essay involves collaborating your thoughts and ideas with the ideas of others, it must be reviewed carefully before the final revisions are made. As with most types of writing, allow for time between drafts. This will help you bring a fresh eye to the piece. If you have the benefit of another editor, this can be extremely helpful. Another person can notice many things. For this stage, ask a teacher or a parent, or try peer editing if possible.

When it is time to revise and edit your draft, read it slowly while focusing on audience, purpose, and thesis. Assess your research. Check to see if the results stand up to your analysis. Are all the data accurate and your conclusions warranted? Do you need additional material? Are your quotations longer than necessary? Evaluate your introduction, body, and conclusion. Are they appropriately organized? Do you transition between ideas? Sometimes outlining the paper as you read helps aid with organization. Also, be sure to check documentation at this stage. Have you included all the appropriate citations? Are the citations consistent?

When you are finished editing and revising your paper, go back once again and proofread your final draft for surface errors. If possible, have someone else check for these errors as well. Also create the works cited page using the sources that you have included in your final draft. There are several styles for citations; the two most common are MLA (Modern Language Association) and the APA (American Psychological Association) styles. More about these styles are in the following sections.

Lesson 8-3: Citation

Citation is when a writer uses someone else's words, ideas, or research. Any words or ideas that come from someone else must be documented. There are several different methods for citation. Although most methods require the same basic information, they differ in the order of information recorded, as well as punctuation. With most research papers, the Modern Language Association, or MLA, style is used for documenting sources. In both high school and college, teachers expect this type of citation. However, with some fields, such as psychology, sociology, or education, the American Psychological Association, or APA, style is used. When the teacher or professor does not specify style, use MLA.

MLA Format for Parenthetical Citations

MLA style uses parenthetical citations in the text of an essay to document. This means that within the body of your paper, credit is given to different sources. Parenthetical citations are brief notations within the text that refer to full bibliographic entries found in the works cited page at the end of the paper. This is done for every quotation, paraphrase, summary, or other material requiring documentation.

Remember to keep parenthetical citations as brief as possible. All your reader really needs is enough information to find the completed citation in the works cited list. Place a parenthetical citation as close to the relevant material as possible without disrupting the flow of the sentence. In most cases, this is before the punctuation mark at the end of the sentence or phrase containing the material. Here are a few rules for MLA parenthetical citation:

▶ Place any punctuation mark after the closing parenthesis.

Example:

> The research indicates a direct change in temperature over extended periods of time (Lee 661).

Notice that the author's name is included in the citation. Do this when you do not name the author within the text. Make sure to include the first name if you have more than one author with the same last name.

▶ If your citation refers to a quotation, place the citation after the quotation mark but before any other punctuation mark.

Example:

> The author uses irony to describe the brutality of imperialism, which *The New American Webster Dictionary* defines as "the policy of expanding national territory" (348).

▶ For works with more than one volume, such as journals and periodicals, note the volume number first and then the page number(s), with a colon and one space between them.

Example:

> According to Williams, there is no direct link between these symptoms and the disease itself (3: 42).

▶ For literary works that are separated by acts, chapters, books, or scenes, first cite the page number followed by a semicolon, and then give other identifying information that will lead readers to the passage indicated.

Example:

> In *The Merchant of Venice*, Bassanio confronts Antonio by saying, "You shall not seal to such a bond for me: I'll rather dwell in my necessity" (15; sc. III).

If this were a part or chapter in a novel, the citation would be: (123; ch. 4). For a poem, instead of page numbers, the citation would include the part and line(s), separated by a period: (6; 33–38).

▶ For an indirect source, use the abbreviation *qtd. in* to show that you are using someone else's secondhand source (conversation, letter, interview, and so on).

Example:

> Mr. Johnson's attorney stated, "Mr. Johnson has no intention of retiring at this time" (qtd. in Ellis 87).

▶ To document two or more sources in the same citation, separate the information with semicolons.

Example:

> Several researchers have discovered the connection between headaches and job-related stress (Anderson 34; Graham 968).

MLA Format for a List of Works Cited

The **Works Cited** list is an alphabetical list of the sources used and documented in MLA style in your essay. This list begins on a separate page after the text of your essay. This list is part of your paper, so it should have continuous page numbers. The sources are listed alphabetically by the author's last name. If the author is unknown, alphabetize the work by the title, omitting the article (*a, an,* or *the*). The first line of a citation is flush with the margin. After that, the lines are indented five spaces. Here is a list of the various ways to cite sources on your works cited page.

Books

▶ The basic entry for a book includes *the author, the title*, and *the publication information*. The author's last name comes first, followed by a comma, and then the first name. The title is underlined or italicized and all major words are capitalized (see Lesson 5-11 on page 215). The city of publication is followed by a colon, a space, and the publisher's name (the publisher's name sometimes can be shortened). A comma and the year of publication follow the publisher's name.

Example:

> Hamilton, Edith. *Mythology: Timeless Tales of Gods and Heroes.* New York: Penguin Books, 1969.

▶ If the work has more than one author listed, list the first author as in the previous example (last name first, then comma and first name), and then list the name(s) of the other authors in regular order, with a comma between authors and an *and* before the last author. For more than three authors, use only the first author followed by *et al.*

Example:

> Abrams, Eliza, June Blakely, and Hanna Smith. *The Virtues of Truth.* New Windsor: Washingtonville Press, 2002.

▶ If the work has a corporation or group as the author, use the name of the group listed on the title page as the author, even if the same group published the book.

Example:

> Society for Financial Freedom. *Handbook of Key Guidelines and Principles.* New York: Society for Financial Freedom Press, 1998.

▶ For books with an editor in lieu of an author, cite the editor the same as you would an author, but add a comma and *ed.* (or *eds.* for more than one editor).

Example:

> Schneider, Elizabeth W., Albert L. Walker, and Herbert E. Childs, eds. *The Range of Literature.* New York: D. Van Nostrand Co., 1973.

▶ If you use one selection from an anthology or collection, list the author of the selection; its title; the title of the volume; *Ed.* and the name of the editor(s); the publication information; and the inclusive page numbers. For numbers higher than 99, note only the last two digits for the second number.

Example:

> Malamud, Bernard. "The Magic Barrel." *The Range of Literature.* Ed. Elizabeth W. Schneider, Albert L. Walker, and Herbert E. Childs. New York: D. Van Nostrand Co., 1973. 206–18.

▶ When citing a translated book, give the translator's name, preceded by *Trans.*, after the title.

Example:

> Camus, Albert. *The Stranger.* Trans. Matthew Ward. New York: Vintage International, 1989.

▶ If you use one volume of a multi-volume work, put the volume number (using the abbreviations *Vol.* and *vols.*) after the title, and list the number of volumes in the complete work after the date.

Example:

> Townsend, Paul. *The Definitive Answer to the Questions of the Universe.* Vol. 2. Trenton: Funston Press, 2004. 7 vols.

Periodicals

▶ The basic entry for a periodical includes *the author, the article title,* and *the publication information.* The author's last name comes first, followed by a comma, and then the first name. The article title, including any subtitle, is enclosed in quotation marks. Remember that the period goes inside the closing quotation mark and that all major words in the title are capitalized. The article title is followed by the publication title, which is underlined or italicized. The volume number, issue number if applicable, and the date of publication come next. For magazines, list the month or the day and month before the year, and do not use parentheses. For journals, list the year in parentheses followed by a colon, a space, and the inclusive page numbers. Do not use *p.* or *pp.* before the page numbers.

Examples:

> Coleman, Barbara. "Low-Impact Dance Steps with a Twist."
> *Dancers' Interest Journal* 11 (1996): 124–49.

> Parsons, Robert. "Dickinson vs. Whitman – A Clash in Style."
> *Poet's Monthly* Apr. 1984: 23–40.

▸ For newspapers, give the name as it appears on the cover but without any initial article (*A*, *An*, or *The*). Add the name of the city if it is not included in the publication. Also, give the edition (if listed), followed by a colon, a space, the section number or letter (if listed), and the page number(s). If the article appears on discontinuous pages, give the first page followed be a plus sign.

Example:

> Ferrell, Constance. "The Hazards of City Living – One
> Woman's Story." *New York Times* 8 Sept 1952, early
> ed.: L1+.

▸ For an editorial or a letter to the editor, use the label *Editorial* or *Letter*, without underline, italics, or quotation marks. Place the word after the title and before the name of the publication.

Example:

> Humphrey, Harold. "Speed Bumps Are a Safety Hazard."
> Letter. *Enterprise* [Cincinnati] 17 Feb. 2004: 26–27.

Electronic Sources

Sources such as CD-ROMs and Internet sites require the same basic information as print sources, but some of this information is not always available. Web pages are created, updated, and deleted on a daily basis. Also, some postings have no author or title listed. The best you can do is to cite what information is available. At the very least, you will have the URL for a Website and a title and publisher for a CD-ROM. Here are a few examples on how to cite electronic sources:

▸ Cite a basic CD-ROM as you would a book or a part of a book. Include the title of the article in quotation marks (where applicable), the title of the CD-ROM, the edition, the medium (CD-ROM), the place of publication, and the publisher.

Example:

> "Civil Rights Movement." *Grolier's Multimedia Encyclopedia.*
> 2nd ed. CD-ROM. New York: Grolier Interactive, 1999.

▶ To document a general Website, include the name of the person who created the site, if possible; the title of the site, underlined or italicized, or, if there is no title, a description of the site; the name of the organization associated with the site; the date of access; and the URL, in angle brackets. If a URL within a works cited list will not all fit onto one line, it should be broken only after a slash.

Example:

> *Selected Topics: Irish Literature.* Blackmore Library, Capital
> University. 27 Dec. 2003. <http://www.capital.edu/cc/
> library/irish/lit.1>

▶ Cite an online book or periodical the same way you would a printed document. Add the date you visited the site, followed by the URL address.

Example:

> Hamilton, Edith. *Mythology: Timeless Tales of Gods and Heroes.*
> New York: Penguin Books, 1969. 16 Dec. 2001. <http://
> www.ddsd.org/mythology/hamilton/.html.>

For more about Modern Language Association style documentation, visit the MLA homepage (*www.mla.org/*).

APA Format for Parenthetical Citations

American Psychological Association, or APA, style requires parenthetical citations in the text to document quotations, paraphrases, summaries, and other material from a source. These in-text citations correspond to full bibliographic entries in a list of references at the end of the text. Here are some examples of how to use APA style for parenthetical citations:

▶ In general, use the author's name in a signal phrase to introduce the cited material, and place the date, in parentheses, after the author's name. For a quotation, the page number preceded by *p.* appears in parentheses after the quotation. For electronic texts or other works without page numbers, paragraph numbers may be used instead.

Examples:

In his fiscal study, Miller (1993) proposes a connection between the initial financial gains from the mutual fund and the amount later invested.

Peterson asserts that this is due to "an unrealistic view of the market's potential brought about by the sudden fluctuation" (p. 94).

▶ When using a specific part of a source, use abbreviations (*chap., p.*) in a parenthetical citation to signify the part of the work you are citing.

Example:

In his fiscal study, Miller (1993, chap. 6) proposes a connection between the initial financial gains from the mutual fund and the amount later invested.

▶ When you do not name the author in the text, give the name and the date, separated by a comma, in parentheses at the end of the cited material.

Example:

One study proposes a connection between the initial financial gains from the mutual fund and the amount later invested (Miller, 1993).

▶ With two authors, use both names in all citations. Join the names with *and* in a signal phrase, but use an ampersand (&) in the parenthetical reference.

Example:

Klinger and Matthews (1995) assert a different reason for the increase. A relatively recent study attributes the rise to resurgence in the overall market (Klinger & Matthews, 1995).

▶ For more than two authors, list all of the authors in the first reference, but for any subsequent references use the first author's name plus *et al.*

Example:

Bellesheim, Hossler, Linden, and Ryan (2000) confirm the latest findings and attribute the fluctuation to an unstable market base combined with a wary consumer unit.

The next phase, according to Bellesheim et al. (2000), is to "balance the variation by combining resources" (p. 39).

▶ If the author is an organization or corporation, spell it out the first time you use it, followed by an abbreviation in brackets. For any subsequent citations, use the abbreviation only.

Example:

First citation: (American Medical Association [AMA], 2005).

Later citations: (AMA, 2005).

▶ If the author is unknown, use the title in a signal phrase or a parenthetical citation.

Example:

Consumer spending increased between the months of October 1999 and January 2000 (*Market Report,* 2003).

▶ If you cite more than one source at the same time, list the works in alphabetical order by the author's last name, separated by semicolons. If citing more than one source by the same author, list them chronologically, separated by commas.

Examples:

(Friedman, 1986; Wilson, 1991)

(Friedman, 1986, 1988)

APA Format for a List of References

The list of works used in a research paper using APA style is called **References**. This list begins on a separate page after the text of your essay, but before any appendices or notes. This list should have continuous page numbers as it follows the last page of your paper. The sources are listed alphabetically by the author's last name. If the author is unknown, alphabetize the work by the title, omitting the article (*a, an,* or *the*). The first line of a citation is flush with the margin. After that, the lines are indented five spaces. Here is a list of the various ways to cite sources on your references page.

Books and Journals

▶ The basic entry for a book includes *the author, the publication date, the title,* and *the publication information.* The author's last name comes first, followed by a comma, and then the first initial. The date of publication is enclosed in parentheses; use only the year for books and journals. The title is underlined or italicized and only the first word, any proper nouns, or any proper adjectives are capitalized. The city of publication is followed by a colon (include the state if the city is not obvious), a space, and the publisher's name (drop any Inc., Co., or Publishers). If numbers are needed, place them in parentheses following *p.* or *pp.*

Example:

Hamilton, E. (1969). *Mythology: Timeless tales of gods and heroes.* New York: Penguin.

▶ For more than one author, separate the names with commas, and use an ampersand (&) before the last author's name.

Example:

Abrams, E., Blakely, J. & Smith, H. (2002). *The Virtues of Truth.* New Windsor, NY: Washingtonville.

▶ If the work has a corporation or group as the author, use the name of the group listed on the title page as the author, even if the same group published the book.

Example:

Society for Financial Freedom. (1998). *Handbook of Key Guidelines and Principles.* New York: Society for Financial Freedom.

▶ For books with an editor or editors in lieu of an author, cite the editor the same as you would an author, but add *Ed.* or E*ds.* in parentheses following the name.

Example:

Schneider, E. W., Walker, A.L & Childs, H.E. (Eds.). (1973). *The Range of Literature.* New York: D. Van Nostrand.

▶ If you use one selection from an anthology or collection, list the author of the selection; the date; its title; the word *In*; the name of the editor(s) followed by (Eds.); the title of the volume; the inclusive page numbers; and the publication information. For numbers greater than 99, note only the last two digits for the second number.

Example:

> Malamud, B. (1973). The magic barrel. In. E. W. Schneider, A. L. Walker, & H. E. Childs (Eds.). *The Range of Literature.* (pp. 206–18). New York: D. Van Nostrand.

▶ When citing a translated book, give the translator's first initial and last name, followed by *Trans.*, all in parentheses after the title.

Example:

> Camus, A. (1989). *The Stranger* (M. Ward, Trans.). New York: Vintage International.

▶ If you use one volume of a multi-volume work, put the volume number (*Vol.*) after the title.

Example:

> Townsend, P. (2004). *The Definitive Answer to the Questions of the Universe* (Vol. 2). Trenton, N.J.: Funston.

▶ For an article in a journal, include the volume number (and edition, if applicable) before the page numbers.

Example:

> Coleman, B. (1996). Low-impact dance steps with a twist. *Dancers' Interest Journal, 11*, 124–49.

Periodicals

▶ The basic entry for a periodical includes *the author, the publication date, the title*, and *the publication information*. The author's last name comes first, followed by a comma, and then the first initial. Separate the names of multiple authors with commas, and use an ampersand (&) before the last author's name. The date of publication is enclosed in parentheses. For periodicals other than journals, use the year, a comma, and the month or month and day. Do not abbreviate the month. The title of the article follows the date. It is not underlined or italicized, and only the first word, proper nouns, and proper adjectives are capitalized. The title of the publication is underlined or italicized and all major words are capitalized.

Example:

> Parsons, R. (1984, April). Dickinson vs. Whitman – A clash in
> style. *Poet's Monthly,* 23–40.

▸ For newspapers, give the name as it appears on the cover. For the
date, include the year, a comma, the month and the day.

Example:

> Ferrell, C. (1952, September 8). The hazards of city living: One
> woman's story. *The New York Times,* p. L1.

▸ For an editorial or a letter to the editor, write *Editorial* or *Letter to the
editor* in brackets after the title and before the name of the publication.

Example:

> Humphrey, H. (2004, February 17). Speed bumps are a safety
> hazard [Letter to the editor]. *The Enterprise,* pp. 26–27.

Electronic Sources

Electronic sources such as CD-ROMs and Internet sites require the
same basic information as print sources, including author, date of publication, and title. These are also cited in the same order and using the
same punctuation as printed resources. In addition, for Websites you
should include the URL and the date you visited the site.

To document a general Website, include the name of the person who
created the site, if possible; the title of the site or, if there is no title, a
description of the site; the name of the organization associated with the
site; the URL, in angle brackets; and the date of access. If a URL within
a References list will not all fit onto one line, it should be broken only
after a slash.

Example:

> Simmons, B. (1997). Introduction to poetry. *Contemporary
> English Literature.* <http://www.lit.edu/cc/library/poetry/.1>
> (1999, April 12).

For more about American Psychological Association style documentation, visit the APA homepage (*www.apastyle.org/elecref.html*).

Most Common Errors

The content of text is essential. It consists of research, ideas, opinions, and/or emotions. It deserves to be presented in the clearest way possible. A portion of this clarity is achieved through outline and the structure of your piece, and part is accomplished through the proper use of language and conventions. Writers have the opportunity to revise what they want to say *before* they say it. Writers also have the opportunity to proofread their work for errors in tense, tone, phrasing, vocabulary, and punctuation. These errors are frequently referred to as **surface errors**. They do not affect the content of your writing; they affect the ways in which your ideas are presented and interpreted. This chapter deals with the some of the most common surface errors related to spelling, grammar, tone, and punctuation.

Lesson 9-1: Fragments and Run-Ons

Each sentence must be complete, meaning it has to contain a subject and a predicate. If a sentence does not contain both of these parts, it is a **fragment**. A sentence must also contain one idea. This idea can be presented in a variety of sentence structures, but it must be contained. If it is not, or if there are several independent clauses separated by commas, the sentence is considered a **comma splice** or a **run-on.**

Fragments

A fragment is an incomplete sentence. There are several ways for a sentence to be incomplete and deemed a fragment. If the clause is missing a subject, if it contains an incomplete verb, or if it begins with a subordinating word, it is a fragment.

Because I am allergic to peanuts.

This subordinating clause is a **fragment**; the independent clause is missing from the sentence. This sentence will become complete by adding an independent clause either before or after the subordinating clause.

Because I am allergic to peanuts, I cannot eat the candy.

This sentence is complete. You can also complete the sentence by simply dropping the subordinating conjunction.

I am allergic to peanuts.

Either choice is correct. To avoid this error, look to see where you use subordinating conjunctions, and make sure you have two clauses that relate to each other.

The fundraiser helped many politicians. Aided the entire Democratic Party.

This fragment lacks a **subject.** This sentence can be corrected by adding a noun or a pronoun as the subject.

The affair aided the entire Democratic Party.

This sentence is now complete. Another choice is to connect the two clauses with a semicolon.

The fundraising benefit helped many politicians; it aided the entire Democratic Party.

The well-dressed man sitting on the bench in front of City Hall.

This fragment lacks a **complete verb.** In this case, the present participle (*sitting*) acts as an adjective, not a verb. It can be corrected by changing the tense of the verb *to sit*, or by adding an auxiliary verb. A simple correction is to use the present tense of the verb.

The well-dressed man sits on the bench in front of City Hall.

This sentence is now complete because the verb is complete. Another solution is to conjugate the verb in past progressive tense by adding an auxiliary verb.

The well-dressed man was sitting on the bench in front of City Hall.

Now the sentence is complete because the verb is complete.

Run-Ons

Run-on sentences occur when two or more groups of words that could be written as independent sentences are grouped together with either incorrect punctuation or no punctuation at all.

Examples

> The day was hot, he decided to go swimming.

This is an example of a **comma splice**. A comma splice occurs when a comma is used to separate two independent clauses. This sentence can be corrected by replacing the first comma with either a semicolon or a period. This will make two sentences.

> The day was hot; he decided to go swimming.

This example is now correct. Another option is to connect the two clauses with a coordinating conjunction.

> The day was hot, and so he decided to go swimming.

These are two examples of the several ways to correct a comma splice. Choose the method that brings the most variety to your writing.

> She decided to go to the store she needed milk.

This run-on contains two independent clauses. This run-on can be corrected by adding either a semicolon or a period between the two clauses.

> She decided to go to the store. She needed milk.

Another solution is to connect the two clauses with a coordinating adjective.

> She decided to go to the store because she needed milk.

All of these options are correct. When dealing with simple clauses that are related, the best option would be to connect them with the coordinating adjective.

Exercise 9-1

Determine whether each of the following sentences is a fragment, a run-on, or a complete, and write the answer in the space provide.

Example: He needs.   *fragment*

1. The large, flowering tree on the hill.   _____

2. The cat rests.   _____

3. After dinner, the young child played with his toys.   _____

4. My friend took the job, she wanted a challenge.   _____

5. Because driving racecars is exhilarating.   _____

6. People garden.   _____

7. I have a new car and my sister went shopping.   _____

8. Today, we are going to the zoo, we will see animals.   _____

9. After the concert is over.   _____

10. He seems.   _____

Lesson 9-2: Subject/Verb Agreement

The subject and verb must always agree. This sounds easy, but it can sometimes be problematic. For instance, the subject of the verb may not be the noun closest to the verb; words between the subject and the verb can lead to an error. Compound subjects, fractions, nouns that are plural in form but singular in meaning, and indefinite pronouns can also lead to disagreement between the subject and the verb.

Examples

The pile of magazines are on the table.

This sentence is incorrect because the subject is singular but the verb is plural. The modifier (*magazines*) comes between the subject and the verb.

The pile of magazines is on the table.

The singular subject (*pile*) matches the singular verb (*is*).

The piano and the table is moved to the new house.

This sentence is incorrect because it contains a compound subject. A compound subject is plural and therefore needs a plural verb.

The piano and the table are moved to the new house.

The plural subject (*the piano and the table*) now matches the plural verb (*are moved*).

Mathematics are difficult to understand.

This sentence contains a subject that is singular in meaning but plural in form. In other words, we think of mathematics as one thing, one field of study. Therefore, it is incorrect.

Mathematics is difficult to understand.

There are few words such as this, but we do encounter cases such as this.

The same problem may occur with fractions or *part* of a collective noun. Always think about your subject. Is it one, or more than one, person, place, or thing?

Either one of them have the right experience for this job.

The subject does not match the verb in this sentence. *Either* is an indefinite pronoun and takes a *singular* verb.

Either one of them <u>has</u> the right experience for this job.

In this example, the singular subject (*either of them*) matches the singular verb (*has*). Remember: The singular case is correct for most indefinite pronouns.

Neither one of the candidates <u>are</u> suitable for the position.

Although *candidates* is plural, neither is an indefinite pronoun. The verb here must be *singular*.

Neither one of the candidates <u>is</u> suitable for the position.

In this example, the singular subject (*neither*) matches the singular verb (*is*). This mistake occurs frequently, so look for it.

Two-thirds of the money <u>are</u> spent.

This is incorrect. In this example, the fraction represents part of one thing, so the verb should be *singular*.

Two-thirds of the money <u>is</u> spent.

Here, the singular verb matches the singular fraction of the money. Fractions are not always singular, however.

Two-thirds of the employees <u>was</u> fired.

The subject does not match the verb. In this example, the fraction represents more than one person. Therefore, the verb must be *plural*.

Two-thirds of the employees <u>were</u> fired.

This sentence is correct. The plural subject matches the plural verb.

Exercise 9-2

For each of the following sentences, underline the correct form of the verb in parentheses.

Example: Apartments in my neighborhood (is, <u>are</u>) expensive.

1. My friends from school (is renting, are renting) a new apartment.

2. Each one (has, have) his own bedroom.

3. The carpet and the floor (looks, look) old and worn.

4. The furnishings (need, needs) to be replaced.

5. One-half of the rent (is, are) paid by Sandy.

6. Everyone (buys, buy) his own groceries.

7. Three-fourths of the roommates (is, are) female.

8. Mary and Tom (debates, debate) frequently over differing beliefs.

9. Politics (is, are) a constant topic for their arguments.

10. The others in the apartment (ignores, ignore) the discussions.

Lesson 9-3: Comma Errors

Comma errors frequently occur in writing because of the many rules involved. Sometimes commas are mistakenly omitted; other times, commas are unnecessarily inserted. This section reviews the more widespread comma errors.

Missing Comma After Introductory Words or Phrases

Introductory words and phrases are separated from the main clause of a sentence by a comma. The phrase can be long or short; it can be adverbial, verbal, adjective, or prepositional.

Examples

Frankly, I have seen enough reality television shows.

This sentence contains an adverb that is separated by a comma from the independent clause.

In order to prevent the grass in my yard from reaching my waist, I mow it.

In this sentence, the prepositional phrase is much longer than the independent clause. For purposes of clarity, a comma is used.

Missing Comma in a Compound Sentence

The independent clauses in a compound sentence are separated by a coordinating conjunction. In most cases, a comma follows the coordinating conjunction. The comma is necessary to demonstrate a pause or separation between two thoughts.

Examples

The night is full of stars, but my heart is full of clouds.

In this sentence, the coordinating conjunction (*but*) is preceded by a comma. It helps with the contrasting ideas in each part of the sentence.

I was tired of eating leftovers, and so I went to the supermarket.

In this example, a comma comes before the coordinating conjunction (*and so*). The comma allows for a pause to help show the relationship between the two clauses.

Missing Comma in a Series

A series consists of three or more parallel words, phrases, or clauses that appear consecutively in a sentence. Traditionally, a comma is used to separate all of the items.

Examples

The scented soap is available in vanilla, musk, lavender, and berry.

In this sentence, a comma is used to separate all of the words in the list.

I found the child's toys on top of her bed, inside her shoes, between her blankets, and under her clothing.

A comma separates each prepositional phrase listed in this sentence. Some people are flexible about the use of the final comma. You may discover it missing in some publications. Technically it belongs, but English is an ever-changing entity.

Exercise 9-3

Fill in the missing commas in each of the following sentences.

Example: We had dinner with family, friends, and neighbors.

1. Kathy likes pears but she does not like plums.

2. Usually I have coffee after dinner.

3. Missy's favorite colors are purple red and blue.

4. Greg washed the floors in the kitchen in the bathroom and in the laundry room.

5. After work my friends and I went to the movies.

6. The library the bank and the school are all within walking distance.

7. We need a new dryer or we will have to repair the old one.

8. Allison played soccer and she performed in the school play.

9. Fortunately I have never lost my keys.

10. She must water the plants feed the pets and turn out the lights.

Missing Comma With a Nonrestrictive Element

Sometimes referred to as a nonessential element, a nonrestrictive element is a word, phrase, or clause that gives additional information about the preceding part of the sentence but does not restrict the meaning of that part. In other words, it is a follow-up explanation or modifier to what precedes it. It can be deleted from the sentence without changing the sentence's basic meaning.

Examples

> Regina, <u>who ran a 10K last year</u>, is running the marathon in October.

The nonrestrictive element is set apart with commas. If removed, it would not change the meaning of the rest of the sentence.

> Chris wore jeans to the celebration<u>, a casual affair at the marina</u>.

The nonrestrictive element is at the end of the sentence, but it is still separated by a comma. The use of commas helps to highlight the main idea of the sentence.

Unnecessary Comma With a Restrictive Element

It is important to know where commas belong. Otherwise, unnecessary commas are sometimes added. Commas are simply inserted where they do not belong. Frequently, the error is the placement of a comma with a restrictive element. A restrictive element limits the meaning of the sentence. Therefore, it should not be separated from the rest of the sentence.

Examples

People, who are interested in space exploration, should visit Johnson Space Center in Houston, Texas.

This sentence incorrectly uses commas to separate relevant information from the rest of the sentence.

People who are interested in space exploration should visit Johnson Space Center in Houston, Texas.

This sentence is correct. The main information is not separated from the rest of the sentence.

The student will earn academic honors, if he maintains at least an A- average.

This sentence is incorrect. The inaccurate use of commas separates the restrictive element from the main part of the sentence.

The student will earn academic honors if he maintains at least an A- average.

This example is accurate. The main idea of the sentence is connected.

Exercise 9-4

For each of the following sentences, add a comma if the word or clause is nonrestrictive, and leave words and clauses that are restrictive as is.

Example: Research, an important element in education, is addressed in history class.

1. The history class which meets on Thursdays is working on term papers.

2. Students must visit the library during class hours.

3. One student a freshman is researching the Middle Ages.

4. The professor will guide her if she needs help.

5. Students who are researching must cite sources.

6. Several people working on English history worked together.

7. The librarian who was working alone aided six students.

8. The professor called a meeting which was held in her office.

9. The printer located in the library will be used throughout the afternoon.

10. All papers are due from the students by next Friday.

Lesson 9-4: Pronoun Errors

There are several ways to commit errors with pronouns. In some cases, the pronoun does not match its antecedent. In other cases, the pronoun is either unclear or unnecessary. Also, it is not unusual to accidentally switch from one pronoun case to another. This section highlights the most common errors found with pronouns.

Pronoun/Antecedent Agreement

The antecedent is the word that the pronoun replaces. For purposes of variety, you would not reuse the same noun several times within a sentence. For instance, it would be awkward to say: The dog is in the dog's house. You would replace the word *dog's* with *his*. The noun to which *his* refers is the antecedent *dog*. They must match according to pronoun case. Some common pronoun/antecedent errors occur with special case singular pronouns and collective nouns. This is especially prevalent in speech. Always take a second look at your writing for pronoun agreements.

Examples

Each of the mothers provided juice for their child.

This sentence is incorrect. Each is a singular antecedent and requires a singular pronoun.

Each of the mothers provided juice for her child.

The sentence is now correct. *Her* is a singular pronoun. It was easy to determine which third-person singular pronoun to use because of the word *mothers*. However, a gender must be assigned to an androgynous singular pronoun.

Anyone visiting the museum had to show their identification.

This sentence is incorrect. *Anyone* is a special singular antecedent. Therefore, we must use a singular pronoun.

Anyone visiting the museum had to show his or her
identification.

The sentence is now correct. The antecedent agrees with the third-person singular pronoun.

The home team lost their lead against the visitors.

This sentence is incorrect because team is a collective noun. It usually takes a singular pronoun.

The home team lost its lead against the visitors.

This sentence is now correct. Team takes a *singular* pronoun because the sentence is about the unit and not the individuals on the team.

After the first game of the double header, the team changed
their uniforms.

In this sentence, the plural pronoun is correct because the antecedent really means the members of the team. Therefore, a plural pronoun is needed.

Vague or Repetitious Pronoun

In some sentences, there is difficulty determining to which noun the pronoun refers. In other words, the pronoun is either vague or ambiguous. Other sentences contain unnecessary pronouns because they are repetitious. The key to good writing is to be as succinct as possible. This is especially important with the use of pronouns.

Examples

Tom told Arthur that his car needs repair.

Whose car needs repair in this sentence? The pronoun is ambiguous.

Tom told Arthur that Arthur's car needs repair.
Tom told Arthur that the latter's car needs repair.

Both of these sentences clearly state that it is Arthur's car that needs repair.

The radio played contemporary music. It played songs by
my favorite artists.

The radio and *it* are vague references. Writing should always be as precise as possible.

The disc jockey on station 101.3 fm played contemporary
music. She played songs by my favorite artists.

This sentence is specific. It is clear who is playing the music.

In the newspaper, it predicts that we will have rain tomorrow.

This pronoun is repetitious. We already have the noun newspaper.

The newspaper predicts that we will have rain tomorrow.

This sentence is correct because we eliminated the unnecessary pronoun.

Vandalism is so out of control at the park that they destroyed the swings and ruined the sandbox.

The pronoun is vague in this sentence. Who are *they*?

Vandalism is so out of control at the park that the teenage residents destroyed the swings and ruined the sandbox.

In this example, we know who committed the vandalism.

Inconsistent Pronouns

Sometimes writers change pronouns within a sentence. This occasionally happens when the writer is struggling with tone. Fortunately, writing can be edited. A writer must always proofread for consistency.

Examples

When one first enters the building, you see the office directory.

The pronouns do not match in this sentence. *One* is third-person singular, and *you* is second person.

When one first enters the building, one sees the office directory.

Both pronouns in this sentence are third person. Notice the change in the verb *to see* to the third person. The sentence can also be changed to second person. It all depends on your tone.

When you first enter the building, you see the office directory.

In this sentence, both pronouns are second person. The verb *to enter* is changed to second person in this example.

Exercise 9-5

Each of the following sentences contains a pronoun error. Underline the error and write the change in the space provided.

Example: The author struggled as <u>they</u> wrote the novel.   *he / she*

1. In the store, they have a wonderful variety of produce. _____

2. Ellen told her sister that she needed milk. _____

3. The book group gave their leader a gift._____

4. Each of the sales representatives created their displays. _____

5. If you want to succeed, one must work hard. _____

6. Someone left their scarf on the bus. _____

7. The boy told his father that he needed to rest. _____

8. On television, it says our economy is improving. _____

9. When one is injured, you must seek medical attention. _____

10. The school lost their funding for sports programs._____

Lesson 9-5: Tense Errors

Tense is an ongoing challenge. When writing an essay, analyzing literature, and/or discussing authors, the present tense is always used. However, with different types of writing it is sometimes necessary to demonstrate two time periods at once. Other times, a sequence of events is presented. Tense errors occur when the verb is inconsistent within a sentence or a paragraph, or when modifiers are unnecessarily added and change the tense. Always review writing for tense consistency. Here are the two most common tense errors.

Inconsistent Verbs

Verbs must be consistent as long as the writer is focused on one passage or idea. Be careful not to switch tenses within a sentence.

Examples

Charlie <u>was watching</u> television when he <u>stands up</u> and <u>fixes</u> a snack.

The tense in this sentence changes from *past progressive* to *present*. The appropriate tense change here should be *past tense*.

Charlie <u>was watching</u> television when he <u>stood up</u> and <u>fixed</u> a snack.

In this example, the entire sentence is in past tense, with the *past progressive* showing the continuing action.

> Each student <u>will complete</u> a reading project. He or she
> <u>reads</u> a book, <u>creates</u> a visual based on the assigned
> book, and <u>presents</u> it to the class.

In this example, the tense jumps from one sentence to the next. The assignment will take place in the future. Therefore, the work will be completed in the future.

> Each student <u>will complete</u> a reading project. He or she
> <u>will read</u> a book, <u>create</u> a visual based on the assigned
> book, and *present* it to the class.

This example is correct. All of the action will take place in the future.

Wrong Tense or Verb Form

Some verb errors occur simply because modifiers are needlessly added. In these cases, the tense is altered without reason. In other cases, the wrong case is accidentally used.

Examples

> I <u>had learned</u> to read at a young age.

In this sentence, the use of *had* is gratuitous. The tense is *past perfect*, when it should be simple *past tense*.

> I <u>learned</u> to read at a young age.

In this example, the use of *past tense* is appropriate. Remember that past perfect involves more than one time period in the past.

> I <u>had learned</u> to read <u>before</u> I turned 5 years old.

In this sentence, the use of past perfect is appropriate. Keep in mind that the use of auxiliary verbs changes the tense.

> Laurel <u>has spoke</u> French and English since childhood.

In this case, the verb *to speak* is conjugated incorrectly. The use of perfect tense is the correct choice, but instead of the past tense, the past participle is needed.

> Laurel <u>has spoken</u> French and English since childhood.

Here, the verb is conjugated properly.

Kim <u>drunk</u> three glasses of cranberry juice.

This example is incorrect because the *past participle* of the irregular verb *to drink* is substituted for *the past tense*.

Kim <u>drank</u> three glasses of cranberry juice.

This sentence correctly uses the *past tense* of the verb *to drink*.

Exercise 9-6

For each of the following sentences, correct the underlined tense error and write the answer in the space provided.

Example: Charlie <u>is needing</u> a new car.　　*needs*

1. Margaret <u>had studied</u> today. _____

2. The rain poured down, and then the sun <u>comes</u> out. _____

3. I walked and then I <u>was studying</u>. _____

4. The young girl accidentally <u>had tore</u> her dress. _____

5. My son <u>has wrote</u> his first story. _____

6. The job <u>will have been completed</u> by tomorrow._____

7. Mary <u>has broke</u> the school's track record._____

8. He will <u>be carrying</u> the flag and march in the parade. _____

9. She ate the banana and he <u>has eaten</u> the apple. _____

10. Gary <u>had shook</u> hands with my father. _____

Lesson 9-6: Preposition Errors

Prepositions express time, space, or direction. Sometimes these expressions are blatant, and other times they are subtle. Changing the preposition can alter the meaning of the sentence. Errors occur when the chosen preposition does not match the intended meaning.

Examples

The catcher threw the ball <u>to</u> the pitcher.

The catcher threw the ball <u>at</u> the pitcher.

These two sentences are similar, except for the preposition. The meaning of each sentence, however, is very different.

She compared her boss <u>with</u> a vicious dictator.

The preposition *with* is not accurate in this sentence. The boss and the vicious dictator are not together, or *with* each other.

She compared her boss <u>to</u> a vicious dictator.

This sentence now makes sense. We do not compare *with*, we compare *to*.

His software program complied <u>to</u> licensing regulations.

This preposition is incorrect. Regulations are not complied *to*.

His software program complied <u>with</u> licensing regulations.

This preposition is accurate. Regulations are met *with*.

Exercise 9-7

For each of the following sentences, choose and underline the correct preposition.

Example: The new safety measures complied (<u>with</u> / to) current automobile standards.

1. Audrey attended the conference to speak (with, to) the audience.

2. He spoke (with, to) me about our mutual safety concerns.

3. This dinner is similar (with, to) the one you cooked last week.

4. Many people rely (in, on) others for financial assistance.

5. Emma compared her little brother (with, to) a bear cub.

6. We are all meeting (at, in) the restaurant.

7. The award-winning roses are (at, in) the city's largest public park.

8. Harry and Ian have an archery competition (at, on) three o'clock.

9. Billy is charmed (by, with) Emily's beauty.

10. Emily is captivated (by, with) Billy's wit.

Lesson 9-7: Homonym Errors

Homonyms are words that sound the same, but are spelled differently and are different in meaning. They are frequently mistaken for each other. Be aware of these homonyms. They are **not** usually caught by spell check.

▶ **Accept / Except**

Accept is a verb meaning *to receive with approval*. **Except** is used as a preposition meaning *excluding*, or a verb meaning *to leave out*.

Examples:

> I <u>accept</u> responsibility for breaking the dishes. I will replace them all <u>except</u> for the ones you broke.

▶ **Adapt / Adopt**

Adapt is a verb meaning *to change in order to fit or be more suitable*. **Adopt** is a verb meaning *to take something and make it one's own*.

Examples:

> I <u>adapt</u> to my new job. The office decided to <u>adopt</u> new policies regarding vacation days.

▶ **Affect / Effect**

Affect is mainly used as a **verb**, meaning *to influence* or *imitate*. It is rarely used as a **noun**, meaning *feeling* or *emotion*. **Effect** is most often used as a **noun**, meaning *a result* or *something that follows as a consequence*. It is less frequently used as a **verb**, meaning *to produce a result* or *to make happen*. These words sometimes overlap in meaning, so be careful. As a rule, try **affect** as a verb and **effect** as a noun.

Examples:

> The drought will <u>affect</u> the crops. The <u>effects</u> could include high produce prices.

▶ **Allusion / Illusion**

Allusion is a noun meaning *reference*. **Illusion** is a noun meaning *fantasy or false impression*.

Examples:

> He made an <u>allusion to</u> Harry Houdini, the great magician. Houdini was known for his magical <u>illusions</u>.

▶ **Buy / By / Bye**

Buy is a verb meaning *to purchase*. **By** is a preposition meaning *near* or *way*. **Bye** is slang for *goodbye*.

Examples:

> I must <u>buy</u> a camera. The store is <u>by</u> the post office. <u>Bye</u>, see you later!

▸ **Emigrate / Immigrate**

Emigrate is a verb meaning *to leave a country and settle elsewhere.* **Immigrate** is a verb meaning *to come to a new place and settle there.*

Examples:

My grandparents emigrated from Ireland. They immigrated to the United States at the end of the nineteenth Century.

▸ **Farther / Further**

Farther is an adjective or adverb meaning *more remote or extended.* It is related to measurable distance. **Further** is an adjective or adverb meaning *more remote or extended,* but it is related to a figurative sense. The distance cannot truly be measured.

Examples:

I jogged underline{farther} today than yesterday. I pushed my body underline{further} than ever before.

▸ **Its / It's**

Its is a third-person singular possessive. **It's** is a contraction of the words *it* and *is.*

Examples:

The cat has something in underline{its} paws. underline{It's} a small acorn he found outside.

▸ **Than / Then**

Than is a conjunction used for comparison. **Then** is an adverb meaning afterward or at that time.

Examples:

Michael is more athletic underline{than} Richard. First they tested strength; underline{then,} they tested agility.

▸ **Their / There / They're**

Their is the third-person plural possessive. **There** is an adverb or introductory word to show place or time. **They're** is a contraction of the words *they* and *are.*

Examples:

underline{Their} car broke down at the mall. They left it underline{there.} underline{They're} walking home.

▶ **To / Too / Two**

To is a preposition that shows space, time, or degree. **Too** is an adverb meaning *in addition* or *also*. **Two** is the number.

Examples:

> I went <u>to</u> the movies. Adam came <u>too</u>. We bought <u>two</u> tickets and went in.

▶ **Weather / Whether**

Weather is a noun meaning the state of the atmosphere regarding heat, cold, or precipitation. **Whether** is a conjunction used to show alternatives.

Examples:

> The <u>weather</u> for our vacation was perfect. We could go swimming <u>whether</u> it was morning, noon, or night.

▶ **Were / We're / Where**

Were is a past tense form of the verb *to be*. **We're** is the contraction of the words *we* and *are*. **Where** is an adverb, conjunction, or noun that designates place.

Examples:

> They <u>were</u> hungry. <u>We're</u> buying food. That is <u>where</u> they eat.

▶ **Who's / Whose**

Who's is the contraction of the words *who* and *is*. **Whose** is a possessive pronoun.

Examples:

> <u>Who's</u> in the bathroom? The boy, <u>whose</u> mother left, is in the bathroom.

▶ **Your / You're**

Your is the second-person possessive. **You're** is the contraction of the words *you* and *are*.

Examples:

> Where is <u>your</u> coat? Sometimes, <u>you're</u> so forgetful.

Exercise 9-8

Each sentence contains an incorrect homonym. Underline each incorrect word and write the correction in the space provided.

Example: Bring <u>you're</u> coat to the movies.   *your*

1. Their are many people registered for the class._____

2. The store excepts all major credit cards. _____

3. I will be there weather or not you approve. _____

4. Its not reasonable to expect special treatment. _____

5. The shoppers all had they're hands full._____

6. An affect of precipitation is poor visibility. _____

7. The mother bought too ice pops for her children. _____

8. I can tell your tired when you slump in your chair. _____

9. Tara can swim all strokes accept the butterfly. _____

10. Maura saw her sister's book and wanted one, two._____

Lesson 9-8: Spelling Errors

Due to the widespread use of computers, spelling errors occur with less frequency. Nevertheless, there is no device other than editing that can catch spelling errors when the text is handwritten. Also, spell-checking software does not notice misspelled words that are actually other words spelled correctly. Here is a list of more than 250 commonly misspelled words.

A	adviser	anonymous	*B*
abridgment	aerial	antecedent	beginning
absence	aisle	antidote	believing
accessible	allotted	anxious	beneficial
accommodate	allotment	arctic	biscuit
accountant	all right	arguing	bulletin
ache	amateur	argument	business
acknowledge	ambitious	ascend	*C*
addressed	analysis	attendance	cafeteria
additional	analyze	autumn	calendar
advantageous	annihilate	auxiliary	campaign

catastrophe
changeable
chiefly
chocolate
college
colonel
column
commercial
commissioner
committee
commotion
comparative
compatible
competence
conceivable
condemn
conscience
conscientious
conscious
consensus
consistent
contempt
convenience
corporal
corporeal
corroborate
counterfeit

D
dealt
deceive
decision
defense
deficient
dependence
desperate
dilemma
disappointed
discipline
disease
disastrous

dominant

E
efficiency
eighth
elementary
embarrass
emphasis
endeavor
environment
equipped
essentially
etiquette
exaggerate
exasperate
excessive
excellent
exhilarated
existence
experience

F
facility
familiar
fascinated
fatigue
feasible
February
fictitious
fiery
foreign
forty
fourteen
funeral

G
gaiety
gauge
ghetto
government
grammar
guarantee
gymnasium

H
handkerchief
harass
height
heroes
hindrance
hoarse
hoping
humorous
hygiene
hypocrisy
hypothesis

I
idol
immediately
inconsistent
inconvenience
incredibly
ingenious
insistent
interference
irrelevant
irresistible

J
jealousy
jeopardize
jewelry

K
kerosene
knowledge

L
laboratory
leisurely
library
license
lieutenant
lightening
lightning
likelihood
literature

livelihood
loathsome
loneliness
lovable
luxury

M
magnificent
maintenance
management
maneuver
mathematics
meager
medieval
millionaire
miniature
miscellaneous
mischievous
misspell
mosquitoes
municipal

N
naïve
necessary
neighborhood
neither
nickel
niece
noticeable
nuclear
nuisance

O
occur
occurrence
omitted
omnipotent
opponent

P
parallel
paralysis
paralyze

parentheses	psychology	safety	through
parliament	*Q*	schedule	twelfth
peaceable	query	scissors	tyranny
permanent	questionnaire	seize	*U*
permissible	*R*	sergeant	unanimous
perseverance	receipt	separate	unnecessary
petroleum	receive	shepherd	*V*
phenomena	reciprocal	sincerely	vacuum
picnicking	recognize	souvenir	vengeance
plaintiff	recommendation	sovereign	vinegar
playwright	referred	specimen	*W*
pneumonia	reign	strength	Wednesday
pollution	relevant	subtle	weigh
precede	religious	succeed	weird
precedent	remembrance	sufficient	wintry
preferable	reminisce	superintendent	wrench
preference	restaurant	syllable	*Y*
prevalence	rhyme	synonym	yacht
privilege	rhythm	*T*	*Z*
proceed	ridiculous	tangible	zealous
procedure	righteous	technique	
professor	*S*	thorough	
pronunciation	sacrilege	though	

Periodically review the words that give you trouble. Also, use your dictionary to check spelling; that is the purpose of reference books.

Exercise 9-9

For each of the following words, determine if the spelling is correct. If the word is misspelled, write the correction in the space provided.
Example: Wensday *Wednesday*

1. absense _____

2. acsesible _____

3. accomodate _____

4. accurasy _____

5. acknowlgement _____

6. adjascent _____

7. allright _____

8. analyse _____

9. antecedent _____

10. apparant _____

11. artic _____

12. attendence _____

13. autum _____   22. eighth _____

14. begining _____   23. enviromental _____

15. busness _____   24. excellant _____

16. changable _____   25. Febuary _____

17. comissioner _____   26. forteen _____

18. convenence _____   27. jeopardize _____

19. conscience _____   28. labratory _____

20. counterfit _____   29. neccessary _____

21. desision _____   30. tangeble _____

Lesson 9-9: Tone

Tone is the register of the written voice, and it is of utmost importance. When you speak to someone in person, you have the benefit of appearance and countenance. When you write, you have tone. The reader forms his or her opinion of the author through tone. It makes an impression on the reader and it sets a level of formality. Tone depends on the writer's choice of words. The most common error is the use of colloquial or trite expressions. The use of vernacular, hackneyed expressions, and contractions sets an informal tone that is inappropriate for most writing.

Examples

Mary <u>couldn't find</u> the keys.

The tone of this sentence is casual. For use in speech, this is adequate. In most cases, however, it is not appropriate for writing. By simply removing the contraction and changing one word, the tone becomes more reserved.

Mary <u>could not locate</u> the keys.

This sentence is less relaxed. The tone is more suitable for writing.

You might <u>cry your eyes out</u> after seeing the movie.

This sentence uses a cliché to convey sentiment. The tone improves with the use of original language.

The <u>poignant film is emotionally moving</u>.

In this example, the tone is formalized by removing the trite expression.

<u>They didn't have any</u> peaches at the store.

This sentence contains a vague pronoun as well as a contraction. A simple rewording makes the tone more decorous.

<u>The store does not have</u> peaches in stock.

In this sentence, both tone and clarity are improved.

Another problem related to tone is the use of double negatives. The use of two negative terms together is not only confusing to the reader, it sets a casual tone. The use of words such as *but, hardly, scarcely, no, not,* and *nothing* should not be used in combination.

Example

I <u>can't hardly wait</u> until summer.

Hardly is a negative, and so it should never be used with *not.*

I <u>cannot wait</u> until summer.

This sentence is correct because it eliminates one of the negatives. The tone is also improved with the removal of the contraction *can't.*

Exercise 9-10

Revise each of the following sentences in order to improve the tone.

Example: It's kind of scary. *I find it frightening.*

1. You can't eat spicy foods before bed.

2. Pam was green with envy over my new car.

3. My kids didn't get any dinner.

4. That's not cool.

5. Judy is a tried and true friend.

6. There isn't any food in the fridge.

7. I can relate to that.

8. In the office they work like a dog.

9. Melissa is as pretty as a picture.

10. They don't make record players any more.

Answers to Exercises

Exercise 9-1

1.	The large, flowering tree on the hill.	*fragment*
2.	The cat rests.	*complete*
3.	After dinner, the young child played with his toys.	*complete*
4.	My friend took the job, she wanted a challenge.	*run-on*
5.	Because driving racecars is exhilarating.	*fragment*
6.	People garden.	*complete*
7.	I have a new car and my sister went shopping.	*run-on*
8.	Today, we are going to the zoo, we will see animals.	*run-on*
9.	After the concert is over.	*fragment*
10.	He seems.	*fragment*

Exercise 9-2

1. My friends from school (is renting, <u>are renting</u>) a new apartment.
2. Each one (<u>has</u>, have) his own bedroom.
3. The carpet and the floor (looks, <u>look</u>) old and worn.
4. The furnishings (<u>need</u>, needs) to be replaced.
5. One-half of the rent (<u>is</u>, are) paid by Sandy.
6. Everyone (<u>buys</u>, buy) his own groceries.
7. Three-fourths of the roommates (is, <u>are</u>) female.
8. Mary and Tom (debates, <u>debate</u>) frequently over differing beliefs.
9. Politics (<u>is</u>, are) a constant topic for their arguments.
10. The others in the apartment (ignores, <u>ignore</u>) the discussions.

Exercise 9-3

1. Kathy likes pears, but she does not like plums.
2. Usually, I have coffee after dinner.
3. Missy's favorite colors are purple, red, and blue.
4. Greg washed the floors in the kitchen, in the bathroom, and in the laundry room.
5. After work, my friends and I went to the movies.
6. The library, the bank, and the school are all within walking distance.
7. We need a new dryer, or we will have to repair the old one.
8. Allison played soccer, and she performed in the school play.

9. Fortunately, I have never lost my keys.

10. She must water the plants, feed the pets, and turn out the lights.

Exercise 9-4

1. The history class, which meets on Thursdays, is working on term papers.
2. Students must visit the library during class hours.   *restrictive*
3. One student, a freshman, is researching the Middle Ages.
4. The professor will guide her if she needs help.   *restrictive*
5. Students who are researching must cite sources.   *restrictive*
6. Several people, working on English history, worked together.
7. The librarian, who was working, alone aided six students.
8. The professor called a meeting, which was held in her office.
9. The printer, located in the library, will be used throughout the afternoon.
10. All papers are due from the students by next Friday.   *restrictive*

Exercise 9-5

1. In the store, <u>they</u> have a wonderful variety of produce.   *the store has*
2. Ellen told her sister that <u>she</u> needed milk.   *Ellen, the younger girl, etc.*
3. The book group gave <u>their</u> leader a gift.   *its*
4. Each of the sales representatives created <u>their</u> displays.   *his / her / his or her*
5. If <u>you</u> want to succeed, one must work hard.   *one wants*
6. Someone left <u>their</u> scarf on the bus.   *his / her / his or her*
7. The boy told his father that <u>he</u> needed to rest.   *the father, the older man, etc.*
8. On television, <u>it</u> says our economy is improving.   *The television newscaster*
9. When one is injured, <u>you</u> must seek medical attention.   *he or she*
10. The school lost <u>their</u> funding for sports programs.   *its*

Exercise 9-6

1. Margaret <u>had studied</u> today.   *studied*
2. The rain poured down, and then the sun <u>comes</u> out.   *came*
3. I walked and then I <u>was studying</u>.   *studied*
4. The young girl accidentally <u>had tore</u> her dress.   *tore*

5. My son <u>has wrote</u> his first story.   *has written*

6. The job <u>will have been completed</u> by tomorrow.   *will be completed*

7. Mary <u>has broke</u> the school's track record.   *has broken*

8. He will <u>be carrying</u> the flag and march in the parade.   *carry*

9. She ate the banana and he <u>has eaten</u> the apple.   *ate*

10. Gary <u>had shook</u> hands with my father.   *shook*

Exercise 9-7

1. Audrey attended the conference to speak (with, <u>to</u>) the audience.

2. He spoke (<u>with</u>, to) me about our mutual safety concerns.

3. This dinner is similar (with, <u>to</u>) the one you cooked last week.

4. Many people rely (in, <u>on</u>) others for financial assistance.

5. Emma compared her little brother (with, <u>to</u>) a bear cub.

6. We are all meeting (<u>at</u>, in) the restaurant.

7. The award-winning roses are (at, <u>in</u>) the city's largest public park.

8. Harry and Ian have an archery competition (<u>at</u>, on) three o'clock.

9. Billy is charmed (<u>by</u>, with) Emily's beauty.

10. Emily is captivated (<u>by</u>, with) Billy's wit.

Exercise 9-8

1. <u>Their</u> are many people registered for the class.   *There*

2. The store <u>excepts</u> all major credit cards.   *accepts*

3. I will be there <u>weather</u> or not you approve.   *whether*

4. <u>Its</u> not reasonable to expect special treatment.   *It's*

5. The shoppers all had <u>they're</u> hands full.   *their*

6. An <u>affect</u> of precipitation is poor visibility.   *effect*

7. The mother bought <u>too</u> ice pops for her children.   *two*

8. I can tell <u>your</u> tired when you slump in your chair.   *you're*

9. Tara can swim all strokes <u>accept</u> the butterfly.   *except*

10. Maura saw her sister's book and wanted one, <u>two</u>.   *too*

Exercise 9-9

1. absense	*absence*	4.	accurasy	*accuracy*
2. acsesible	*accessible*	5.	acknowlgement	*acknowledgment*
3. accomodate	*accommodate*	6.	adjascent	*adjacent*

7.	allright	*all right*	19. conscience	**correct**
8.	analyse	*analyze*	20. counterfit	*counterfeit*
9.	antecedent	**correct**	21. desision	*decision*
10.	apparant	*apparent*	22. eighth	**correct**
11.	artic	*arctic*	23. enviromental	*environmental*
12.	attendence	*attendance*	24. excellant	*excellent*
13.	autum	*autumn*	25. Febuary	*February*
14.	begining	*beginning*	26. forteen	*fourteen*
15.	busness	*business*	27. jeopardize	**correct**
16.	changable	*changeable*	28. labratory	*laboratory*
17.	comissioner	*commissioner*	29. neccessary	*necessary*
18.	convenence	*convenience*	30. tangeble	*tangible*

Exercise 9-10

1. You can't eat spicy foods before bed.
   (possible answer) *Eating spicy foods at night might cause indigestion.*

2. Pam was green with envy over my new car.
   (possible answer) *Pam demonstrated enormous envy after she saw my new car.*

3. My children didn't get any dinner.
   (possible answer) *My children barely had enough time to eat.*

4. That's not cool.
   (possible answer) *I do not approve of your actions.*

5. Judy is a tried and true friend.
   (possible answer) *Judy is a supportive and reliable person.*

6. There isn't any food in the fridge.
   (possible answer) *Your refrigerator does not contain any food.*

7. I can relate to that.
   (possible answer) *I sympathize with your emotion.*

8. In the office they work like a dog.
   (possible answer) *The employees of this company are overworked.*

9. Melissa is as pretty as a picture.
   (possible answer) *Melissa is a striking young woman.*

10. They don't make record players any more.
    (possible answer) *Companies no longer manufacture record players.*

Glossary

Absolute phrase: See *phrase*.

Active voice: See *voice*.

Adjective: A word that describes, identifies, or quantifies a noun or a word or phrase acting as a noun. Most adjectives precede the noun or other word(s) they modify, such as *good food*. A predicate adjective follows the noun or pronoun it modifies. For example: *The food is good.*

Adjective clause: See *clause*.

Adjective forms: Changes in an adjective from the **positive degree** (*tall, good*) to the **comparative** (comparing two; *taller, better*) or the **superlative** (comparing more than two; *tallest, best*). Longer adjectives usually form the comparative by adding *more* (*more special*) and the superlative by adding *most* (*most special*). A few adjectives have irregular forms (*good, better, best*), and some adjectives do not change form.

Adverb: A word that modifies, qualifies, limits, or defines a verb, an adjective, another adverb, or a clause, frequently answering the questions *when?, where?, why?, how?, or to what extent?*

Adverb clause: See *clause*.

Adverb forms: Changes in an adverb from the **positive degree** (*eagerly*) to the **comparative** (comparing two; *more eagerly*) to the **superlative** (comparing more than two; *most eagerly*). Most adverbs add *more* to form the comparative and *most* to form the superlative, but a few add *–er* and *–est* or have irregular forms (*little, less, least*).

Agreement: The correspondence of a pronoun with its antecedent in person, number, and gender or a of a verb with its subject in person and number. *He needs his homework. They need their homework.* Also see *antecedent, gender, number, person.*

Angle brackets (< >): An Internet symbol used to surround an e-mail address or a Website location within other text. For example: < http://www.careerpress.com/>

Antecedent: The specific noun that a pronoun replaces and to which it refers. A pronoun and its antecedent must agree in person, number, and gender. *The woman moved her suitcase to the train platform.*

Appositive: A noun or noun phrase that identifies or adds identifying information to a preceding noun.

Article: *A, an,* or *the,* the most common adjectives. *A* and *an* are **indefinite**; they do not specifically identify the nouns they modify. *I have a hat and an overcoat. The* is **definite**. It identifies a particular noun. *The hat is blue.*

Auxiliary verb: Also called a **helping verb,** it is a verb that combines with the base form or with the present or past participle of verb to form a verb phrase. The most common auxiliaries are forms of *do, have,* and *be. I do not dance. He has a puppy. She is eating.* **Modal auxiliaries** such as *can, may, shall, will, could, might, should,* and *would* have only one form and show possibility, necessity, obligation, and so forth.

Base form: The form of a verb that is not conjugated, such as *listen* and *walk.* It is also the form cited in the dictionary. For all verbs except *be,* it is the same as the first-person singular form in the present tense.

Case: The form of a noun or pronoun that shows its grammatical role in a sentence. Nouns and indefinite pronouns can be **subjective, possessive,** or **objective.** *The cat sleeps. Here is the cat's toy. She fed the cat.* In these three sentences, the

noun *cat* is in the subjective, possessive, and objective cases, respectively. The only change to the noun is in the possessive case. Personal pronouns usually change for each case. *He talked to him. He* is the subjective case and *him* is the objective case of the third-person singular pronoun. *His brother listened. His* is the possessive case of the same pronoun. Also see *pronoun.*

Clause: A group of words containing a subject and a predicate. An **independent clause** can stand alone as a sentence. *The boy sang.* A **dependent clause,** or **subordinate clause,** cannot stand on its own; it must be connected to an independent clause by a subordinating conjunction or a relative pronoun. A dependent clause can function as an adjective, an adverb, or a noun. *The boy who was next to the microphone sang* (adjective clause). *The boy sang when the music began* (adverb clause). *The boy sang whatever came to his mind* (noun clause).

Collective noun: See *noun.*

Comma splice: An error resulting from joining two independent clauses with only a comma.

Common noun: See *noun.*

Comparative degree: See *adjective forms, adverb forms.*

Complement: A word or group of words completing the predicate in a sentence. A **subject complement** follows a linking verb and renames or describes the subject. It can be a

predicate noun (*Jay is a student*) or a **predicate adjective** (*Jay is studious*). An **object complement** renames or describes a direct object (*We considered him a genius*).

Complete predicate: See *predicate.*

Complete subject: See *subject.*

Complex sentence: See *sentence.*

Compound adjective: A combination of words that functions as a single adjective (*ten-foot pole, high school graduation, mushroom-pepperoni pizza*). Many compound adjectives require a hyphen to separate the individual elements.

Compound-complex sentence: See *sentence.*

Compound noun: A combination of words that functions as a single noun (*in-law, oil well, windshield wiper*).

Compound sentence: See *sentence.*

Compound subject: See *subject.*

Conjunction: A word or words that join words, phrases, clauses, or sentences. **Coordinating conjunctions** (such as *and, but, or,* or *yet*) join grammatically equal elements. *Bob and Tammy have two children* (two nouns). *They live in New York, but they have a house at the beach* (two independent clauses). **Correlative conjunctions** (such as *both, and; either, or; neither, nor;* or *not only, but also*) are used in pairs, and they also join grammatically equal elements. *Neither Rob nor Tom had the telephone number* (two nouns). *They needed to either find a directory or locate the address* (two clauses). A **subordinating conjunction** (such

as *although, because, if,* or *when*) introduces a dependent clause and connects it to an independent clause. *He moved to the country, where life is peaceful.* A **conjunctive adverb** (such as *consequently, moreover,* or *nevertheless*) modifies an independent clause following another independent clause. It usually follows a semicolon and is followed by a comma. *The house is spacious; moreover, the scenery is exquisite.*

Coordinating conjunction: See *conjunction.*

Correlative conjunction: See *conjunction.*

Dangling modifier: A word, phrase, or clause that does not logically modify any element in the sentence to which it is attached. *Dancing slowly, the music began to relax me.* This sentence is incorrect because *the music* cannot be *dancing slowly. Dancing slowly, I relaxed to the music.* This sentence is correct because *I* is modified by *dancing slowly.*

Declarative sentence: See *sentence.*

Degree: See *adjective forms, adverb forms.*

Dependent clause: See *clause.*

Direct address: Sentence construction where a noun or pronoun names the person or thing being spoken to. *It seems to me, Bob, that you need a new coat.*

Direct discourse: A quotation that reiterates a speaker's exact words, indicated with quotation marks.

Direct object: A noun or pronoun receiving the action of a transitive verb. It answers the question *what?* or *whom? Ashley threw the ball.* Also see *indirect object.*

Exclamatory sentence: See *sentence.*

First person: See *person.*

Fused sentence: A sentence in which two independent clauses are incorrectly joined without a conjunction or punctuation between them. This is also called a **run-on sentence.** Also see *comma splice.*

Future tense: See *tense.*

Gender: The classification of a noun or pronoun as masculine (*man, he*), feminine (*woman, she*), or neutral (*people, it*).

Gerund: A verbal form ending in *ing* and functioning as a noun. *Cleaning can be relaxing.*

Helping verb: See *auxiliary verb.*

Imperative mood: The form of a verb used to express a command or urgent request. An imperative uses the base form of the verb and may or may not have an implied subject. *Leave now. Let's hurry!*

Imperative sentence: See *sentence.*

Indefinite pronoun: See *pronoun.*

Independent clause: See *clause.*

Indicative mood: The form of a verb used to state a fact or opinion or to ask a question. *Germany invaded Poland. Were they victorious?*

Indirect discourse: A paraphrased quotation that does not repeat someone else's words verbatim. It does not require quotation marks. *John F. Kennedy told the audience not to ask how the country can help them, but to ask how they can help their country.*

Indirect object: A noun or pronoun that answers the question t*o what or whom?* or *for what or whom?* a transitive verbs action is performed. It usually precedes the direct object. *Ashley threw Sarah the ball.* Also see *direct object.*

Indirect question: A sentence pattern in which a question is the basis of a subordinate clause. An indirect question is not an interrogative sentence; it should end with a period, not a question mark. *Patty wondered why Larry was unhappy.*

Infinitive: The base form of a verb preceded by *to* (*to walk, to eat*). An infinitive can function as a noun, an adjective, or an adverb. *To leave would be rude* (noun). *The restless man had no more time to waste* (adjective). *We stopped to talk* (adverb). An **infinitive phrase** consists of an infinitive together with its modifiers, objects, or complements. *We left to see the early show.* Also see *phrase.*

Intensifier: A modifier that increases the emphasis of the word or words it modifies. *I am really excited. I very nearly won the contest.* Although the purpose of an intensifier is to increase the emphasis of the word, the opposite sometimes happens. In formal writing, intensifiers detract from the power of the word.

Therefore, they act as fill. Remember to be concise when writing and avoid term such as *really, very, extremely,* and so on.

Interjection: A word or group of words that is an exclamation or an outburst of surprise, outrage, dismay, and so forth. *Oh my god! Watch out!*

Internet: A worldwide network that links computers to other computers. It provides a means of access to the many sites, sources, and services. Its slang term is *"the Net."*

Interrogative sentence: See *sentence.*

Intransitive verb: A verb that does not need a direct object to complete its meaning; it is a complete action. *Nathan spoke.*

Irregular verb: A verb whose past tense and past participle are not formed by adding *–ed* or *–d* to the base form. It follows an irregular pattern for conjugation. For example: *break, broke, broken.*

Linking verb: A verb that joins a subject with a subject complement or complements. Some common linking verbs include *appear, be, become, feel,* and *seem. Stella became adept at writing. She seemed confident.*

Main clause: An independent clause. See *clause.*

Main verb: The verb that carries the central meaning in a verb phrase, not the modals or auxiliaries. *We could have won the race. Won* is the main verb in the verb phrase *could have won.*

Misplaced modifier: A word, phrase, or clause in the wrong place within a sentence, so that it seems to modify a word other than what the writer intended. *Hesitantly, the man opened the door and embraced his wife. Hesitantly* modifies actions. Unless the writer intended to have the man hesitantly embrace his wife, the modifier is misplaced. The sentence should read: *The man hesitantly opened the door and then embraced his wife.*

Modal: See *auxiliary verb.*

Modifier: A word, phrase, or clause that acts as an adjective or an adverb and changes or qualifies the meaning of another word, phrase, or clause. Also see *adjective* and *adverb.*

Mood: The form of a verb that indicates the writer's or speaker's feeling toward the idea expressed by the verb. The **indicative mood** is used to state a fact or opinion or to ask a question. *The child is hungry.* The **imperative mood** is used to give a command or request. *Feed the child.* The **subjunctive mood** is used to express a wish, a suggestion, a request or requirement, or a condition that does not exist. *If the child were fed, he would go to sleep.*

Nonrestrictive element: A word, phrase, or clause that modifies but does not change the essential meaning of a sentence. It can be removed from the sentence without changing the essential meaning of the sentence. A nonrestrictive element is set off from the rest of the sentence with commas or, in some cases, dashes or parentheses. *My cat, a brown and black Siamese, came from the local shelter.*

Noun: A word that represents a person, place, or thing. Nouns serve as subjects, objects, complements, and appositives. The plural for most nouns is formed by adding –*s* or –*es,* and the possessive with *'s.* **Common nouns** do not name any specific person, place, or thing (*manager, park, bench*). **Proper nouns** name specific persons or things and are capitalized (*John, Delaware, July*). **Collective nouns** refer to a group of people or things (*jury, class, team*).

Noun clause: See *clause.*

Noun phrase: See *phrase.*

Number: The form of a noun or pronoun that indicates whether it is singular (*book, he*) or plural (*books, they*).

Object: A word or words, usually a noun or pronoun, that takes the action of a transitive verb or is connected to a sentence by a preposition. Also see *direct object, indirect object, object of a preposition. I found my keys under the chair. Keys* is the object of the transitive verb *found,* and *chair* is the object of the preposition *under.*

Object complement: See *complement.*

Objective case: See *case.*

Object of a preposition: A noun or pronoun connected to a sentence by a preposition. The preposition, the object, and any modifiers make up a **prepositional phrase.** *The plane is*

above the clouds. Clouds is the object of the prepositional phrase.

Participial phrase: See *phrase.*

Participle: A verb form or verbal with properties of different parts of speech. As can an adjective, a participle can modify a noun or pronoun; as a verb does, it has present and past forms and can take an object. The **present participle** of a verb always ends in *ing* (*dancing, laughing*). It can act as a verb or a verbal. The **past participle** usually ends in *ed* (*danced, laughed*), but many verbs have irregular forms (*eaten, spoken, become*). Present participles are used with the auxiliary verb *be* to form the **progressive tenses** (*I am walking, I have been walking, I will be walking*). Past participles are used with the auxiliary verb *have* to form **perfect tenses** (*I have walked, I had walked, I will have walked*) and with *be* to form the **passive voice** (*I am seen, I was seen*). These combinations of auxiliary verbs and participles are known as **verb phrases.** Also see *auxiliary verb, phrase, tense,* and *voice.*

Parts of speech: The different roles that words play within a sentence. Many words act as more than one part of speech. The parts of speech are *adjectives, adverbs, conjunctions, interjections, nouns, prepositions, pronouns,* and *verbs.*

Passive voice: See *voice.*

Past participle: See *participle.*

Past perfect tense: See *tense.*

Perfect tenses: See *tense, participle, verb.*

Person: The relation between a subject and its verb. **First person** (*I, me*) is when the subject is speaking about itself. *I read the newspaper.* **Second person** (*you*) is when the subject is being spoken about. *You must read the newspaper.* **Third person** (*he, she, it, they*) is when the subject is being spoken about. *She reads the newspaper.* Most verbs change form only in the present tense with a third-person singular subject. (*I read, you read, he reads, we read, you (plural) read, they read*). *Be* has several forms depending on the person (*am, is, are, was, were*).

Personal pronoun: See *pronoun.*

Phrase: A group of words that functions as a single unit but lacks a subject, verb, or both. An **absolute phrase** modifies an entire sentence. It usually includes a noun or pronoun followed by a participle (sometimes implied) or participial phrase. *My grief gone, I looked to the future.* A **gerund phrase** includes a gerund and its objects, complements, and modifiers. It functions as a noun and can therefore act as a subject, an object, or a complement. *Communicating clearly can help any relationship* (subject). An **infinitive phrase** includes an infinitive and its objects, complements, and modifiers. It functions as an adjective, an adverb, or a noun. *She left to answer the phone* (adverb). A **noun phrase** includes a noun and its modifiers. *A lengthy long-distance phone call can be expensive.* A **participial phrase** includes a present or past participle and its objects, complements, or modifiers. It functions as an adjective. *Finishing dinner, the man cleared his plate.* A **prepositional phrase** begins with a preposition and ends with a noun or a pronoun, called the object of the preposition. This type of phrase functions as an adjective, an adverb, or a noun. *The light in the doorway began to dim* (adjective). *The group of girls went to the movies* (adverb). A **verb phrase** contains a main verb and one or more auxiliaries, yet it acts as a single verb in the sentence predicate. *I should never have gone* to town.

Plural: The form of a noun, pronoun, or adjective that refers to more than one person or thing (*we, tables, those*).

Positive degree: See *adjective forms, adverb forms.*

Possessive case: See *case.*

Predicate: The verb and related words in a clause or sentence. The predicate expresses what the subject does or is. The **simple predicate** is the verb or the verb phrase. *She has been working all day.* The **complete predicate** includes the simple predicate plus its objects, modifiers, or complements. *She has been working at the store all day.* A **compound predicate** has more than one simple predicate. *She sold toys and organized the shelves.*

Predicate adjective: See *complement.*

Predicate noun: See *complement.*

Prefix: An addition to the beginning of a word to change its meaning (_unhappy_, _non_-entity).

Preposition: A word or group of words that denotes the relationship of a noun or pronoun, called the object of the preposition, to another part of the sentence. _Her mysterious man disappeared into the night._ Also see _phrase._

Present participle: See _participle._

Present perfect: See _participle, tense, verb, verbal._

Present progressive: See _participle, tense, verb, verbal._

Present tense: See _tense, verb._

Progressive tenses: See _participle, tense, verb._

Pronoun: A word used in place of a noun, usually called the antecedent of the pronoun. **Indefinite pronouns** do not refer to specific nouns. They include _any, each, everybody, somebody_, and similar words. _Many of us had some dessert._ **Personal pronouns** (_I, me, my, mine,_ and so forth) refer to particular people or things. The have different forms depending on their case. _You need your notebook._ **Relative pronouns** (_who, whom, whose, which, that, what, whoever, whomever, whichever,_ and _whatever_) connect a dependent clause to a sentence. _I wonder who will win the race._ Also see _antecedent, case._

Proper noun: See _noun._

Regular verb: A verb whose past tense and past participle are formed by adding _–d_ or _–ed_ to the base form (_stare, stared; jump, jumped_). Also see _irregular verb._

Relative pronoun: See _pronoun._

Restrictive element: A word, phrase, or clause that limits the essential meaning of the sentence it modifies or provides necessary information about it. A restrictive element is not set off from the rest of the sentence with commas or other punctuation. _The movie that I saw was fantastic._ Also see _nonrestrictive element._

Run-on sentence: See _comma splice, fused sentence._

Second person: See _person._

Sentence: A group of words containing a subject and a predicate and expressing a complete thought. In writing, a sentence begins with a capital letter and ends with a period, a question mark, or an exclamation mark. A **declarative sentence** makes a statement. _The sun shines._ An **interrogative sentence** asks a question. _Who took my cookies?_ An **exclamatory sentence** indicates surprise or strong emotion. _That's terrible!_ An **imperative** expresses a command. _Get out, now._ Sentences can be **simple,** containing only a single independent clause; **compound,** with two or more independent clauses; **complex,** with an independent clause and at least one dependent clause; or **compound-complex,** containing at least two independent clause and one or more dependent clauses. Also see _clause._

Sentence fragment: A group of words that is not a grammatically complete sentence but that is punctuated as one. Usually a fragment lacks a subject, verb, or both or is a dependent clause that is not connected to an independent clause. Creative writers might use fragments when writing dialogue, but in most cases sentence fragments are incorrect and should be avoided.

Simple predicate: See *predicate*.

Simple sentence: See *sentence*.

Simple subject: See *subject*.

Singular: The form of a noun, pronoun, or adjective that refers to only one person or thing (*he, table, this*).

Split infinitive: The placement of an adverb between *to* and the base form of the verb in an infinitive (*to better serve* rather than *to serve better*). This is considered an error and should be avoided in formal writing.

Subject: The noun or pronoun and its modifiers that indicate who or what the sentence is about. The **simple subject** is the noun or pronoun. The **complete subject** is the simple subject and all of its modifiers. *The tiny bird flew across the yard.* In the previous example, *bird* is the simple subject and *the tiny bird* is the complete subject. A **compound subject** contains more than one noun or pronoun. *The bird and the butterfly flew across the yard.*

Subject complement: See *complement*.

Subjective case: See *case*.

Subjunctive mood: The form of a verb used to express a wish, a suggestion, a request, a requirement, or a condition that does not currently exist. The present subjunctive uses the base form of the verb. *I asked that you be ready.* The past subjunctive uses the same form of the verb as the past tense except for the verb *be,* which uses were for all subjects. *If you were ready, we could leave.* Also see *mood*.

Subordinate clause: A dependent clause. See *clause*.

Subordinating conjunction: See *conjunction*.

Suffix: An addition to the end of a word that changes the word's meaning or part of speech (*happy, happiness* [adjective, noun]; *think, thinker*[verb, noun]).

Superlative degree: See *adjective forms, adverb forms*.

Syntax: The way in which words are arranged in a sentence.

Tense: The form of a verb that indicates the time when the action takes place. Tenses include **past, present,** and **future**. Additionally, tenses can be **simple** (*I watch television*), **perfect** (*I have watched television*), **progressive** (*I am watching television*), or **perfect progressive** (*I have been watching television*).

Third person: See *person*.

Transitive verb: A verb that takes a direct object, which receives the action of the verb. A transitive verb may be in the active or passive voice. *Melissa flew the kite* (active voice). *The kite was flown by Melissa* (passive voice). Also see *verb*.

Verb: A word or group of words that states what action a subject takes or receives or what the subject's state of being is. Verbs are necessary to form a complete sentence. *Patty made lunch.* Verbs change form to show tense, number, voice, and mood. Also see *auxiliary verb, intransitive verb, irregular verb, linking verb, mood, person, regular verb, tense, transitive verb, verbal, voice.*

Verbal: A verb form that functions as a noun, an adjective, or an adverb. The three types of verbals are *gerunds, infinitives,* and *participles.*

Verbal phrase: A phrase using a gerund, a participle, or an infinitive. See *phrase.*

Verb phrase: See *phrase.*

Voice: The form of a transitive verb that indicates whether the subject is acting or being acted on. When a verb is in the **active voice,** the subject performs the action. *John ate the chips.* When the verb is in the **passive voice,** the subject receives the action. *The chips were eaten by John.* The active voice is used most frequently and is appropriate for formal writing.

Index

About the Author

MAUREEN LINDNER, a faculty member of Dobbs Ferry High School in Westchester County, New York, has been teaching English at all levels for about 10 years. Certified to teach English in the International Baccalaureate Program, she has experience in rural, suburban, and urban schools. Prior to pursuing her teaching career, she worked as an editor for a translation service in Westchester County. Ms. Lindner earned a Bachelor of Arts in English and Secondary Education from S.U.N.Y. New Paltz, and a Master of Science with Distinction from Mercy College. She continues her post-graduate studies in English and education through various programs. Maureen resides in Hastings-on-Hudson, New York, with her husband and three children.